M⬙RATHON

MERATHON

MERATHON

Running from Denial

to

Running a Business

—

Karl D. Klicker

VADE MECUM PUBLISHING GROUP, LLC

Published in the United States of America

by

Vade Mecum Publishing Group, LLC

Tampa, USA

Indispensable

This book is dedicated to God

and Janis Joplin

Also by Karl D. Klicker

INDOC (2013)

INDOC (Indoctrination) – spans the past 30 years of Ideology, Propaganda and Conflict in the Marine Corps and al-Qaida. Dr. Karl D. Klicker, retired Captain of Marines, intelligence officer, and Iraq War veteran explores the internal cultural tensions within the Marine Corps, the roots of division in the Sunni and Shi'a camps; the social psychology of recruiting for war; and the on-going conflict between radical Islamists and America's armed forces.

Tested by Fire:
Recipes for Leaders, with Metaphors on the Grill.
(2012)

TESTED BY FIRE presents the arts, sciences and intuition of backyard grilling as a metaphor for developing new leaders in any industry. Combining theory and real-world experience from 40 combined years in military leadership, industrial training, organizational psychology and backyard grilling, the author presents 13 fundamental, thought-provoking scenarios for middle and senior leaders who own the responsibility for training and educating their organization's next generation of leaders. Examples include tales from the combat zone of Anbar Province in Iraq in 2006-'07 to life post-ENRON; comparing Santa Claus and jihad; and managing the challenges inherent in The 2nd Law of Social Thermodynamics - wrapped around the arts and sciences of spare ribs, potato salad, beer can chicken, and more.

Organization

What's going on here?

MERATHON reads in three intertwined parts. The introduction brings Captain Steele into the story as a story-teller. Captain Steele is a metaphor, an avatar with a mission – who brings his own allegories along to help us understand why organizations behave the way they do. *Laser* chapters are Captain Steele chapters.

Personal musings overlap the *Laser* chapters in the form of a memoire. Much of this experience is analyzed through concepts of the *grief cycle:* denial, anger, fear, shock, creativity and the rest. Through the frustration of seeking non-existent jobs for three years, my catharsis is running marathons.

The final third evolves from Captain Steele's metaphors and my own analysis of ENRON's collapse. This thread evaluates *First Principles:* Quality, Ethics, Leadership, Freedom and more. A discussion in Quality, for example, starts with re-visiting Pirsig's *Zen and the Art of Motorcycle Maintenance.* Evolutionary Ethics derives from the Principia Cybernetica Web Project (see the end notes.) Leadership – the Marine Corps and Sunday School; Freedom – Janis Joplin, running, and unemployment, etc.

All three threads converge in the final chapters. Unified, the sum of these three stories presents a journey of faith and a lens through which to understand the leader's role in any organization.

Table of Contents

Prologue

It takes FOCUS, DISCIPLINE and ENDURANCE
to run a global corporation,
to run a marathon and to survive unemployment.

As of this introduction, 12 years on, ENRON's mythic self-destruction should be a distant bad memory. The book that follows took shape in the first two years after I was laid off from ENRON (December 2001) – along with 4500 other people in Houston, Texas. By the time I had finished the manuscript for this essay in 2004, I had missed the wave of publishable introspections on the ENRON phenomenon. I'm okay with that. Now. Back then it would have been nice to sell the book and have some sort of paycheck. (You reach for what you can...) I put the finished book on the shelf and got on with the rest of my life. Soon (although not soon enough) – I had a lot going on.

More than a footnote: Far from sitting at home, a home I was close to losing, and writing a 90,000-word cathartic essay on "what ENRON did to me," I spent every day of those first two years scrubbing job postings at monster.com, careerbuilder.com, sixfigurejobs.com, the Houston Chronicle on-line and a dozen other resources. I applied for more than 400 jobs in those two years, but the job search process usually exhausted only 5 a.m. to 10 a.m. I sent out 10 or 12, sometimes 15 to 20 job applications a week, each with a tailored resume, for jobs in Houston and any other city or state I would have been willing or able to move to. Done with this process well before noon each day, and accustomed to working eight to ten hours a day for the previous 25 years or so, I had to find something to do. Positively. Productively. It took nearly two years to realize what enron did *for* me.

So I wrote. I painted. I also had unlimited access to time with my then-5-year-old daughter. We went to "the hundred acre wood" and looked for Pooh Bear tracks, and skinks, and flowers and autumn leaves. I had become a single dad a month before starting work at ENRON, had built a new-construction home in the coming year, then lived in the new house 6 months before ENRON collapsed. I had an almost-$2000/month house payment and not enough military pension to cover it. I've been there...that unemployment thing, and I lived through it for three and a half years. I had so much time on my hands through all of this. I had time to run. I trained for the next marathon. And I started my own business. The rest of that story lies in the pages that follow.

The original post-script in the book was, of course, just the first in a series of post-scripts. (I was an English major too many years ago, and I don't know the term for a second post-script. Post-post-script?) Ten years from now I'm sure I'll have another look at this, another set of opinions, but I'll save that for conversations at a back-yard barbecue.

It is indeed 12 years on, and ENRON has etched itself into the vernacular. The books and the movies were entertaining in their own right, and I heard that as of late 2009 there was a "Broadway play" type production about ENRON opening in England. Whatever.

Looking back on this essay, I wouldn't change a word. This is how it happened, although in light of gradual changes and the "great" recession (2008-2011), some of the companies I used to compare to Enron have lost their luster. Yet now I feel a duty to people who have lost their jobs – either because of their own company's corruption or short-sightedness or because their industry has been incidentally but materially impacted by the recession – to recast the experience they are experiencing – on their terms... But this book is not directed only to the unemployed or chronically unemployed. This is a book about leadership and focus, a book about how to run a business – a mom and pop shop or a global corporation.

For those who are unemployed – particularly those who have been unemployed six months to a year or more – this book's message is: Get over it and hang in there. It won't be easy. So? Go into survival mode. One of the most important survival tools is attitude. As it started to become apparent that I could lose my home, my car, and face personal bankruptcy; as I teetered, for a while, at the edge of hopelessness, my brother expressed the idea that contributed to my change in attitude. He said, "You're not un-employed; you're *self-employed.* You're just not making much money. Yet."

The other most significant lesson for me came from Sunday School. That story is told in the essay as well. One may think of it as God is allowing me – my character – to be tested. Most of us don't want to be tested of course. Or we'd like the test to be over. Think of it as a marathon, or as those first two weeks of football practice, or first two weeks of P90X – where everything hurts, and we're tired. Really tired. And it hurts. At the end, we're stronger and what we have gained is both tangible and intangible.

That Sunday School lesson was the reminder that I was not in this experience alone. Thus a possible subtitle: *Freedom's Just Another Word for Nothin' Left to Lose."* At least for a time, if I didn't have to report to corporate America, if I lost my home and my car and the payments that went with them – I would have total freedom, total maneuverability. I could go anywhere I wanted. I could *do* anything I wanted. (How would I get there? Walk if necessary. How would I eat? The Lord would provide...)

For me, that maneuverability translated to the freedom to start my own business – a consulting business. My salary that final full year at ENRON was $106,000. In my first year as an "independent consultant," I made $11,000 (that's $5.28 an hour – in 2002), but I quickly learned to like the working conditions and the freedom of being self-employed better than the self-esteem-artificially-pegged-to-a-six-figure-job. In my second year, I earned $26,000; $45,000 in my third. But that third year was a partial year. I accepted a recall to active duty in the Marine Corps and would soon find myself in Iraq. How the rest of that turned out is captured briefly in my post post-script.

One

...kicking through the charred remains of another of his squadron's gunships. He was outwardly calm but muscularly kinetic. Methodical. Mechanical. Mentally frenetic. Groping in the night for one last battery pack.

Alien warships hovered between 20 and 30 meters off the deck and little more than a hundred meters off, moving slowly to the west. To the East, another smoking hole. Steele could barely make out the tail number in the confused destruction – 32. That would be Captain Purcell and his door gunner, or what was left of them. What was the kid's name – the salty corporal from Brooklyn? Maybe they would have had an extra battery pack. Captain Steele's laser was dry.

The lanky captain sprinted through the night, gun balanced on his good shoulder, taking advantage of the terrain to avoid the invaders' sensors. The light from his own moon would not betray him, but his movement could. The unwelcome ones overhead were waiting on his infrared Doppler shift to give him away. Everything Steele knew from intelligence reports told him they couldn't see him in the visual...but their phased array sensors in IR would. If they could pick him out from the mottled landscape.

Fury pushed fatigue from his body. Adrenaline masked the pain screaming from an oozing hole in his left shoulder, a souvenir from the alien freaks overhead that had shot his own ride out from under him and taken down what remained of his squadron.

Twenty yards...

It wasn't his squadron, really. But hey – his skipper was dead. So was the XO. Steele was the only one left now. That made it his squadron to command, if anyone were alive.

Memories of memories washed over the battle-weary captain. Ancient targets streaked like tracers across the inside of his eyelids as he blinked hard to force out the sweat.

The targets arced over a fighting hole on a distant shore in what seemed to be hundreds of years in the past. Steele found religion in that war. Or maybe it found him. He survived the combat tour, left the Corps for college. Then a seminary. Then his first, and last, congregation.

Back then, he was focused on THE WORD. He was intense. Disciplined. The words flowed naturally. Everything seemed coherent, and he thought, back then, how like a laser was the Word of God. Intense. One wavelength. Focused energy. Supported by values rooted in more than two thousand years of faith. The message had not changed in thousands of years. Now the cockpit was his pulpit. Back in uniform, he could've been a chaplain, but there were plenty of those around. No, his mission now was putting more fire than brimstone down the gullets of this misbegotten horde from the other side of the galaxy. Apparently all they wanted was water. But did they have to waste entire populations to get it? Did they have to take his Kathryn?

Ten yards. Five.

Safe! He leapt into the cratered jumble of twisted aluminum, polycarbonates, titanium and Captain Purcell's scattered flesh, leaned the laser against the hull of the downed Mach M fighter, then reached up to gently pull the kid from Brooklyn out of the gunner's seat. The kid's eyes were closed, face calm. He was dead before his muscles could form a scream. Captain Steele knew he wasn't sleeping, wasn't just unconscious.

Steele's gentleness was out of respect. He looked again into the front seat. There was nothing he could do for the pieces of his fellow captain. He fought tears as he laid the corporal under the wing of the tattered fighter, then checked his six and with his good arm, barrel-rolled over the gunnel. The canopy had been completely torn away. He strained into the aft cargo bay behind the gunner's swivel seat, hoping...groping for success.

At last! Juice in a can! "All I need is one more terawatt-second," he thought. He inserted the four-pound battery canister into the butt-plate of the weapon and hefted it. The 40-pound laser was normally mounted on a tripod ashore, or clamped to a swivel base for a door gunner in the fighters. A lone warrior would tire under the weight of this marvelous neodymium-glass death machine in field conditions, but tonight it seemed light. Steele snorted at the play on words.

Time poised motionlessly, ponderously, on already burdened shoulders. As the alien ships turned toward Steele's movements and now hovered ever closer, scanning Earth's surface for what some sensor must be telling them was a survivor, Steele watched the charging pump indicator on the side of the laser. Thirty seconds. Just thirty sweet more seconds....The laser's active assembly would drain the battery, transform the current, power the internal lamp, and convert neodymium-glass molecules to liquid death by way of coaxing the electrons into an excited state. A photon frenzy. Those released photons, in a higher than normal energy state, would start bouncing around inside the laser tube and reflect off the mirrored surfaces inside. All in the same wavelength, these bundles of energy excited other atoms, and reflected back and forth inside the tube, all in phase, in step – like squads of Marines in parallel columns forming a platoon on the march.

When the gunner squeezed the trigger, it would be as if a tiny door was opening on the business end of the laser – loosing a brief pulse of immensely powerful light on a condemned target. Steele mused how his own team assembled resembled this amazing invention. The acrid taste of the combat mission provided the energy that excited *his* atoms – his troops. In a higher than normal, excited energy state, they too released photons – the war cries of the vicious, and the weapons of pinpoint accuracy and certain destruction. In their excited state, they excited others. They radiated, but all in one direction. All on one mission. They were focused. Sometimes they won. Sometimes they died. But before those photons could even hope to be effective in any battle – whether they would win or lose – they had to be in step with each other, working together. Steele could still hear his drill instructor screaming in his ear, years ago, "Get in step, lads! Work together! Gung Ho!"

In phase. In step. All in the same wavelength. Coherent – all focused on the same mission, all moving in the same direction, all reflecting the same values. It was the history of his Corps that reflected the values, the living heroes and the legends. They all worked together to keep the troops, and the Corps, in line and in step. Intense. Focused. Then...

ZZZzztt! One 40-picosecond pulse and something was gone forever – a man, a gun ship, an alien. It didn't matter. Mission accomplished. Five...

Steele counted down the final seconds as he slid his thumb to the selector switch.

Four.

Like computer code, you're either a one or a zero.

Three.

And today, Captain Steele had no intention of being a zero.

Two.

The switch jerked into the 'on' position.

One.

The lights came on...

and I woke to reality. My job was imaginary; Captain Steele was tangible. The laser as metaphor was more palpable than ever. The concepts of leadership and ethics, personal and organizational psychology, freedom, control, values, decision making, faith and quality all sprang from theory back into reality, where they belong, as enron retreated into myth.

Each of these concepts – leadership, ethics, freedom,

psychology, faith, trust, quality and more – would become my manna, a ticket to my daily bread, as the truth of the company's unreality came into focus. Accepting why and how I had bought in to enron was one issue, but there were other challenges. Like so many others, I needed to understand why the company imploded. I needed to understand, in the context of ex-employee, what the experience would mean for my emerging career decisions. I needed to understand this new reality of being unemployed.

I needed to eat.

Almost immediately and constantly at the edge of personal bankruptcy, I had to come to grips with the former reality of being one of the "best and brightest" on the team identified by Fortune Magazine as *most innovative* six years running, and the latter reality of "sorry, sir, but we don't need someone with your qualifications at this time." Stigma? Unfortunate coincidence with the free-falling economy exacerbated by WorldCom, Tyco, Kmart and others, the 9/11 terrorist attacks and uncontrollable economic cycles? A residual belief by a prospective employer that we had all been paid too much at enron?

What I really wanted to do was either find the company I would be proud to call home, or create that same kind of company and call it my own. There was a me before and I could somehow imagine a better me after. Before I would get close, I would wake to discover I was alone, adrift, with only days, nights, horizons.

Two: I before E
(Emotional Push-ups)

4 p.m., Saturday, November 23, 2001
Holiday Inn, Waveland, Mississippi

I'm wondering if the woman ahead of me, checking in at the Holiday Inn, is a Marine. She's wearing a Marine Corps Marathon long-sleeve "T," so that's an easy entrée. She looks old enough to be maybe a captain or major.

"Jarhead?" I asked.

She looked up from the hotel register, smiling but confused. "Excuse me?"

I realized the reference was lost. She probably wasn't a Marine, but I continued: "Are you in the Marine Corps?"

"No," she said, then looked down from the hotel register to the Eagle, Globe and Anchor and the rest of the Marine Corps propaganda on her shirt, a trophy from the previous year's annual race sponsored by the Marine Corps in Washington, DC. "Oh – this. I ran last year. I'm not a Marine."

"How'd you do?"

"Four-something," she said. She put her MasterCard back into her purse and stepped aside, opening the counter for me to register.

"Was that your first marathon?" I asked, as if I had run hundreds. I hadn't. The desk clerk called up my name on her computer and started filling out the guest card. "No. My 20th. I'm in the 50 States & DC Marathon club..."

I was impressed.

"My husband and I..."

Another guest entered the lobby – a weathered senior

citizen with white hair, in a crew cut, accompanied by a nice looking lady, equally senior. He overheard enough of the conversation between the lady runner and me to invite himself into the conversation. At a place like this, all you need to have in common is 26.2 miles. After that, the conversation is as natural as the aimless-but-friendly chatter amongst strangers at a KOA, who rely on the bond of recreational vehicles, historical markers and interstate highways to generate conversation.

It turned out the old fellow was a Marine Corps veteran, from around the time of Davy Crockett lunchboxes and the final stages of my strategic planning for kindergarten in San Diego. He was a veteran of more than a hundred marathons. Following Saturday's race he and his wife would get back in their RV and drive back to Florida where he would run a Sunday marathon.

Huh?

This would be my second marathon. I had run thousands and thousands of miles since junior high school, but my races had been mostly one-mile, three- mile, five-kilometer (5K), and an occasional 10K. After my first Houston Marathon 10 months earlier, in January 2001, I drove home, dragged my sorry body, five pounds lighter, into the house and lifted my pulverized hips and knees into the Jacuzzi tub, opened a bottle of champagne, and set my *phaser* on 'numb.' Over this weekend, I would learn there are lots of people who have run hundreds of marathons. I had heard of the 50 & DC Marathon club, but had no idea that some of these idiots would run races one week apart, or for that matter – back-to-back races in a single weekend.

If you're not a runner, you might ask, "Why do they do it?" And even if you are a runner, you might ask, "*HOW* do they do it?"

The reality is that the 26-mile, 385-yard event is not a race, except for the rare few dozens in the world who finish with times under two and a half hours. World-class men consistently post times under 2:15; women in the neighborhood of 2:20 to 2:30.

For everyone else, it's a metaphor. The marathon is a symbol of "I can do it." For some, it's a once-in-a-lifetime event. For others, it's a once-a-year self-confirmation. There are those whose passion developed gradually and accidentally after they started walking and jogging to lose weight, and others who purposefully compete with themselves to drive their own times lower and lower. There are as many reasons for running as there are runners.

Depending on a runner's age and conditioning, the physical part of the marathon may last anywhere from eight or ten to 19 or 20 miles. But even with water stations on the course and Ibuprofen and carbohydrate-rich Power Bars in a fanny pack, top runners and novices alike face the mental part of a marathon, when the body doesn't want to accomplish the goal set by the mind. It might be the second half. It might be the last mile. It might even be the whole thing. Something has to keep aching feet moving, pounded knees bending and arc-welded hip joints rotating.

Desire? Determination? Stupidity? A light at the end of the finish line? Free lunch or a $5 mass-produced T-shirt and a $3 'been there' marathon medal in exchange for a $60- to $120 registration fee?

I wouldn't know it then, but even if I had come in first in Mississippi, I would not have won. I wouldn't be done. The race tomorrow was merely another day in a mental boot camp. It was another day of training. I wouldn't realize it until weeks after the next Houston Marathon, in January 2002. That would be the last I would be able to justify the cash for a registration fee. It would also be the *top* of the slope.

I put my credit card in my wallet and bid my newfound friends adieu until race time.

"Aren't you loading?" the running lady asked.

"Loading?"

"Carbo-loading party. Spaghetti dinner. Here in the hotel conference room. Eight o'clock."

Spaghetti is one of the pre-race favorites for marathoners and Ironman competitors (another breed of self-abusing morons who exploit their bodies not only in running-too-far events, but in the additional foreign languages of bicycling-too-far and swimming-too-far). Spaghetti equals carbohydrates. "Sure," I said. "I forgot. But first I need to run out and find some Power Bars." It would take me two hours, but at least I was rewarded with a relaxing drive along Mississippi's incredible coastline. I can remember wishing the race course would be like this: salt air, elegant homes in pastoral communities perched along south-facing hills, overlooking the beach like widows and mothers looking hopefully out to sea, five knots of breeze. This was every coastline I had ever fallen in love with, from Oregon and Okinawa to Kitty Hawk and Padre Island. It was calm. It was easy. (A few years later, after Katrina, the Mississippi coast was a mess.)

Mental Carbo-Loading

The girl from the Northeast, the salty marathoner from Florida, his wife and I joined the running congregation in the Holiday Inn conference room amidst towering altars of running shoes in boxes offered by Nike, New Balance, Asic and other vendors willing enough to find their way to this little out-of-the-way race.

A cup of spaghetti – 44 grams of carbohydrates. At my rate, that would be part of 300 grams of carbs and more than 800 calories twelve hours before the race. I'd be up by 4 a.m. for bagels, yogurt, bananas and high-glucose Gatorade, too nervous to sleep. By race time I'd have taken in more than 4000 calories in 24 hours; over 8000 calories in two days. I would have gained three to four pounds, net, in the week before the race. Tomorrow I'd lose five to six pounds net, with a few water stops included.

The running lady and the old jarhead conversed freely about past races. She was on track to run a marathon in every state and Washington DC. Her husband usually traveled with her, but she freely admitted that her goal was becoming expensive. I excused myself after my third plate of spaghetti to chase down a couple of pieces of peach pie and stopped on the way to check out the shoes. I bought a new pair of Nike 729s. I shouldn't have, but they were marked down $20, and $55 for a top quality shoe is a great price and a good investment for a runner who regularly puts a hundred to two hundred miles on the road each month. I'd start breaking them in next week. Never run a race in new shoes.

When I returned to the table, the New England running lady was chatting with a running lady from Arizona. The veteran and I started in on the Marine Corps...what his job was, where he had been stationed and when. His four years in uniform, after Korea and before Vietnam, overlapped my Dad's career. We used to laugh when people would say, "You're in the Marine Corps? Do you know Sergeant Schmuckatelli?" As big as the Corps is, it wasn't that unusual, especially in a fairly small specialty like my intelligence field, my older brother's electronics and communications field, or Dad's food services field. It was worth asking, but as it turned out, he didn't remember ever running into my father in the Marine Corps, or the few of my Dad's buddies whose names I could remember.

Dad was a cook in the Marine Corps. A darn good cook too. We all grew up with good habits in the kitchen and the dining room – the chow hall – and all five of us can cook respectably well. This skill was serving me well as a single dad. Diet and exercise? Thirty years after high school and I'd gained four or five pounds. There must be something to it. Most of all, Dad was a Marine. Four of us enlisted; two of us made a career and retired. Baby sister's health kept her out of the Corps but she inherited Dad's strength and Mom's way with words. She's a lawyer and a certified high school teacher.

Dad was a grunt too. Before he became a cook, Dad

had enlisted in 1948 with hopes of getting into school to learn heavy equipment – tractors, bulldozers, graders. At the end of boot camp, September, '48, Dad had told me that his company first sergeant had come into his graduating company with the message, "If you take *boot leave* and go back home to see your little sweeties, you'll get orders overseas. If you don't take boot leave, you'll get a stateside assignment. You'll be able to go see your little sweeties any time." Dad's dream of driving heavy equipment faded.

Dad had banked on getting home in a couple of months, so took the stateside assignment to Camp Pendleton, California. Six months later, with little warning, Dad's unit packed up and shipped out to Guam to join the First Marine Brigade.

As things got hot in the Far East, the First Marine Brigade on Guam joined the First Marine Division in Korea. It would be nearly three years from the time Dad left home for boot camp before he would walk in the door at the family farm in Minnesota. He hadn't been wounded. Not shot. But we always knew Dad's days were numbered. The Marine Corps retired him in 1963 on a medical disability, with Reynaud's Disease, apparently brought on by severe frostbite on more than one occasion during the Korean War, just short of 16 years in the Corps and on the selection list for gunnery sergeant.

Mom flew home with Dad's body from their campground in San Antonio in February, 1994. For me at least, there was no denial, no anger, shock, fear or frustration. I jumped right to stress. I had been prepared for Dad's death for years. At the top of my list was concern for Mom's mental and physical well-being.

I had tried to submit my retirement papers to the Marine Corps the year before, in honor of the day the 'commander-in-chief' with the stained blue dress took office, but got talked back into the Corps for another year by a clutter of colonels. Dad died when Son Number One was off to college and Son Number Two was in his senior year of high school. Empty nest. All the while there was another colonel who didn't know how to get a 12-hour-day's worth of work done in less than 16 hours dominating my life. A 15-minute story took four hours. "Where's the Captain?" he would ask.

My answer: "Tell the colonel the captain went for a run." The Marine Corps required it.

Aside from the crew cut and the link to the Corps, that hard-boiled marathoner across the table didn't really remind me of my Dad. Dad was 6-foot-5 and 220-plus; this fellow was maybe 5-foot-7, 5-8 at the most, and 120 pounds in the rain. But he did remind me that I missed Dad, and I told him so.

Mom died with lung cancer in '96. They were married 43 years and I'll always think she died of a broken heart. They were one. Mom was just sad and tried her best to hide it. I'm glad kid sister was home to absorb the work. Eight years later kid sis would master the art of surviving breast cancer, with plans to get back on her Harley. I had just retired from the Corps when Mom joined Dad, and had been working in my first civilian, corporate job in Detroit. I made 11 trips to Minnesota during the year Mom fought cancer. My third child – a daughter – was on the way, 20 years after Number Two Son.

I held Mom's hand when she took her last breath. My brothers and sisters always joked that Mom liked me best. I protested. I actually didn't believe it. I still don't. When I joined three of my siblings at Mom's home a month after the funeral, to decide who should take what home, Sister Number One gave me a slip of paper that had been folded up in one of Mom's wallets. It was a Christmas list. Each of our names was written down with a dollar amount and a check mark. That Christmas, long ago, Mom had made a note to send each of us – grown and married – $25. Next to my name, and only my name, she had crossed out '$25' and had written in '$30.' Kid sister laughed and said, "Told ya so!"

"I didn't know...," I insisted.

"Don't worry about it," sister said. "You probably

needed it that year."

Eventually the running lady wandered back into conversation at our table. Talk found its way to families, kids, jobs. Interesting that people from Vermont, Florida and Texas had so much in common, but I did not want to discuss families, kids and jobs. I had been avoiding this kind of talk. I knew my sons would grow up and move away some day, creating lives for themselves. I had waved goodbye to them at the pier in Bremerton, Washington, when I shipped out for the Persian Gulf Theater during the Iran-Iraq oil war in 1988, leaving 13- and 11-year-old sons to be the men of the family. But did they have to grow up so fast? Did they have to graduate from high school when their step-mom and I went separate ways? Did their step-mom need to leave when my Dad's time ran out?

"So – where do you work?"

"Enron."

Three: The Metaphysical Enron

ENRON never existed.

The *Meta*-ENRON never existed. The *model* enron – the corporation that took up residence at 1400 Smith Street in Houston – existed apart from the possibility for there to exist a perfect ENRON. Conducting arbitrage on energy prices, exploiting their own natural gas pipeline rights-of-way with fiber optics trunks in anticipation of an exploding demand for broadband, sloughing off tangible assets in favor of creating profit in risk derivatives on paper, pulp, gas, electricity and countless other commodities, and introducing dozens if not hundreds of other innovative, *alien*, even rule-breaking concepts to the business world throughout the 1990s made enron look every bit the ENRON we hoped it could be. Yet that look, that appearance, was a façade. enron's storefront window was so papered over with Fortune magazine articles that nobody could see what was going on inside.

This is not a reductionist, house-of-cards, woe-is-me approach to deconstructing enron's collapse. This is a catheter, a release that comes to grips with the impact of getting laid off. The lies, the deceit, the off-shore bank accounts and shadow corporations...let the courts figure all that out. Or – kinda like the slogan on a Marine Corps T-shirt: "Kill 'em all – Let God sort 'em out."

The proposal on the table is that a corporation, by any given state's laws of incorporation, is merely the *model* of an ideal. It's a theory...in action, trying to become a reality. Each company's set of corporate officers in a given industry has a different version of how to approach that ideal. As a consumer, I can envision the possibility of the corporation (or even small company) that responds precisely to my desires for quality products and services. If it's energy, I get not only the energy I need, but when and where I need it, at a fair price, and total transparency on what it costs to produce that energy, with a plain English explanation on what the corporation makes as a profit. The same foundational concepts would hold true with any provider of goods or services – cars, clothing, electronics, furniture, lumber or hardware, the guys who mow my lawn, trim my trees, or lay tile in my kitchen.

As an employee, I can imagine the employing organization of my dreams: work that fits my talents, skills and knowledge; fair pay (perhaps slightly above market) and generous benefits; a chain of command filled with increasingly senior leaders (but most importantly – my immediate supervisor) I can have confidence in; challenging but realistic goals; clear communication; common-sense processes that create what they're supposed to create; co-workers with whom I have a shared sense of mission, and because of that shared sense of mission – put so much energy into work that the inevitable minor differences with co-workers are forgotten on a regular basis.

This organization exists only in the abstract. There is perfect – the metaENRON that enron wanted to be and the perfect organization that you want your organization to become – and then there are lesser forms of ideal, good, not-so-good and I-hate-my-job kinds of organizations.

What determines where enron failed at becoming ENRON, and where all of us can learn, is more complex than a dismissive wave of the hand and a proclamation of "Greed." Yet it is also fundamentally simple. The accounting rules broken are less important than what led to the system that allowed the actual and alleged crimes. To be able to dismiss enron, I need to understand, even if through some pseudoscience, what happened to enron.

enron was a construct. A creation, a fractal, an epiphenomenal derivative of *how to run a global corporation.* My working hypothesis is that the manufactured enron, searching for ENRONness, failed for lack of focus on First Principles. These principles apply whether an organization exists as a non-profit filling some socially redeemable mission, as a government agency, as an educational institution, or as a commercial company created to deliver products and services to the public, to an internal or business-to-business consumer base, or anything in between. These first principles may also be logically applied to individual relationships, such as doctor-patient, attorney-client, husband-wife, parent-child.

enron's leaders apparently drew their own roadmap for enron's extinction, via natural selection, by their e-mails, board decisions, handshakes and back office deals. enron was simulating ENRON. enron as a working hypothesis was simulating the ideal it wanted to become. As a laser – intense, coherent, high-energy, focused light – enron won, or at least appeared to be winning, hands down, on all counts but focus. They were looking in the wrong direction, focused on the wrong thing.

Where is the perfect organization? The one we strive for? Its name is QUALITY. But not simple quality in products and customer service; not just best-in-class in what goes out the door. To understand the metaphysical ENRON, we must understand the metaphysical QUALITY.

Four: QUALITY – the 1st First Principle

Gospel. Law. Business.

If they're all "first principles," why is there a *first* first principle? Because the remaining first principles derive *from* QUALITY.

After reading thousands of pages and dozens of philosophers over close to 30 years, I returned to *Zen and the Art of Motorcycle Maintenance*[i] (ZMM) once again after the fall of enron. I'd read it three or four times before, but each of those events was with a different eye. Robert Pirsig finally offered a small but significant cadre of unifying thoughts to the meaning of *meaning*. He paid dearly for it, as most who have read ZMM well understand. Yet through trips on peyote, explorations of Eastern religions as well as the classic western philosophers, and an introspective motorcycle trip with his son, Pirsig offered tangible, deceptively simple, apparently irrefutable evidence for a metaphysics of QUALITY. The sum of his journey provides part of the answer to why enron was on the *wrong* track to become ENRON.

Pirsig's odyssey through past experiences takes us back to his catalyst, which is relevant in understanding both the ENRON that could have been and Pirsig's struggle with QUALITY. In the present of the book, Pirsig's motorcycle trip with his son is more than a vehicle for telling the story. The trip takes him back through Montana and allows the passage of present time to explain Pirsig's troubled past. He seeks to confront *Phaedrus,* the demon ghost of his former self. In the quest to define quality, Pirsig had gone mad.

Now, after surviving electric shock treatments and years in an institution, Pirsig's passion is to make sense of the notes he left behind, to reconstruct the beginnings of his metaphysics. What was *he* – Phaedrus – thinking? The catalyst came early in Pirsig's career as a professor of rhetoric, a creative writing teacher, at Montana State University in Bozeman. Pirsig grew increasingly frustrated with the lack of satisfactory results teaching writing skills by rote. "Just follow these rules" did not yield the quality he sought from his students. Holding up classic texts as symbols of quality didn't work; many of the writers of so-called classic works broke the rules he had just taught his students to follow. Providing his own writing as an example to imitate would lead the students to produce plastic imitations with little sign of creativity or higher-order thinking.

Eventually, Pirsig pursued an experiment, withholding grades and removing the artificial constraints imposed by the rules of composition and the pressure, reinforced by grades, to conform to an artificial ideal. At the end of the semester, he found that the students' grades were in line with previous grades and entrance exams. Surveying these students, Pirsig found the A students favored the no-grades policy 2 to 1; B and C students were evenly divided; D and F students unanimously opposed. His hunch: "that the brighter, more serious students were the least desirous of grades, possibly because they were more interested in the subject matter of the course, whereas the dull or lazy students were the *most* desirous of grades, possibly because grades told them they were getting by." His students would beg, "We don't know what quality is," and Pirsig would prove them wrong. He offered well-written papers and poorly written papers for the class to judge; he offered as many as four papers at a time, on a continuum from good to poor. In almost all cases, Pirsig writes that he observed unanimous agreement on which papers were of *good quality* and which were of *poor quality*. They couldn't define it, but they too <u>knew it when they saw it</u>. But the experiment only fueled Pirsig's desire to understand what had happened, and in seeking to understand quality, he next ventured to define it. The pilgrimage would be his undoing.

Before taking that next step with Pirsig, the pending question would be: "what does this pre-epiphany of Pirsig's have to do with quality in my organization?" What Pirsig was observing was not the quality that came out in his students' writing – the parallel to your products and services – but the environment in which those products and services were being created. In harsh terms, magnificent works of engineering (the Great Pyramids of Giza for example) can be created by slave laborers.

In less harsh terms, the organizations we work for, or buy books, cars, groceries, hardware or electronics from, all generally emphasize the quality in their products and services. But quality is not restricted to commercial goods and services. Quality also defines processes, working conditions and relationships. If we assume for the moment (and Pirsig will agree in a moment) that part of what *quality* means is "good," or has "value," then non-profit organizations, government agencies, educational institutions, and yes – interpersonal relationships – all have a stake in quality. In the late 1990's, I came face to face with the man who held Pirsig's answer with an iron hand.

At the National Aeronautics and Space Administration (NASA) Johnson Space Center, civil servants and government contractors alike came to understand the *wrong rock* syndrome, sponsored by Center Director George Abbey, but propagated through many directorates and divisions as a legitimate way to do business. The concept was that a senior official would request a plan for some new system, and those both eager and foolish enough to hope for the right solution would scurry off to build their PowerPoint presentations in response to the request. Without specific guidance on what or how the end result should look like, cost, or operate, each succeeding presentation would meet with a response that translated to "Go look under another rock." And the essence of this was, "I don't know what it is, but I'll recognize it when I see it." George Abbey's quality was Pirsig's quality.

In the wake of the Columbia tragedy, in which all seven crewmembers perished as the orbiter Columbia broke apart during reentry on February 1, 2003, NASA was taken to task by the Columbia Accident Investigation Board (CAIB), eventually calling for significant, sweeping changes in NASA's management culture. The *wrong rock* syndrome was a symptom of the culture that allowed both the Columbia accident and the Challenger accident, 16 years earlier. The

CAIB cites culture as a root cause for both incidents in their final report.[ii] While private and commercial space enthusiasts are increasing in number and funding, no other organization on this planet has the mix of talent – in both civil servants and supporting contractor personnel – to create the *quality* or *value* that NASA creates in response to *all of* NASA's missions. NASA's products and services are Safety of Human Space Flight, Mission Success, and concepts like these. They don't sell a thing, but they have customers – nearly every person on the planet has benefited in some way from NASA's work over the past four-plus decades. Responding to those customers, NASA is obligated to give them what they want, which starts with bringing crew members home alive.

NASA's culture focused some people on the rules instead of the values that created the rules. The same evidence surfaces in public education in the United States. The Bush Administration's experiment, the Leave No Child Behind game plan, was designed on the same principles: make rules and test the heck out of everyone. Let's prove success by comparing test scores. And just like NASA and hundreds or perhaps thousands of other organizations, everyone runs off to follow the rules and standardize the evidence of success. The A teachers are feeling constrained, the D and F teachers are grumbling but watching the test scores to prove they are just above the minimum, and the B and C teachers are probably evenly divided on the value of "No Child Left Behind." Gone is the focus on quality in the *process* of education; now we are making *plastic imitations of quality* education and proving our success by the test scores. There is no measure for 250% or 1000% better than "the norm" in a normal school. Think about that. Sure – most of the abnormally exceptional students may be identified early on, but what about those performing at 110% or 120% of "the norm?"

NASA can change, but it will not be easy, in large measure due to the preponderance of engineering talent on the civil service and contractor teams. I worked with these folks for three years and got to know more than a dozen astronauts well enough to use first names. I met John Glenn in the parking lot once, and had two astronauts and two cosmonauts to my home for a cookout with a gaggle of American and Russian space operations trainers. I respect them all and admire them immensely. But there is a screaming tendency with this engineering crowd to analyze, quantify and define, to make scientific in order to make relevant. And as Pirsig discovered, to define is to limit. Does this mean I would imagine a NASA without rules, processes or regulations? Preposterous, I think. Rules, processes and regulations bring order to chaos, don't they? But we need to understand *all* of the rules, including the *cultural* rules of human interaction. NASA's culture became more powerful than NASA's written rules, which is odd....In an engineering environment, the subjective culture overpowered the objective rules.

Pirsig's wanderings took him through classic and romantic logic. If we have a word for it – quality – we must be able to perceive it. If we can perceive it, we must be able to define it. Pirsig exhausted both houses of logic. On the classic side, he determined that quality is not exclusively tangible. The beautiful BMW motorcycle he rode has value or quality in its tangible, quantified existence, but that wasn't all there was to it. On the romantic side of logic, the motorcycle's "excellence, worth, or goodness" offered value or quality to the owner, but these were not measurable by scientific instruments, as Pirsig points out, and what constitutes value or quality for me in a vehicle probably differs from what you like. Dead end.

Unable to define quality in either classic or romantic logic, as objective or subjective, tangible or intangible, form or function, Pirsig was smitten with the idea that "Quality is just what you like." But this troubled him. The idea of "what you like" was an emotional response, and that would place it in the romantic logic camp. Pirsig homed in on how we teach children:

> Little children were trained not to do 'just what they liked' but...what? Of course! What *others* liked. And which others? Parents, teachers, supervisors,

policemen, judges, officials, kings, dictators. All authorities. When you are trained to despise 'just what you like' then, of course you become a much more obedient servant of others – a *good* slave. When you learn not to do 'just what you like' then the System loves you. (pp. 232-233)

Pirsig could not possibly be talking to 21ˢᵗ century American culture, could he? People work of their own free will, don't we? Try this: get in your car and "forget" to put your seat belt on. Drive around town. The first time you see a cop, what happens? What clicks in your head? Is there an *indoctrinated* urge to reach for your seat belt? Keep driving. Pull alongside the police cruiser and match speeds. When you get to the first stop sign or traffic light, do you come to a *complete* stop and look both ways before moving on? What's going on here?

Once a month or so I notice other drivers reach for their seatbelts when they see a police car. Every day I see people run red lights and roll through intersections with stop signs when there is no police officer in sight. The trigger is the police officer as a symbol. The stop sign can't write you a ticket, but the cop can. The same thing is happening in your organization. People are fixated on the laws, rules, policies and processes. Because we emphasize the rules and not the values that created the rules, we get two categories of responses: those who try to follow the rules but don't have a clue when something comes up that isn't covered by the rules, and those who go along with the rules while "under surveillance." Those in the latter set, when faced with a decision not covered by the rules, will base their response on their own values. If those values coincide with the company values, we're in luck. If we have a training program that focuses on values and we *know* that company values will guide decision-making, we can treat our employees like adults and turn decisions over to them. enron wasn't breaking the law, at first, because there was no specific law that said they were breaking the law.

The stop sign doesn't mean stop. The stop sign means

save lives and *protect property.* These phrases are *not* equivalent. "The law says *stop,* so we stop and we save lives" does not equal "The human desire to save lives has led to the installation of the stop sign." One has to create the other; one has to come first. The company's ISO9000 or 6 Sigma processes are intended to standardize output in order to ensure quality, but industrial accident after industrial accident, we find that it is impossible to write 100 percent of the possible rules, laws, policies or processes that would govern any given operation. This is true from community symphonies and grocery stores to emergency rooms and sixth grade classrooms, from nuclear submarines to submarine sandwich shops to gun control laws.

It's not just the worker bees, the grunts, who are stuck on the rules. Managers do it. Directors do it. Vice presidents and corporate CEOs do it. (Notice I did not write that 'everyone' is doing it.) Those who are stuck on the rules are the low C worker bees, grunts, managers, directors, etc., and all of the Ds and Fs. They rely on the rules because they've been indoctrinated that way.

And here I'll diverge and expand on Pirsig, who asked, "But suppose you *do* just what you like? Does that mean you're going to go out and shoot heroin, rob banks and rape old ladies?" Pirsig handled this quandary by delving into what he calls scientific materialism and classic formalism. I understand his premises and conclusions, but will take a different track. I'll ask, "Who do we perceive to own the rules?" In civil society, it seems to be the legislatures that create them and the courts and constabulary that enforce them, aided and abetted by the executive branch that appoints and has the appearance of leading. It is in their best interest and ours for a civil population to obey traffic signals, wear seat belts, refrain from shooting hand guns into the air at 4th of July picnics and so on.

But we're talking about the government. We elected them. If I turn left on a red light when there is no on-coming traffic, I'm making a decision outside of the rules because I think the traffic signal isn't smart enough to judge all possible traffic permutations, and by extension – I put that traffic signal and its enforcement there anyway because I voted for the legislators who wrote the laws and the government that hires the police officers.

Perhaps this means I think that people should judge when to take the law into their own hands based on expediency or whatever the current situation seems to dictate. Or perhaps this means I think laws are meant to be broken. Neither is the case. What I mean is that people fixate on the rule and forget the *reason*, the value that led to the creation of the rule. When it comes time to solve a problem that isn't covered by the rules, they freeze. Or they get stuck in a "this is the way we've always done it" feedback loop that fails to address the problem.

In the corporate world, and this includes corporate bodies that are not commercial, maintenance of the status quo is most easily accomplished by rules, laws and policies, not unlike civil society. But unlike the civil world, the relationship between employer and employee has more of a voluntary character to it. It's always been amazing that at the intersection of employer and potential employee, at the interview, both are marketing themselves; both are customers and both are selling. Once the transaction is sealed and the candidate accepts a job offer, the relationship changes from horizontal and equal power to vertical and unequal power. Ask any one of your employees to draw an organizational chart and I would bet 90 percent or more would start with a series of boxes arranged in some vertical hierarchy. My seminar participants do it. My undergraduate students in Bachelor of Management or Bachelor of Business Administration all do it. My graduate students in Organizational Dynamics do it. Why? They've been indoctrinated and have accepted that the people who have more senior positions in the company are "upper" management. The relationship is now parent-child instead of equal-equal. Don't we elect and pay for the President of the United States and members of Congress? They work for us. Shouldn't they be at the *bottom* of the "org chart?"

How do parents control their children? Most of them

establish rules. Wear your seat belt. Brush your teeth. Look both ways before crossing the street. Clean your room. Don't drink, smoke or use drugs. Finish your homework. Be in before 10. Failure to comply typically comes with a punishment, just like in civil society. *Of course* each of these rules has a purpose. As parents, most of us take seriously some kind of mission to help our children establish decent personal grooming standards, learn basic academics so they can become productive members of society, and avoid harmful situations. This is a process of moving the child from externally imposed discipline, by rote, to internally motivated self-discipline. But because *punishment is efficient and yields quick results, we forget the purpose and focus on the rules that grew out of the purpose.* It's quicker and easier to punish infractions against the rules than to figure out how to reward expressions of the values that created the rules. Most companies do a great job spelling out the punishments.

Pirsig's experiment showed that the A students were not only more creative and less apprehensive in the no-rules environment; they were internally driven to excel. When I quiz my seminars or my college students, "How many of you are in the ideal job? Everything is exactly the way you want it?" The positive responses range from zero to around 25 percent. The ones who love their jobs describe them as something they would do whether they got paid or not.

If we're all free to leave any time we wish, and those who love their jobs do not wish to leave, what does this say about those who hate their jobs? What they say is they feel trapped. I interpret that to mean they feel they are being controlled or have lost control. In other words, they don't perceive the freedom to move to another career. It may be their education, their location, the job market, fear of starting that interview process all over again. If they feel limited, they must also feel defined. To define is to limit. They may feel defined by their gender, their racial background, and their initial financial or cultural conditions. All of these are artificial restrictions that can be overcome, with endless evidence to contradict "but my *chances of* becoming a successful...." Whatever the reason, not only do they feel trapped and controlled, many also hate their jobs because they believe their bosses are controlling, the internal processes are controlling and leave no room for personal initiative. These are like the people Thoreau was talking about, leading lives of quiet desperation.

If the end results are identical, is it possible that the weight of influence from written rules is matched or even exceeded by the weight of influence embedded in values or culture...the unwritten rules? One person stops at a stop sign because of an indoctrinated sense of altruism, safety and concern for other drivers and property. The next driver stops at a stop sign because it's the law and he seeks to avoid punishment. Outwardly, there is no possible way to determine which driver is which. The results are the same.

Flash back to NASA, which not only has an immense library of documented rules, laws, processes and procedures for some of the most complex systems on – and off – the planet, but a deeply ingrained (emotional) corporate sense of responsibility to the men and women who 'strap on the rocket' and enter the microgravity world of orbit. The laws of physics are no less laws, and in parallel with the processes leading up to launch and the prime directive of Safety of Human Space Flight, we follow the rules and we launch. But riding shotgun on the laws of physics and the rules for safety, are a set of cultural givens that bear the weight of law. Junior engineers don't question senior engineers. Junior engineers don't embarrass their supervisors, especially in public. Contractors are subordinate to civil servants.

In true NASA fashion, when NASA responded to the Columbia Accident Investigation Board's stern recommendation to fix its management culture, NASA finally released a Request for Proposals (RFP) on exactly how to accomplish this monumental task. The RFP was made public on December 19, 2003, with a deadline of January 6, 2004. The message was, "You aspiring contractors can work your asses off over the holidays; we're on vacation." Of course I was pissed off – post-enron I was aspiring to build a consulting business offering training seminars in leadership and organizational development. I wasn't the only one who was pissed off. Someone who knew the system requested an extension and got a one-week reprieve.[iii] We can figure out the physics; the real challenge is understanding the impact of attitudes, culture and values.

At NASA, at your company or the company down the street, in your married life, going through the motions can produce what everyone on the outside perceives as quality end results, quality products and services – a successful Mars probe, a fine wine, outstanding cigar or best-seller video game, or a marriage that appears to be letter perfect. But the internal human framework can be dysfunctional, broken or just plain wrong. The human part of doing business can lack quality even though the end results can *appear* to be just fine.

For a while. Like enron.

Pirsig wanted to know why. He could not define quality in purely subjective terms; could not define it in purely objective terms. For a time he felt comfortable with what he called a trinity of mind, matter and Quality, without defining the relationship amongst them. As he probed deeper into *Phaedrus'* sequestered memories, he observed:

> I don't know how much thought passed before he arrived at this, but eventually he saw that quality couldn't be independently related with either the subject or the object but could be found *only in the relationship of the two with each other*. It is the point at which subject and object meet.

> That sounded warm.

> Quality is not a *thing*. It is an *event*.

> It is the event at which the subject becomes aware of the object.

> And because without objects there can be no subject – because the objects create the subject's awareness of himself – Quality is the event at which

awareness of both subjects and objects is made possible.

Hot.

Now he knew it was coming.

This means that Quality is not just the result of a collision between subject and object. The very existence of subject and object themselves is *deduced* from the Quality event. The Quality event is the *cause* of the subjects and objects, which are then mistakenly presumed to be the cause of Quality! (p. 239. original italics)

What Pirsig is telling us is that we can't grab a pile of sheet metal, an engine and a bucket of paint, follow some rule book on how to build cars, slap a plastic badge that's supposed to look like chrome on the front of the finished product and call it Quality. Almost every car out there is an imitation of one before. Some dealers are brazen about it – showing the higher priced look-alike next to their own and extolling the virtues of smaller monthly payments for "just as much car."

When it comes to quality in a finished product or service...*just* the product or service, the only vision of quality that matters is the customer's. Every time we try to imitate quality, we get an imitation.

For every car that truly earns the title of "classic," for beauty, comfort, performance, speed or heart-pounding excitement, there are 99 cheap imitations of "classic." The car manufacturers know this, but they're feeding the masses so they can get away with it. The average joe can't afford a Bentley, Ferrari or Maserati, so the manufacturers mass produce tens of thousands of less expensive imitations of sexy, expensive vehicles – and are successful at selling them (because they are more affordable). Some are very well-made and serve basic transportation needs, but not on the scale of Bentley, Ferrari or Maserati. The masses have no control over what the manufacturers create unless the manufacturers actually listen to them. We generally seem to have no hope of shaping what the manufacturers create. A line from a 1980's children's story makes the point: "People who have no hope are easy to control."[iv]

For our purposes, Pirsig's final epiphany came in accepting Quality as prime, independent of mind or matter, form or function. Pirsig says Quality is indefinable; it just *is*. Beyond that, we accept Quality as good.

And while Pirsig touched on it, he did not specifically fill in the blanks on *qualities*. As Pirsig fought for territory in this battle of mind, he asserted that we cannot assemble Quality inductively by bolting on qualities. I would counter, however, that we can come to understand what our customers' view of Quality is – the "Just what you like," by coming to understand deductively what *qualities* or attributes define their view of "good." For many people, the price of the car, the cost to maintain, insure and operate the car, are significant, if not the most important qualities. (And price fits into the category of *quantitative*.). An inexpensive car has car-ness to it, typically with four wheels, an engine and transmission, seats and a radio – all of that quantitative 'car stuff' that makes it a car. Cost is one of those qualities. 'Just what you like' has a continuum. More quality, more of 'just what you like,' such as speed, roominess, color options, entertainment consoles and other options – comes at a price.

Pirsig is nearly exhausted. His final realization is that Quality exists before we are aware of it. There is a preconscious awareness for the possibility of an ideal car, marriage, corporation or computer. Not a perfect one; an ideal one. And I'll defend that in a moment. Shall we test it...Pirsig's view of quality? I've never seen a rebuttal to Zen and the Art of Motorcycle Maintenance, although there is a text, "Guidebook to Zen and the Art of Motorcycle Maintenance,"[v] that offers to help explain it. To test the validity of what (I believe) Pirsig *means* for our organizations, or even our personal relationships, in the context of quality, it should be useful to post his model as a null hypothesis and attempt to prove it wrong. In other words, let's hypothesize that Pirsig was wrong. Can we find an example – mathematical, metaphysical or mystical – that disproves the null? That he was right?

When I first read Zen and the Art of Motorcycle Maintenance, I was about 24, in undergraduate studies, and reading about 100 books a year as an English major with a history minor. ZMM seemed like a bunch of mumbo jumbo. I'm sure I wasn't mature enough or well-read enough. Five or six years later, after a 'low quality' event in my life had settled itself out, I read it again and found Pirsig's metaphysics brilliant. Ten more years passed and I was teaching college courses in English Composition – rhetoric – when the subject of writing *quality* papers came up. As a professor, I scored an educational discount with a local bookstore and assigned ZMM as required reading. This worked fine two semesters running, until one of my students brought up Pirsig's challenge with the trinity of subject-object-Quality. (One of my students had actually read the book!) Pirsig had written:

> Although there's no logical objection to a metaphysical trinity, a three-headed reality, such as trinities are not common or popular. The metaphysician normally seeks either a monism, such as God, which explains the nature of the world as a manifestation of one single thing, or he seeks a dualism, such as mind-matter [subject-object or intangible-tangible, yin-yang, male-female], which explains it as two things, or he leaves it as a pluralism, which explains it as a manifestation of an indefinite number of things. But three is an awkward number. (pp. 238-239; my parens)

Like a heat-seeking missile, this astute A student of mine had zeroed in on the concept of God as a monism. Although I was teaching as an adjunct professor for a secular college, my students were certainly not restricted from discussing topics in religion or faith. I have to stay neutral because of my position as influencer-instructor, and have my own convictions. I let her proceed, with interest.

She offered, "What if we take Quality, as a metaphor,

in comparison to God. Pirsig tossed out the idea in the first place. Didn't Pirsig say, 'The sun of quality does not revolve around the subjects and objects of our existence. It has created them."? In the Christian sense of a *triune* God, there *is* one God...but in three persons. If God the Father is comparable to Quality, then Jesus Christ, manifest in human flesh, is matter; the Holy Spirit is mind. That's one way to look at it anyway..."

I was stunned.

She might be right and I might be excited, but the temptation to get deeply involved as a peer was swept away. The class debated the idea, and other excellent and not-so-excellent ideas surfaced as well. For years after this experience, I kept coming back to this metaphor. Or was it a metaphor? A few years later I read ZMM once again, convinced Pirsig was *all wrong* because I decided he was a heathen and had taken his lessons from what he called *The Church of Reason.* I was convinced Pirsig had no God other than his own mind.

Now I'm entering middle age and enron comes along with the answer. Another rebuttal to the null hypothesis. Pirsig was right! It started as a trickle, then washed over me like a flood. In my own Christian upbringing, I've been attached to a Law-Gospel faith since birth. The last 40-something years have not been without question. Martin Luther had questions. I still plan to ask God how he pulled off that creation thing. It's one of the first questions I intend to ask when I get to Heaven.

What Christianity teaches is: "Believe that Jesus Christ died and was resurrected for your sins," and you will be saved. So – what if we pair Quality to Faith in Jesus Christ, and then ask, where is Law? A song by the Cavaliers from the late 50s or early 60s plays on the oldies station, and tells the story of a boy and a girl out on a date who have a car accident. The girl dies; the boyfriend mourns: "She's gone to heaven so I got to be good, so I can see my baby when I leave this world."

The suggestion is that good people, people who follow the rules, go to heaven. Are some people in the business world uncomfortable thinking about this? Why? In December, 2003, one of those little pop-ups on my computer announced that more than 80 percent of Americans said they believe in God and think life after death, in Heaven, is real. But what the Bible tells us is that we can spend a lifetime not crossing one of the 10 Commandments and still not be saved from eternity in Hell if we don't have faith that Jesus Christ died for our sins. So. What came first? The law or the gospel. Which is prime? Which is paramount?

If we proceed *from* the gospel (Jesus, faith, quality) first, and follow the rules (10 Commandments, ISO 9000 processes, 6 Sigma processes) *because* of that faith or quality – we're doing the right thing for the right reason, not fixated on the law, but acting according to the values that created the laws. Gospel, then Law, *then* business. In other words get the values and ethics part down first and you'll need fewer "laws" to run your business.

One more point to nullify the null hypothesis: Some of the enron defendants will testify that what they did from an accounting point of view was totally legal – because it was not illegal. The Bible provides another example, but only as a metaphor if you like. In the times of Jesus, some 2000 years ago, there was an educated class of clerics who sought to maintain the sanctity of the Jewish faith. They were the Pharisees. If the 10 Commandments said, for example, "Remember the Sabbath, to keep it holy," they would go one better and define *how* to keep it holy. God rested on the seventh day, so the Sabbath was a day of rest. The Pharisees listed do's and don'ts for the Sabbath, like not walking more than a mile, or not working in the fields, or cooking food the day before so that no one would have to cook on the Sabbath.

But once these rules, meant to clarify the 10 Commandments, were published and well understood, the people could then skirt the rules by nuance. If I go 200 meters down the road and place something I own in my friend's home, then that home has my property and is part of my home. If I go another 200 meters down the road and place another of my possessions in the next friend's home, that too is part of my home. And so on. If I have enough knick-knacks, I can walk all the way to Cairo and not break the Sabbath, technically.

Generally accepted accounting practices?

The sad thing is, enron believed ENRON was possible. But an ENRON would have been the perfect corporation. Perfect in every sense. Back off and consider the perfect car. Someone gives it to you free of charge. It costs nothing to operate and converts ambient hydrogen in the air to energy. Nothing on this car ever wears out. It's got dynamic curb appeal, can do 0 to 60 in 4 seconds, and yet it's street-legal. Heated leather seats and incredible comfort. Superb handling. Theater-quality surround sound. It's sexy, sporty and fast – and you can change the color at the push of a button. There are no maintenance costs, and because it's so safe in every respect – insurance is $1 a year. God's car? Perfect doesn't exist, as the Walgreen drug store commercials of 2004 once reminded us. So – we're left with "pretty good," "ideal" or "best in class."

Perhaps some of the fault lies with enron's senior executives. Some responsibility may be attached to a look-the-other-way Securities and Exchange Commission, or a conservative federal government that favored business because the more successful business is, the better it is for people who need jobs and the nation's economy as a whole. Creating the *perfect* corporation by a set of rules without starting from a set of ethics is doomed to failure.

ENRON always was impossible, but enron wasn't even headed in the right direction. We *can't* write enough rules to cover every possible contingency, and enron was creating some weird businesses. The staggering cost of litigation in the enron mess is due in large measure to the complexity of the legal and accounting entanglements created at 1400 Smith Street. The simple answer would have been, like the faith of a child – a simple test of ethics. In other words – Quality behavior. But that's another chapter...

In sum, the First First Principle is QUALITY. Whether we are filing a dba and launching a mom and pop shop tomorrow, or reengineering an organization that has existed for more than 100 years, everything starts *from* the possibility for there to exist quality. Most of us have the product and service part down well – or at least the cognitive and technical ability: find out what the customer wants (quality defined in customer terms), then create and deliver.

It's the rest of the business that needs attention: Identify employees as customers (that's what they were when we were selling them on the idea that our company is a great place to work), then learn what constitutes quality in the employee-employer relationship. In addition to reading that more than 80 percent of Americans believe in God, I've also read that more than half of the employed adults in the U.S. don't like their jobs, and of those who do leave – most leave because of problems with their managers. Conversely, most of us hire based on technical skills and credentials, and fire because of interpersonal problems. We know the technical side of doing business; we don't do well creating the mind-matter/subject-object environment that responds to the need for a quality work environment.

Identify everyone else as customers: competitors, banks, the government, stock holders, the environment, suppliers, the general public. If the ideal organization can be visualized, Quality as an imperative defines every process, every deal, every transaction, every decision. We can't post Respect, Integrity, Communication and Excellence as core values on the company web site then turn around and make millions on insider trading, while screwing the employees who helped build the company in the first place. That's not QUALITY.

To this point I haven't written a word about revenue or profit. The *focus* is on Quality; revenue is the *result* of achieving Quality. How effectively and efficiently we run our organizations determines how much of that revenue becomes residual profit.

enron lost focus.

Five: Laser Chapter 2 - Pseudoscience

Every machine in the universe had to have some signature. Captain Dave Steele lay motionless, listening, feeling the Earth through every tendon for a signature, a sound or vibration. Nanoseconds wore into seconds. Minutes. Nothing seemed to be moving in his hemisphere. Finally inhaling with certain exhaustion, Steel gained his feet and surveyed the mess he had created.

As he all-but tiptoed to the first of the totaled alien warships, smirking, he thought of the '58 Chevy his older brother had wrecked in his first race.

"Don't tell Dad," John whined, as if younger brother Dave had to worry about whether their Dad would notice the smashed windshield and crumpled sheet metal. Right here in front of Steele was a totally wrecked '58 Chevy from the other side of the galaxy. Difference was – it probably wasn't a '58. It definitely wasn't a Chevy. And...there were no survivors.

John was lucky back then. Bold, but lucky. And he didn't really get in much trouble with Dad. In fact, Dad took him back to the stretch of highway where he had raced and walked through the whole event to help John figure out what went wrong.

John didn't win his next race either, but he didn't wreck. He just kept getting better until he did start winning, and Dad stayed out of his way until he was needed. He just seemed to know some guys are going to race, no matter what you do. When he got away from school and away from the house, racing was John's destiny. There was value in racing, because it led to other things.

Steele apprehensively approached the defeated fighter. The craft had the shape of a shark. As Steele prodded inside the alien cockpit with his K-Bar, poking through the melted bubble canopy for any sign of life, he noted the charred remains of the two aliens. They had uniforms, just like us. They had rank insignia, just like us. He wondered if this crew had responded automatically or if they were a detachment operating independently from the main arm. That was a scary thought. There just wasn't enough intelligence in this war. We hadn't even figured out how they fly these contraptions yet.

This ship's carcass was done. Steele moved on to the second of three. Caution guided the wary captain as he sought foothold in the darkness. The next beast had spiraled into the pavement nose first. No likely survivors in this one either.

How do you measure the reward in a war like this, Steele wondered, not that he was taking the aliens' side. Where's the motivation? But damn – you put a couple million miles on the car you expect to get something out of it. Maybe a babe. Especially if you can find a spectacular beach. And planet Earth had some great beaches...

John was that way. He was single-minded on "gettin' some." His view of the world was built around a '58 Chevy with a high-performance engine. In John's case it was girls and his car. Because John believed his car was the ticket to the right girls, it had to perform. There it was... a 348 bored 40 over, with trips – triple two-barrel carburetors. Hard to do 20 years ago, keeping up with a 50-year-old car. To John, the only thing 'verbs' translated to was top quality performance. Action verbs. Doing things. And performance translated to only two things. Gettin' some, and going fast.

After a perfunctory inspection, Steele moved on to the third wrecked bird. This machine had skidded in on its belly. Like coming in to the carrier on bingo fuel and missing the 4-wire, hoping for the brakes. Didn't look like there was any joy in number three either. Even though Steele had his guard up, he kept thinking about his brother John taking chances. That eerie feeling of Dad always watching in the past tense meant something unhealthy was lurking not far off in the present tense. Dad helping John learn to race signaled that he had probably raced when he was our age, although he never mentioned it. He was watching to coach. Mentor. If there were aliens around the corner, they probably weren't interested in coaching anyone. He shrugged off the wisdom not to, and temporarily divided his attention between this incapacitated warship and a glance over his left shoulder. He winced at the pain.

Nothing.

Here Steele had to step up on the wing root, the stubby pectoral fin, to probe around inside the alien cockpit. Another glance – over his right shoulder. Whispers of danger again suggested caution. There were always four ships in an alien section. It was a characteristic of their TTPs – tactics, techniques and procedures.

Nothing.

This fighter done, Steele jumped down squarely on his heels, then regretted it. His left shoulder screamed out, "STOP!" and Steele did. With his immediate work done, he reached into a zippered pocket and pulled out a fresh battle dressing, unwrapped it, and stuffed the bundle between his shoulder and his flight suit – the zoom bag – to sop up the coagulating blood. A good shot or two of Wild Turkey would go great right now. Before chow or anything to drink, he had to get comm and see who was up on the net. With hours yet to daylight, Steele set off in the direction he had launched from...what, a day ago? Was the fighter base even there? It was certain none of the carriers were aloft anymore.

Steele winced as he hefted the laser and strode off in the general direction of South, out of what used to be a nondescript industrial area of some sort, now almost unrecognizable, and into a sparsely wooded countryside with a mostly pancake landscape. He consciously avoided putting himself on the occasional skyline, anxiously aware the intruders would be scanning for his infrared signature. On the scale of opportunities, he might find Starboard Delta on the radio and call in his own med-evac. Next down the list, if search and rescue didn't reach him, he could end up walking all the way to the rear. That didn't sound like fun but was preferable to the bottom of the options – running into the boogie man. The intruders. Now that just wouldn't be fair.

On the move, Steele opened his handheld and started the passive scanner looking at the 5,000 or so frequencies in which he might find a friendly signal. If a voice freq opened he might be able to get a passive fix. Once he transmitted in voice or data however, a new clock would start. He'd have to assume the bad guys would copy his transmission and triangulate from just about anywhere this side of the moon. Any free ride home for Steele would have to be closer or at least faster than intruder gunships.

With the handheld set on scan, Steele tapped the display and selected GPS to get a position update, then oriented on the constellation Orion, turned to his right, and continued his trek. Even on a crystal night in July there weren't any brilliant constellations in the southern sky. But navigation to Corpus Christi seemed natural enough without solid astronomy or digital support. He'd flown that approach hundreds of times.

Reoriented, and with a hundred miles to trek, Steele folded the display closed with his free hand, slipped the device into a zippered flight suit pocket, then positioned the wireless receiver in his ear. No sooner done, the receiver crackled. In a second, he retrieved the handheld and verified a hit in the 6 gigahertz range. Couldn't be comm, he thought. Must be a radar, but we haven't heard the intruders using anything we'd recognize as radar. It's all passive infrared.

Steele froze. First he sensed it. Then he felt it. He refused to believe it until he saw it.

"Geez, it's about time you guys," Steele said to the night wind as the lone Marine Corps Mach M fighter came into focus to the southwest. As the hovering fighter closed on his position at 8-10 knots, about 30 meters above tree-top level and dropping, Steele tapped the display on his handheld to call up the 4-digit transponder code and prepare to ping his ride home. "Thanks for taking the initiative, guys," he thought. "But then, you probably don't know I'm here...yet."

Steele's spirits lifted. The low-slow profile could mean they were on SAR – search and rescue – or it could mean they were approaching the battle space with caution, wary of intruders. But there should be at least two fighters in this section. The more he thought about it, something wasn't right. Someone is out on his own....Not our tactics.

Steele's mind flashed back to old Corps doctrine. This was an organization, more than 250 years old that had survived by, among other things, building a spirit of initiative and leadership into even the youngest, most junior Marines, and the reliance by middle and senior leaders on a concept called delegation. How did that paragraph go? – The page was etched into his memory: "...the Corps' style of warfare requires intelligent leaders with a penchant for boldness and initiative down to the lowest levels. Boldness is an essential moral trait in a leader, for it generates combat power beyond the physical means at hand. Initiative, the willingness to act on one's own judgment, is a prerequisite for boldness. These traits carried to excess can lead to rashness, but we must realize that errors by junior leaders stemming from over-boldness are a necessary part of learning. We must deal with such errors leniently; there must be no zero defects mentality."[vi] It was a system that worked, and worked well for generations. Recruit deaths at the Marine Corps Recruit Training Depots in the 1950's and '70's led to crushing scrutiny from Congress, the media and the American public. The Marine Corps is a public institution, and if we're going to send you our sons and daughters, you damn well better take care of them.

The Marine Corps indeed had problems to clean up, and it wasn't merely the harsh treatment of recruits. The 1956 court-martial determined in part that the six recruit deaths were a symptom of a larger problem – overworked and under-appreciated drill instructors. More drill instructors were added to each training unit; more supervision by officers was added to complement the change; and the body of regulations expanded exponentially. Recruit training became a system. Yet superseding volumes of official doctrine and regulations about what time recruits should rise, when they should be allowed to read a newspaper, how often they should be allowed to make head calls, brush their teeth and hundreds of other details, the essence of training Marines still boils down to Quality, an ethic that drill instructors are expected to live by. The violation of any of hundreds of specific regulations can be tested against a simple creed, and Steele knew it well:

These recruits are entrusted to my care. I will train them to the best of my ability. I will develop them into smartly disciplined, physically fit, basically trained Marines, thoroughly indoctrinated in love of the Corps and Country. I will demand of them, and demonstrate by my own personal example, the highest standards of personal conduct, morality, and professional skill.

With the code inserted, he prepared to send the burst message to his fellow pilot, then hesitated. Again he sensed a presence. Oh shit. Sure enough, he twisted around, and hovering just above the tree line one or two clicks to the north was a lone intruder, closing on his position at about 10 knots. "There you are, number four. We're gonna have a fur ball and neither one of these two cowboys knows I'm here." Thoughts raced. "If I signal, it should distract the goof in the intruder ship. That's a good. But if my guys read me right, know there's a soul on the ground, and are aware of the intruders, they may think they have to make a choice. That's a bad. If I can get a clear shot through the trees, I could take the alien bastard out of the equation. I've got 10 minutes..."

Six: Denial

8:40 a.m. Saturday, November 24, 2001
Mississippi Welcome Center
Interstate 10, two miles east of Louisiana

I've got 10 minutes to make a head call. Waiting on the porta-potties before the Houston Marathon is insane...worse than women having to wait for the bathroom at an Astros baseball game. Here at the rest area, in sight of Interstate 10, there were two men's heads, two women's and two porta-potties. Hardly any wait at all at this marathon venue.

The old salt and his wife are standing with another elderly couple near the sign-in table, talking about the course. (Don't let that 'senior citizen' or 'elderly' moniker fool you, though. I know guys in their 60s running 5k races under 17 minutes.) According to the flyer, we were supposed to run several miles alongside idyllic Stennis Space Center, just north of Interstate 10. Barely two months after the 9/11 terror attacks in New York, D.C. and Pennsylvania, NASA exercised caution and asked race organizers to change the route, eliminating the space center from the venue. The new course would be almost a straight line, 11 miles southeast along route 607 toward Waveland, away from Stennis, then 11 miles back to the rest area, then under and past Interstate 10 for two miles, then back to the finish at the rest area.

I stopped by for morning greetings, then jogged off for my fourth visit to the men's room in thirty minutes. It's been the same since high school track – a combination of nervous anticipation and Gatorade. The lines aren't too long and I start wondering how many people are signed up for this event. I hadn't considered it until now. My only experience in a marathon was 10 months earlier in Houston, where 8,000 to 10,000 people show up for the marathon, a half marathon and a 5K. Each runner pins a number, a bib, to his or her shirt or shorts, with races of different distances assigned numbers in different colors. I notice different-colored numbers here at the rest area too. In Houston it takes planning and patience to make head calls in time for the race.

Relieved, I trotted off to warm up with a jog around the rest area – maybe half a mile. There's a parking area south of the main building, but it's not even full. Can't be more than a few hundred people here this morning. Maybe I'll be able to take home some hardware – a medal for placing in my age group – back to Houston to show my Enron Running Club buddies.

Running lady has joined the veteran and his wife by the time I get back. They're discussing the weather. A hostess in the rest area says there is a chance of rain. It was already overcast, and the breeze had picked up. Where was my sunny, placid Mississippi coastline? My visually stimulating nature trail through beautiful Stennis Space Center? It wasn't the race organizers' fault, but we would be running an up-and-back course with no protection from the weather. Whoever had built Highway 607 had cleared the southern coastal pines in a swath wide enough to lay down two 10-lane, Texas-size interstate highways side by side. Nothing but trees and power lines. Snorezzzzzzzzz. In Houston, the course is urban and even the limping, straggling runners don't have time to get bored. Nearly half a million people line the course each year, many with hand-lettered signs, some with hard candy, some with orange slices, some with beer, all with encouragement. Here, the few hundred spectators, clustered at the finish line, would almost match the number of runners.

8:50

A rented loudspeaker on a pole announces: "Runners! It's time to get to the starting line. You know the drill: 5-minute pacers up front, then 6-minute, 7, 8, 9 and so on."

Several of us laugh. "There's a 5-minute miler in this crowd? A world-class runner? I asked someone near me. (There are no strangers at the starting line.)

"Maybe not world class, but national class for sure – someone who paces at 5-something. Five minutes a mile is a 2:10 marathon. They send invitations to runners around the country. Someone up there," he says, pointing toward the actual starting line, "will break 2:30... maybe 2:20."

I'll be glad to break 4 hours. Jim, my Enron Running Club buddy, always asks, "What are your marks? I'll be delighted with...I'll be happy with...I'll be satisfied with..."

Today I'm going to run a smarter race. Pace myself. Miss Lisa, my running buddy from days working at NASA in Houston, told me about the Power Bars and Ibuprofen. I've got both. I'm full of carbs; my shoes have only 50 miles on them; not too far gone and not too new. I feel great. I'll be delighted with 3:25 – my age group's qualifying time for the Boston Marathon. I'll be satisfied if I break 4 hours. My first race was 4:10, so that seems realistic. I guess that puts my 'happy with' mark somewhere around 3:45 – 3:50.

9:00

"Runners! Take your marks!"

"Bang!"

In retrospect, the major differences between that start and the Monday exodus at enron nine days later were that the enron employees were carrying books, papers, family photographs and coffee cups, and enron's morbid, slo-mo race to the parking garage had more media. Oh – and in Houston, there were around 4500 people getting screwed and in Mississippi on this Saturday after Thanksgiving, there were only a few hundred runners. But the pain in Mississippi was voluntary.

The first half-mile to mile at the start of most marathons, runners in the back of the pack spend more time moving up and down, jogging in place, than going forward. In Houston, even if you line up with the 4-hour runners a hundred yards from the start – the 9-minute-per-mile pace – you can walk all the way to the starting line and it takes a mile or two more after that before the gaggle of runners starts to thin out.

No one spoke. The runners all had something in common, but there was nothing to talk about. Talking takes energy. Oxygen. The enroners – ex-enroners – all had something in common too, but there was nothing to talk about. Our energy company, the darling of the Fortune 50, would suck out our own life's energy through the proxy of vice presidents and directors, in conference rooms all over the building, in meetings small and large, between 9 a.m. and noon: "Leave the building by one o'clock; take all your personal possessions. Do not re-enter the building. You'll be contacted."

9:07:30

One mile. Seven and a half minutes. Too fast. Can't keep this up. I need to slow down to a 7:45 pace. When I was 16, 18, even 25 or 30, I'd start right at the front and do my best to stay there. A 4:20 mile at the end of high school. Or was it 4:30? A 16:10 three-mile at the end of Marine Corps boot camp. But that was another, younger, invincible me a long time ago.

9:15:15

Two miles. I can barely make out the lead runner. If he's turning a 5:30 pace, he's covered nearly three miles by now. I've cut my rate slightly, but not the length of my stride. Don't know how it works, but after 35 years of running I can settle into a stride at a specific pace, like six and a half minutes, or seven, or eight minutes per mile, and hold it. The pace depends on whether I'm training or racing, and of course – the distance. Two weeks earlier I had finished a 20K in ninety minutes – close to a 7:30 pace. I was determined to hang on to 7:45 today as long as I could.

9:22:58

Three miles. Starting to feel comfortable. Muscles are warmed up. Joints are working fine. I settle into a dream state and let my body do the work. Calories are loaded and my legs are on autopilot. Three and a half to four hours is plenty of time to write a book in your head, plan a vacation, sail to St. Thomas or build a house.

One by one I'm passing runners who started too fast and are already feeling it. As I'm closing in on mile four, I can count 15 to 20 runners ahead of me, not counting that national class rabbit who scorched the highway when he took off. Fifteen to twenty people? I get excited. That means there are a couple of hundred behind me. Thousands finished ahead of me in Houston, and I would have been happy to come in in the top hundred in my age group. All of the runners ahead of me are men except two. It looks like one of the women is in a husband-wife team running side-by-side. I wouldn't catch them until the last four or five miles. They appeared to be in their early 20s.

By the time we had started, I'd found out there were close to 300 registered for the marathon and another couple of hundred running the half and a 5K. I was only concentrating on male marathoners between 45 and 49. In our age group, if you're running competitively and trying to catch up to and pass guys in the same age group...look for those bald crowns and silver hair.

Laugh.

I do.

9:30:44

Four miles. I'm on cruise control. Light breeze from the south, but the sky looks threatening. I'm not going to worry about coming storms. My next paycheck from enron will be the break-even point following my divorce in the summer of 2000. After we split up the 401k from my previous employer to pay off joint bills and sold the house near Johnson Space Center, I contracted to build my own home, starting in January, 2001. I would finally be in the position to pay off the last of the credit cards – one each month for six months. All that would remain would be a car payment and a house payment, utilities, phone, groceries and cable. With a comfortable salary from Enron and a comparatively small pension for my 22 years on active duty in the Marine Corps, I was starting to enjoy this bachelor life.

9:38:30

Five miles. I couldn't decide if I was going to buy a look-at-me yellow Porsche or that magnetic red Vette that came out in the first C-5 body a few years ago.

Then I couldn't decide if I wanted a hard top or a convertible. Should I get a sailboat that's big enough to live on, or a day sailer that's just big enough to overnight on? No mid-life crisis...just rewarding myself for raising three kids.

My mind wandered back to the house. I had moved in two weeks after tropical storm Allison dumped on Houston. Flood management experts in my area of Harris County did a great job, and my new subdivision was spared the flooding that ruined homes, cars and businesses in other locations around the city.

This time, the house was mine. And, whereas my ex-has a great eye for decorating, her tastes are too formal and traditional for me. Maybe that's one of the places we didn't connect. I planned to do all of the decorating myself. Why pay someone to paint or install hardware for draperies if you can do it yourself?

9:46:12

In five months, I had managed to paint all of the main walls downstairs and the hallways and common areas upstairs. No builder-grade off-white for me. I went with 'Eldorado Tan.' I painted the formal dining room scarlet and put all my 'me' stuff on the walls – college diplomas, plaques and photographs from days in the Marine Corps. The room rarely gets used, so it's less like a 'me' room because it's not on display. My daughter's room took a little more effort. She wanted a Wizard of Oz theme in a pink and purple bedroom, with a loft bed. So, I painted bands of "bubble gum," "grape" and white on three walls, and on the long wall painted a floor-to-ceiling rainbow, a field of poppies, and hand painted

Dorothy, the Tin Man, Scarecrow and Lion strolling down the yellow brick road.

9:54:02

Seven miles. I lost five seconds. I sprinted for about 15 seconds to catch up to one of the silver-haired runners ahead of me, then realized when I glanced sideways that this fellow was at least one if not two age groups senior to me. I complimented him on his endurance. He returned the kindness before we both fell silent.

He reminded me of one of the few people over 50 that I knew at enron. At my previous employer, contracting at Johnson Space Center, I felt like a kid in my mid-40s. At enron, I felt like an octogenarian. My department's vice president was perhaps in his mid 30s. I had asked him once or twice after Jeff Skilling left if there was any need to start looking for another job. Following Skilling's departure and enron's announcement of a billion dollars in losses and accounting errors, the stock had sunk to a third of the value posted when I joined the company a year earlier.

"No," my boss replied. "The best thing we can do is close contracts and contribute to the financial health of the company. The only thing wrong is the investors' perceptions." My boss was a smart guy. He was telling us what his leaders were telling him. And he apparently believed them.

My department was responsible for throwing probabilistic models over the wall to the deal-makers. My colleagues created tools that statistically predicted the revenue a particular deal would generate, given the energy savings enron could muster, the size of the customer's facilities, the age and condition of their energy-using capital assets – heating and air conditioning, boilers and steam systems, refrigeration, air compressors and so on – and a host of other factors including enron's discounted price for energy, based on oil or natural gas futures, reduced to mathematical values plugged into a Monte Carlo simulation. My job was to create training in these tools and on the audit processes for energy savings in categories of equipment. I pulled my own energy – a peanut butter Power Bar – out of my waist band, unwrapped it on the run and stuffed it into the energy-using asset – me, then grabbed water at the water station, and downed 1000 milligrams of Ibuprofen for dessert.

10:01:40

Eight miles. Nearly one-third done. On pace. Feeling fine. Weather's holding.

As September, October and November melted away, and enron's stock value with them, I started taking on this probabilistic outlook in terms of my eventual lay-off. enron was home to about 20,000 people, around half of them in Houston as far as I knew. How bad could it be? A couple of hundred people at the most?

My boss – that young VP – told our department during weekly staff meetings that our team's contribution to enron energy services (EES) was critical, even up to two weeks ago. All the lunches were still catered. We had taco soup, or pizzas. We had salads, soft drinks. Some people in the department flew back and forth from homes in California, Colorado or Illinois weekly, at enron expense. But the week before Thanksgiving was a different story. Talk of lay-offs. Massive layoffs.

I spotted a four-wheel-drive Ford pickup in a driveway along the course. The truck seemed strangely divorced from its chassis and huge tires, separated by a lift kit. In the rear window, a sticker: "I ain't skeered."

10:09:30

Nine miles. Up ahead I see the lead runner, headed toward me and back to the finish. That means he's about 30 minutes and four miles ahead of me at the nine-mile mark. It doesn't matter. We have different goals.

10:17:14

Six more runners are headed the opposite direction;

six other runners are between me and the 11-mile turn-around. I'm still on pace.

enron and I had different goals too. Actually, enron's newly discovered reality differed from the goals of about 4500 employees that December 3rd. Case by case, as allegations become mature investigations and ultimately indictments, the twin, mirrored enron towers assume the identities of those accused or those copping a plea, like Andy Fastow and Michael Kopper.

I didn't want the freedom to search for a new job. I didn't want the freedom to write my own ticket, start my own business. I knew freedom was even more valuable when you have to work your tail off to keep it, and I remembered that saying allegedly scrawled on the helmet of some Marine in Vietnam a few short years before my time: "For those who fight for it, Freedom has a meaning the protected will never know." I didn't want the freedom to learn software I had always wanted to learn. I didn't want the freedom to write and publish children's stories. I didn't want the freedom to get up when I wanted, shave when I wanted, create a web site, create two web sites, paint murals all over my house, go for 12-mile runs every day on my terms. I wouldn't have the money to get started on this life of freedom I had always talked about – unless enron made good on its published severance package. When the time came, I was in denial. I was dead certain I'd have a job in a week.

10:25:04

Eleven miles. Turn-around. Wind, about 10 knots, out of the northwest. Where the heck did that come from? I must not have noticed it at my back. I caught one guy, maybe 40, and someone who was probably in my age group passed me at the turn. Net zero. The only thing at the turn-around besides the guy with a walkie-talkie and a clock was a porta-potty. Didn't need it. Where were the Three Elvises from Houston? The Dolly Parton Twins? The Belly Dancers? The Tuba Band? Where were the radio stations playing Queen, Aerosmith and Mexican polka music? This Mississippi race was a well-put-together event, but a guy could go to sleep out here.

Years after Saigon fell, still an enlisted Marine, I would go around my Army lieutenant colonel boss to get orders for a three-month assignment with the Joint Public Affairs Bureau in Beirut, Lebanon. I was a journalist. I wanted this assignment for the adventure of it. I was still in my 20s. My boss got a hold of the orders when they came in, before I did, and called me into his office to chew on me. I stretched the limits of the officer-enlisted relationship as far as I thought I could and protested, "Colonel, you had your chance. You were a 20-year-old warrant officer flying helicopters in Vietnam. You got to take the final exam and you passed. You're here. It's my chance, damn it. Sir."

He said he'd think about it. It was September 1983. The eventual compromise was to rearrange the journalism instructors' schedules so that I could have an open window for the assignment that would start in April, 1984 (a year after terrorists had bombed the U.S. Embassy in Beirut, killing 63, including 17 Americans). Then on October 23, 1983, terrorists drove a truck packed with explosives into the building housing U.S. forces at the airport, killing 241 Marines, soldiers and sailors. The resulting outcry from Congress and the American public caused an about-face in U.S. policy, and by April 1984, there were few Marines left in Lebanon. Marine infantry units had been redeployed and the remaining public affairs staff from previous months, under the leadership of Captain Dale Dye, stretched their assignment to cover clean-up operations. I stayed in Indiana.

10:33

Twelve miles. I lost 20 seconds. I started doing mental calculations on the impact that would have on my overall time. Less than two seconds per mile for the first twelve. Eight minutes per mile for the remaining 14 miles would still put me in reach of the Boston qualifying time. I looked down the highway. Single runners and packs of three, five and more, headed for the turn, strung out seemingly all the way back to the start. Over their heads storm clouds were rolling in from the West. It didn't look pretty. I put my head down and fought for pavement.

Funny what you find along the highway...things you'd never notice in this drive-everywhere generation. Coins, keys, shoes, sunglasses. I found a wallet once while running, and tracked down the thankful owner. He said he must have left it on top of his car. Why would someone put a wallet on top of a car in the first place?

Coins on the road became dollars in my mind and I started doing some mental math on my financial reserves, just in case we did get laid off. I wasn't worried but the exercise helped pass the time. It didn't take long anyway, because I didn't really have financial reserves, just a couple lines of credit and two credit cards I could get cash out of. Besides – if I got pink-slipped, I'd be back to work in no time. Heck, I've got a bachelor's degree in English, a master's and a doctorate in education. I've got a great track record with Fortune 500 corporations. I'm employable. No sweat.

10:40

Thirteen. The knees are complaining, but I'm hanging in there under eight minutes a mile. Ahead I can see someone walking. Not walking toward me...one of the 12 ahead of me is walking. I shouldn't have looked. I shouldn't have let the thought get in my head. I told myself this would be a chance to pass one more person – probably my last. The front 20 or 30 runners were spaced pretty far apart at the halfway point.

10:48:20

Fourteen. The hips have joined the knees and now they're doing harmony. Grinding. Crunching. I passed that walker at the half-way marker, then he found new energy and strolled back up next to me, asking rhetorically, "Why the hell are we doing this?"

I just grinned. I was out of witticisms. I set my sights on passing the woman ahead of me, whether this guy ran along or not. The husband-wife team was slowing down, but were still at least a mile away. I pulled out a chocolate Power Bar and another 1000 milligrams of Ibuprofen.

The wind was picking up.

I felt the first raindrops.

I was running into a storm and I was losing seconds nearly as fast as enron stock was losing pennies. Stock that was once trading at more than $80 a share was now around $10.

10:56:39

So I never made it to Beirut... probably a good thing. I didn't really want to leave the journalism school. It had been the best duty station in my career up to that point. And in reflection, it probably was one of the best overall. My personal affairs were in good shape and I had great relationships with my sons – both under 10. I was working on my doctorate at Ball State University, and although the two-hour round trip four nights a week was exhausting, the opportunity to finish a terminal degree while in the military is rare. Everything was working.

11:05:10

Sixteen. Rain. Headwind. I made the decision to walk for a while at the next mile marker. Everything wasn't working the way it was supposed to. My knees and hips were screaming at me.

Nearing the end of doctoral studies, I was well on the way to getting accepted for a commission in the Navy. I headed to Naval Aviation Officer Candidate School in Pensacola, Florida. The boys went to live with my folks in Minnesota for a few months, and our mail continued to go to a black hole in Indiana until we got things sorted out.

11:14:14

Seventeen.

That hundred-yard walk turned into two hundred yards and a 9-minute mile.

11:25

I'll just walk, fast, from the start of this guard rail to the end.

I'll just walk a little farther.

A few more steps, then I'll start running again.

The next tree.

No, the next one.

A few more...

11:37:07

The two years in Korea turned out to be almost as good as the two and a half in Indiana. A much different mission – working in Naval Intelligence – and it would set me up for the remainder of my career. The parallel was lots of research and lots of writing.

11:49

Twenty.

I'm walking almost half of each mile. My knees haven't felt this good since that 20-mile hike back in boot camp, with a 60-pound pack, steel helmet and M-14 rifle. I'm not going to think about it. I'm not going to think about it. I'm not going to think about it. I'm going to think about my grinding hip joints instead. And whether the rain will wash the salt off my body.

I read recently about a sailor found off the East Coast of the United States, adrift for nearly four months. He survived by collecting rain and catching fish. Tough old salt. Determined. Ahead I can see Interstate 10 and the underpass for the local highway, and I think about the invisible community of people in Houston who stand at major intersections in their mismatched shoes, tattered clothes, missing teeth, holding signs that read, "Praise the Lord," and "Four Children. Jobless. Anything You can Give Helps," and "Will Work for Food." Some of these people are missing limbs. Who's the survivor – the guy who survived enron's performance appraisals, made million-dollar bonuses and parks his silver Porsche in the enron parking garage, or the guy under the highway overpass? Sure, some of the "homeless" aren't homeless; they're alcoholics and drugs addicts looking for a free ride. Some might even rake in a respectable wage panhandling. But there are indigent homeless, and they are hungry, and they are survivors. They figure it out one day at a time, and they're my heroes.

Six miles and 385 yards to go.

12:00:05

Twenty one miles in three hours. Boston is gone for next year, unless I can figure out what I'm doing wrong in time to make up the difference in Houston in January.

I had 19 years combined in the Marine Corps-Navy-Marine Corps by the time the ex- left, and she was the closest I had come to combat. Next closest was a six-month "West-Pac," or tour of duty onboard the USS NIMITZ, keeping an eye on North Korea during the 1988 Olympics, and monitoring reflagging operations at the straits of Hormuz during the Iran-Iraq oil war. Nothing was predictable. Not the Iraqis; not the Iranians; not the Pakistanis; not the Russians. At sea, we had highs and lows – the adrenaline rush of buzzing Vladivostok's perceived airspace on a Monday morning, 200 miles off the coast, when they apparently had no idea we were in the Sea of Japan, and the 18 Soviet Bear and Badger bombers running practice bombing runs on the NIMITZ battle group the next morning to say, "Spacibo," or "Thank You." I'd bet some Soviet wing commander lost his job over that.

Our low: the NIMITZ crew fought a fire on the flight deck in the middle of the night, in the middle of the Indian Ocean. It was 13 years and a day before this race. We lost three crew members and half a dozen aircraft.

As I start running again, a younger runner passes, slowly. He caught up while I was walking. It doesn't matter.

Never look back.

12:11:30

Twenty two. I want this thing to be over. I'm wet. I hurt. I can't remember any good jokes. The same dumb song keeps going through my head...something from the 5th Dimension, from the 1960s. I catch the husband and wife, but two other runners pass me. At least one of them is surely in my age group and determined to steal my medal.

12:23:33

Twenty Three. I'm walking too much. I don't care. I just want to hang on to four hours if I can. My stomach is growling. I laugh. I want a steak. A 2-pound, 2-inch thick, Ruth's Chris Steakhouse steak, with soy sauce on the side. Broccoli spears. Beer. Crunchy stuff...radishes. Celery. And I want cheesecake for dessert, and shrimp cocktail. And another beer.

I laughed in survival training in the Navy too. My team had one cup of rice for 10 officer candidates – for four days. We scoured our training area in the Hurlburt Field, Florida, panhandle for prickly pear cactus and with it made 'potato chips.' We found palmetto shoots, caught a snake and turned it in to the instructors for a cup of oil to cook the cactus, palmetto and rice. We each had one canteen of water for the four days. The exercise is supervised by trained Navy hospital corpsmen – medics – who know well enough that the lack of food for four days isn't going to damage anyone. None of this was funny until the final day. We were reaching natural highs, living off endorphins.

One of the enlisted Navy instructors thought he would be helpful and catch us a squirrel. The squirrel didn't want to be caught. The instructor, a second-class petty officer, would chase the squirrel until it ran up a tree. Then he would chop down the small tree with his machete, which took about 15 minutes. As the tree was falling, the squirrel would jump from tree top to tree top, and the petty officer would start chopping down the next tree. We watched five or six small trees fall. No squirrels. My team, 10 candidate officers due to be commissioned in a week, was entertained. The petty officer was not one to give up. We never did get any squirrel meat...just a lot of firewood for the next class, due to arrive the following Monday. The Marine drill instructors had watched the circus from their camp, 50 or 60 yards off through the woods. One of them finally rescued the petty officer, calling him over to their campfire.

12:36

Twenty four. The second turn around.

I'm glad this is not on videotape for the evening news back in Houston. I'm sure by now my running looks like the race to the dining room in an assisted living retirement center.

Two miles to go. I can't see the finish, but I know it's around the corner. About 3500 steps. Mentally I'm invigorated and search for the strength to get my legs moving. They're stiff and uncooperative. I can hear Gunnery Sergeant Holtry at Naval Aviation OCS in Pensacola, "Ladies, you can do this with your eyes closed, standing on your head. It's only 14 weeks. Do what you're supposed to do; don't do what you're not supposed to do. How hard can it be?"

I think most Marines, and those Navy officers who have had the pleasure, would agree that many Marine Corps drill instructors should be awarded honorary PhD's in psychology.

Holtry was my introduction to the Navy. I can only assume it was a little bizarre for the 10 or 12 Marine drill instructors at Pensacola at the time to find an officer candidate in their midst who had been a Marine staff sergeant the week before. Gunnery Sergeant Holtry and I didn't exactly go out for chicken and beer after work every afternoon to discuss it. I had heard later that he did not want me to become the class leader; he didn't want to compete with me for the class' attention.

The Marine captain who owned our class persuaded him to let the class take its own course. I was voted in as the class leader, and the drill instructors – even the drill instructors from other classes – had a toy. I did more pushups in 14 weeks than steps I took in a marathon. I certainly did more pushups in Navy OCS than I ever did in Marine boot camp. The truth was spelled out on a plaque behind the chief drill instructor's desk: "Adversity Tempers Steel."

The Navy and I were good to each other for six years. It was a good run, but the play was over when I couldn't get the Navy to send me to Desert Shield or Desert Storm in 1990-'91, so I applied for an inter-service transfer back to the Marine Corps. They'd send me. That's what I had originally enlisted for so many years earlier.

12:48

Twenty five miles.

Four hours ago I was accelerating toward the speed of light. Therefore my mass must have increased...so THAT's why I'm now moving at the speed of heavy. I'm a slug. I'm old. I hate this crap. I am NEVER doing this again.

Would you like to ride...in my beautiful balloon?

I'm thinking the old fart a hundred yards in front of me is too old to be in my age group so I don't care. I don't care about much right now. I don't care if I smell bad. I don't care if I hallucinate.

We can ride among the stars together, you and I....

By the time my paperwork got through Navy channels and was approved by the Marine Corps, Desert Storm was over. What the heck?! Six Months? I got to the 2nd Marine Aircraft Wing at Cherry Point, North Carolina, in June, 1991. Entire squadrons had already been sent back from Saudi Arabia and Kuwait, and from ships in theater, home on leave.

1 p.m.

Twenty six miles. I'm weightless and numb. Four hours and I'm at the door. The finish line...

1:01:48

There's denial, and then there's clueless.

How could anything go wrong? I finished 11th in a marathon! I was invincible once again. It didn't matter that there were only a few hundred people in the race. It didn't even matter that I wasn't taking home a medal, finishing 'out of the hardware' at 4th in the 45-49 age group. People around me, people at the finish line, people younger than me were awed by a 4-hour performance. They obviously had never seen people my age do it an hour and a half faster. An HOUR and a HALF!

MORE than an hour and a half faster.

Today I didn't care. I was done. I found my share of Mississippi barbecue sausage, black beans and rice, a Bud Lite, bananas, bagels and orange slices. Great diet, eh? Truth is, by the time I got back to Houston, I felt great. A little stiff in the knees and hips, but great overall. I joined the old Marine's wife at the finish line and waved him in, some minutes past 4 hours - twenty. The running lady from New England had admitted the night before that she shouldn't be running, a week before some unspoken surgery. Still, she finished around four hours-thirty, and we waved her in too.

Before we all parted company, they wished me well with Enron.

Marathon registration - $40. Hotel in Waveland, Mississippi - $69. New running shoes – $50. Carbo loading party – $10.50 plus gratuity. Four Power Bars – $10 plus tax.

Gas for the old Ford truck – $63. Finishing 11th in a marathon – well, you know how the commercial went.

I climbed into my red Ford truck, turned the key, backed out of the parking space, and headed off into the sunset to go face what I had been running from.

Seven: First Principle Two –
Evolutionary Ethics and
The 2nd Law of Organizational Thermodynamics

Understanding enron's fall, Pirsig's Quality can send us to Ethics or Leadership – the human side of the business – or off into the structure of the organization. Captain Steele whispers 'ethics and leadership,' but I sense that developing a context for leaders to work in will help things run more smoothly.

There's a system to this running thing. Jim offered a short seminar at one of the monthly Enron Running Club lunches, about *training heavy* and *racing light*. If you watch a marathon from a single vantage point, you can see a seemingly endless continuum of running strategies. Some runners pin their bibs – their race numbers – to their shorts and wear nothing but shorts, socks and shoes, even when the temperature is in the low 40s at start time. Others turn out in racing tights, plastic bags or sweat suits, then strap on bottles of water, or liquid carbohydrates like Gu, Power Gel or Carb Boom. So we did the math on the extra weight. This applies to a half pound of water or gel as much as to 4 ounces extra per shoe: A marathon, 26 miles and 385 yards, is 138,435 feet. If you carry an extra half-pound that distance it's roughly like forcing your body to perform an extra 69,217.5 foot-pounds of work (assuming you lift your feet 6 inches on each step. The math is "rough"...). Converting foot-pounds to Newton-meters, we could calculate the horsepower required to perform the work, and the calories necessary to generate that horsepower. The results were startling. Made me want to leave the gel behind *and* go on a diet.

Sometimes strategies like this backfire. Back in high school, some of my fellow varsity wrestlers would struggle to drop enough weight to qualify in a lower weight class. Otherwise healthy 155-pounders were dropping to 145; 145-pounders were going to 138. Some dropped two weight classes, and often this was at the secret or not-so-secret urging of the wrestling coach. But if the guys on other high school teams were doing the same thing – where was the advantage? We would just be watching two 145-pounders from different schools competing for the medal at 138 or even 132 pounds, but in a weakened state from unnecessary dieting. I fought the trend. At 159 pounds, I could easily cut 4-5 pounds and wrestle at 155, but usually wrestled on varsity in the 167 or even 180-pound class. I had a good string of wins and had steak, eggs and potatoes for breakfast on the day of a tournament. I liked my system better.

Running, wrestling, writing, music, painting or teaching – all of these had quality for me in the Pirsigesque sense of Quality, and they all seemed to have a system of rules, which Pirsig seemed opposed to. Music is a perfect example. At its core, music has both an objective side (the physics of sound and the mathematical relationships between notes and rests) and a subjective side (the perception of *art* and the emotional response music generates). At the level of "Quality is just what you like," Pirsig's argument holds true, which explains why the world has more than one song, more than one kind of instrument. You may like classical; I like rock 'n' roll.

But now we get to the question of how that music is created. I spent years creating plastic imitations, following the rules. I started in the band in 5th grade, played trombone for 2 years, then tuba through junior high and high school. I played music other people had written. After high school, I played an audition tape to enter the Marine field bands, skillfully reproducing the scales and arpeggios in the prescribed book. After Marine Corps boot camp, I studied music theory in greater depth at the Armed Forces School of Music in Norfolk, VA. For the next two years I played tuba, on the Marines' Hymn, the Star Spangled Banner, The Stars and Stripes Forever, the Colonel Bogey March (at the 2nd and 3rd Marine Division bands) and countless other well-worn martial tunes over and over and over and over, which was part of the reason I eventually left the band. Enough was enough.

Music is about innovation. Check with the Beatles, Styx, Billy Joel, Elton John, The Rolling Stones, the Beach

Boys, Jimmy Buffet. Audiences want something new, something *innovative* and new. I always had the freedom Pirsig spoke of, to innovate and create something different, something unique. But the reality was, if I were to check the market there would be few people who would identify a preconscious awareness for the possibility of Quality to exist in a tuba serenade. Jethro Tull got away with a flute in rock 'n' roll, but he also had a band and they could sing.

I would later be told, entering the multi-media field of Marine Corps public relations, that I had a face made for radio and a voice made for print. How many rock 'n' roll tuba bands have we seen since the 50's?

But what if Pirsig had been a music teacher instead of an English teacher? Would he object to teaching *any* rules? *Any* music theory? Would he avoid playing the classics and shy away from music appreciation? In individual lessons, would he *not* demonstrate how to place the hands on a piano, or an optional fingering for a high C on a trumpet? Or what if he had been teaching rhetoric and composition to 3rd or 4th grade writers? Pirsig never addresses this.

Quality doesn't give us the tools, principles or building blocks *with which to innovate.* If a cave man or an alien came upon a saxophone or a trombone – would it be useless, a weapon, or a musical instrument? So is Pirsig wrong after all? I'm not ready to recant. Pirsig's metaphysics seems defensible, but he never clearly states that you don't walk into a Quality, shopping for a Quality. You don't wake up in a Quality, having dreamed of a Quality. Yes – Quality just is. But until it causes something to be, or to happen or to be felt, those objects and subjects won't reflect the Quality from which they are supposed to emanate. Quality therefore must be descriptive of the events Pirsig writes about. Things and events are the lenses through which we perceive quality after we've started looking for it. Pirsig is so far just half right.

Each succeeding generation produces a few savants who, without benefit of formal instruction, sing beautifully, or compose, or just sit at the piano for the first time and play as if they had been playing for decades – with no instruction. For the rest of us, a little inspiration is required to get the interest going, at least a little competence and success is necessary to build confidence, and someone or something is necessary to show us the essential techniques or tools – before we can hope to move from externally imposed discipline to internal motivation or self-discipline. This holds in music, in writing, gymnastics or rebuilding engines.

I don't need "a Quality." I need a quality pickup truck. I need a quality relationship. I need a quality employer. A quality energy company.

If we take this not as a rebuttal but a footnote to Pirsig, then Pirsig's desire to have his students exercise their freedom to innovate plays right into enron's hand. That's how enron fooled Fortune Magazine and the rest of us – innovation. The fundamentals of how to start a business, how to form a corporation, were well established long before enron was born, even long before Ken Lay and Jeff Skilling were born. America's corporate models today reflect much of ancient Roman law on the concepts of property:

> Property rights belonged not only to natural but to corporate or juridical persons. The Roman law on corporations, in fact, is the foundation of medieval and modern corporate law. From it we retain the idea that what is done by the majority of the members of a corporation (in the Roman law, if two-thirds of the membership, a quorum, attending the meeting) was done as if it were by all the members and therefore by the corporation as a person....In the thirteenth century, canon lawyers advanced the theory that since only a natural person could have a soul and could be excommunicated, a juridical person or corporation was soulless and hence could not be punished. But the Roman idea persisted, and exists now, that while the corporation is not subject to punishment for a delict [offense against the law], the officers can be punished.[vii]

Not only did the early fathers of modern enron have more than 2000 years of legal canon upon which to base their innovations; even better, starting in 1985 the new CEO, Ken Lay, had a PhD in economics and Harvard Business School wizard Jeff Skilling as a side- kick. I would guess powerhouses like that had already been through the fundamentals, were already internally motivated and already felt the freedom to innovate. But still – isn't there a structure, a set of minimum standards that defines what a corporation is and how it operates? enron was registered as a corporation in the state of Oregon, an artifact of the natural gas pipeline history of the original companies that came together to form enron. But rather than explore the specifics of Oregon legal codes – or Texas or U.S. Federal laws relating to corporations – I want to get to the question of whether enron (or any other company) was doomed to fail. Wasn't there a general structure to guide enron? Something to prevent failure?

The chapter's title suggests business entropy, that enron, as a closed system, follows an analogous path to increasing chaos because that is the natural order of things. Of course, enron was not closed in the sense of a sealed mechanical system, and people in a corporate body do not follow the laws of physics. But enron presents a case for examining it with this metaphor through systems theory:

There was enron and not-enron, so we could see a system-environment boundary. (This gets a bit touchy however with the subsidiary and contractor workforce who got pushed aside when enron was forced to pay a symbolic severance package of $13,500 during 2002. Those employees who did enron work on proxy but were not enron employees were still fighting for a severance check two years after the bankruptcy.)

enron's inputs and outputs were legion, particularly when the company headed in the direction of selling derivatives. enron had process, goal-directedness, state, information and hierarchy. We can study it as a system. The Principia Cybernetica Web tells us that:

Systems theory was proposed in the 1940's by the

biologist Ludwig von Bertalanffy (General Systems Theory, 1968), and furthered by Ross Ashby (Introduction to Cybernetics, 1956). von Bertalanffy...emphasized that real systems are open to, and interact with, their environments, and that they can acquire qualitatively new properties through emergence, resulting in continual evolution....(Thus,) the same concepts and principles of organization underlie the different disciplines (physics, biology, technology, sociology, etc.), providing a basis for their unification. Systems concepts include: system-environment boundary, input, output, process, state, hierarchy, goal-directedness, and information.[viii]

So enron was a system. The system broke. Why? Go back to the arguments in Pirsig and ask again if the perfect corporation is possible. Perfect in every sense of the word. A perfect human world in some people's imagination might have no war and no hunger, no disease, but necessarily also would have a manageable birthrate. Natural resources would be equitably (not equally) distributed. Imagine the perfect food, perfect car, perfect house, perfect spouse or perfect children.

Imagine the *perfect* corporation.

enron, like every other organization, was a replica, a living simulation. enron was a model; one possible variation on what a corporation should be or could be. We could finish the chapter by focusing on the word "should," and proclaim that "should" is a function of Pirsig's "Just what you like," as determined by the people who built the company. But because a corporation has inputs and outputs that significantly impact people and organizations (stock holders, vendors, banks, secondary and tertiary businesses that rely on the corporation for their existence) that are *not* internal parts of the corporation – the corporation has responsibilities that theoretically prohibit it from doing any darn thing they please.

So we are left with what enron *could* have been. Our

knowledge of what constitutes a business, a corporation, fits within a relatively small cache of doctrine. All states have some sort of mechanism for creating and identifying companies, from sole proprietorships to "C" corporations, from limited liability companies, partnerships, and "S" corporations, to permutations in between. The essence of understanding what we know about a given model resides in our knowledge of knowledge – epistemology, just as Pirsig was searching for the qualities of quality.

Before returning to the Principia Cybernetica Project (PCP), a word on what cybernetics means: cybernetics studies *organization, communication* and *control* in complex systems by focusing on circular *(feedback)* mechanisms.[ix] I will offer it as a given that enron was an organization with features of communication and control, complex systems and feedback mechanisms, thus one variation on a cybernetic system.

At the PC Project, we enter the domain of knowledge about knowledge (epistemology) much as Pirsig did, on a metaphysical level, relying on logic and abstracts. PCP offers the guiding philosophy of MST – the Metasystem Transition Theory. PCP notes that, "Its most salient concept is [of course] the Metasystem Transition (MST), the evolutionary process by which higher levels of complexity and control are generated."[x]

Paraphrasing the essential elements of MST, as I understand it, brings us directly back to Pirsig. If QUALITY *must* exist (definable or not) and there are both the preconscious awareness for pure QUALITY, and inferior approximations pretending to be quality, then the imitations (no matter how inferior) are subsets of or pretenders to the throne of QUALITY. The PCP explains Metasystem Transition: Consider a system S of any kind [perhaps a perceived perfect ENRON]. Suppose that there is a way to make some number of copies from it, possibly with variations. Suppose that these systems are united into a new system S' which has the systems of the S type as its subsystems, and includes also an additional mechanism which controls the behavior and production of the S-subsystems. Then we call S' [enron?] a metasystem with respect to S [ENRON?], and the creation of S' a metasystem transition. As a result of consecutive metasystem transitions [enron energy services (EES) (?), a wholly owned subsidiary of enron] a multilevel structure of control arises, which allows complicated forms of behavior.[xi](my parens)

In the context of enron, this says that there exists a process for creating corporations (systems). Every enron, shell, general motors, microsoft, wal-mart is a copy of the abstract system for creating corporations (corporate systems). enron becomes its own metasystem $(S^{1)})$, creating subsystems (enron energy services – a wholly owned subsidiary that I worked in, or enron partnerships with names like LJM_1, LJM_2, Chewco, Jedi) with multilevel structures of control – which allowed complicated forms of behavior. In a business climate with less government regulation, each corporation is comparatively free to evolve on its own. Corporations reinvent themselves all the time. Breakfast cereals sport new packaging; dishwashing liquids are new and improved; this year's car model is better than anything you've ever seen before. Superlatives abound. Pirsig would support this; in the absence of grades and artificial rules the actor is free to innovate. Freedom to innovate is the path to competition. Freedom is the path; QUALITY is both the starting line and the finish.

On closer inspection, however, the very *process* of system evolution, according to the PCP, is a process of trial and error. America's business histories are littered with road kill. Larger companies swallow smaller companies whole. Litigation and class-action law suits kill others. Lack of quality products and services, in the pedestrian sense of quality, has certainly killed off others. The market takes an active role in otherwise "natural" selection, and in a Darwinian sense, less (government) regulation and more competition will determine which corporations survive.

Our *knowledge* of what enron could have been is based on enron as a model. The PC Project further explains:

...knowledge is understood as consisting of models that allow the adaptation of a cybernetic system to its environment, by anticipation of possible perturbations. Models function as recursive generators of predictions about the world and the self. A model is necessarily simpler than the environment it represents, and this enables it to run faster than, i.e. anticipate, the processes in the environment. This allows the system to compensate perturbations before they have had the opportunity to damage the system. Models are not static reflections of the environment, but dynamic constructions achieved through trial-and-error by the individual, the species and/or the society. What models represent is not the structure of the environment but its action, insofar as it has an influence on the system. They are both subjective, in the sense of being constructed by the subject for its own purposes, and objective, in the sense of being naturally selected by the environment: *models which do not generate adequate predictions are likely to be later eliminated.* Thus, the development of knowledge can best be understood as an evolutionary process characterized by variation mechanisms and selection criteria. There is no "absolutely true" model of reality: there are many different models, any of which may be adequate for solving particular problems, but no model is capable to solve all problems..[xii] [my italics]

enron's senior managers seemed strangely divorced from this reality – that no model can solve all problems. As a simulator, enron could serve both as a training environment, which it did, and as an incubator. enron paid handsome bonuses to employees who submitted winning ideas for new businesses – new perturbations. My very own department, with its Monte Carlo simulations, was central to testing new models. During the final years, as enron shrugged off the old image of "America's best pipeline company" and even the more recent image of "America's best energy company," the banners went up, proclaiming enron's new goal: to be "America's Best Company." The meaning could not have been lost on even the most blinded. Enron sought to become number one on the Fortune 500, and by extension – the most powerful company in the world. To fight entropy – inevitable decay – enron was obliged to continue feeding the system with a source of energy. The more complex the control systems – the more energy the system required.

That energy was money.

In April 2002, lawsuits led by the University of California's Board of Regents on behalf of its pension fund, and crafted by William Lerach and a team of lawyers from Milberg Weiss Bershad Hynes & Lerach, alleged that nine banks or financial institutions (J.P. Morgan Chase, Citigroup, Credit Suisse First Boston, Canadian Imperial Bank of Commerce, Bank of America, Merrill Lynch, Barclays, Deutsche Bank and Lehman Brothers) were complicit in enron's charade:

> Keeping Enron's stock price aloft was the crucial imperative for all these parties. The company was borrowing billions in the short-term money market to finance its expansions but had to issue long-term debt securities to pay off the short-term paper. If the share price faltered, Enron could lose its investment-grade credit rating and access to long-term credit. The banks would lose their ability to sell more debt and their own commercial loans to Enron might even be imperilled. With its distinctive circular logic, Enron was in effect creating "profits" from its own soaring share price--and vice versa. The fatal flaw, however, was embedded in the deals themselves. To reassure outside investors and presumably the bankers, these special entities included a promise that if things went poorly and the share price fell, the entities would be made whole again with--guess what?--new issues of Enron stock, a consequence sure to drive the share price still lower. This bind gave insiders a strong motive to maintain the deception. If they stopped pedaling, the bicycle would fall over.[xiii]

I have this recurring dream of *Fiddler on the Roof,* with Topol dancing down the street singing "Tradition." Then enron comes along and blasts tradition in favor of "Innovation!" But when Andy Fastow and Jeff Skilling do "the perp" walk, led away in handcuffs, I picture Ken Lay dancing down the street singing "Deception!" At Skilling's trial, Ken Lay is called as a witness. The prosecuting attorney asks Lay what he was doing if he wasn't watching the store. Lay breaks out in song: "If I were a rich man, all day long I'd daidle deedle daidle daidle daidle deedle daidle dum...."

A more straightforward syllogism was never writ.

Why didn't I just write a single sentence and say what I believed – that enron failed for a lack of ethics? It's not that simple. Enron failed for a lack of *evolutionary* ethics.

The PC Project explains that its view of "evolutionary philosophy can be used for developing an ethics or system of values. The basic purpose... would be *the continuation of the process of evolution,* avoiding evolutionary 'dead ends'."xiv This evolutionary philosophy, borrowing from concepts also found in The Selfish Gene,xv suggests that an organism will do whatever it must to ensure immortality of the organism's species. For humans, this means procreation. For corporations, this means innovation (no one wants to listen to the same tuba song over and over and over...). Everything enron's officers did seemed to point the way to corporate immortality, which in the United States is quite rare.

What went wrong? Enron's immortality determined the immortality of the corporation's officers. With tens of millions of dollars in compensation tied to stock, keeping the stock price buoyed not only benefited the corporation – it benefited anyone who held shares. The more shares you hold, the more you benefit. In the few years before enron filed for bankruptcy, Lay and Skilling combined reportedly sold more than $150 million in enron shares, at prices ranging from $31 to $86 a share.

In 2002 testimony to a congressional panel, Harvard-grad Skilling (one of the few enron officers who did *not* take the 5th Amendment) claimed he was ignorant of the rule that prohibits a company from using its own stock to generate a gain or void a loss. "I am not an accountant," he said. Less than 6 months before bankruptcy, Enron employees were locked out of over $100 million in company-matched stock due to company restrictions, while company executives were dumping stock left and right.

The original goal of corporate immortality was forsaken for corporate survival. Corporate survival was forgotten in favor of individual immortality.

That's the flaw.

The courts will decide who operated with conflicts of interest, who benefited while screwing their stock holders and employees, but there is a lesson far simpler than jail time, and I'm sure they've heard it before: You can't take it with you.

In 2003, Susan Stamberg, one of my favorite National Public Radio (NPR) voices, was working on a series about *Power*. Although most of the segments are interesting and relevant in the context of enron, a brief, simple interview with Newt Gingrich, former Speaker of The House of Representatives, tells volumes. In this interview, Gingrich discusses what Stamberg calls "Life after Power."[xvi]

Stamberg postulates that Power defined the person – Gingrich as Speaker. Gingrich denies it.

Gingrich explains his point of view: He points out that his view of power is filtered through his experience as an "Army brat." He'd grown up on military bases, observed general officers being driven about in cars with flags on them, being saluted and treated with respect and deference. But then those generals retire; they wear civilian clothes and play golf. Someone new becomes the "division commander" or the "base commander."

Power is on loan, Gingrich says. "You'd be a much smaller person if you were defined by your job." The Greeks, he said, believed power centered on the person; the Romans believed it centered on the institution (or the office). And this is how Gingrich says he came to view his role as Speaker: "This Power is on loan to me from the American people."

General officer, corporate executive, husband or wife, student or lemonade stand operator – the roles we play are only temporary. We are judged by our stewardship in those roles. For those who accede to positions of leadership, stewardship demands more.

The Second 1st Principle holds: *Profit is not a legitimate fuel to keep a corporation from internal chaos, disorder and destruction.* Quality is. The concepts of private property, legal entities and corporations have existed for more than two thousand years. Humans collectively have determined that the notion of a business, the idea of a corporation is good – people have jobs, customers' needs are met. It's a self-sustaining system. Yet the inevitability of decay in the system is real. Energy is required to keep the system alive, to fight entropy. Regulations stifle creativity and innovation; conversely – freedom encourages creativity and innovation, which generate energy (or market activity).

The customer's view of quality is the only view of QUALITY that matters. The CEO's view of quality as a $10 million home in Houston, one in Aspen, and three others scattered around the world do not add value to the corporation's struggle for immortality. Again – *Profit is not a legitimate fuel to keep a corporation from internal chaos, disorder and destruction.* Quality is.

Revenue, thus potential profit, both proceed *from* QUALITY.

The banner *should* read: "To become the company that meets or exceeds our customer's needs better than any other company in the world."

Eight: Laser Chapter 3

Time to roll the dice. Steele quickly surveyed the scenario and estimated the time remaining until either fighter would have to get a lock on the other, barring temporary stupidity in either cockpit.

Ten minutes. Tops.

These guys were creeping along like helo jocks doing rooftop-by-rooftop searches. Steele passed on his first plan and opted to encode his handheld with an expired transponder code instead of the current one. Next he set the timer to release the signal in eight minutes. Finally, hefting the laser that was about to save his, and hopefully his fellow Marines' lives – and maybe all of mankind (well, he could dream, couldn't he?) – the captain stepped off quickly to the northwest, perpendicular to the apparent collision course of the two fighters. There wouldn't be a collision, of course, but Steele had to do something to negate the coin-toss predictability of who would gain visual – and shoot – first. It seemed like a good idea to get out of the probable path of destruction.

Steele scratched along the side of an embankment running the direction he needed to go, with only a minimum of visibility toward the intruder. That would cut his infrared signature, but it would also mean only occasional clear shots on his target through the stand of pin oaks and pines running the ridgeline. He had what was left of eight minutes. Under the circumstances, that would be about half a mile.

"Now if only I can get these guys to do what I want them to do...," Steele muttered. That's the problem with new guys. The intruders just didn't want to get with the program...wanted to do everything their way. It was just like boot camp. When you're in the middle of it, you never think about it. In retrospect, his drill instructors' daily mission was to get 60-odd recruits to conform. And this wasn't just any old conformity. It wasn't even conformity to something the DI's thought up. It was conformity to mental and physical behaviors that defined Marines. It was conformity to values that guided those mental and physical behaviors. We were all thinking the same thing back then. Escape from boot camp. Escape the wrath of the DI. Freedom from pushups and jumping jacks and endless running. Now it was combat.

While Steele moved in relation to the alien fighter, he checked his six to verify his own teammate's progress. Still on target. "They must both be on passive listening across the spectrum," Steele thought. "At this rate, whoever picks up the other guy's IR first is going to have the advantage. Crap! If this goes south, somebody in a nearly new Mach M fighter is going to be royally pissed off!"

There was no way to tell if either fighter was mapping straight ahead, ahead and up, ahead and down, or 360. Steele checked his watch as he moved into position. Four minutes. He hoped the bogus code his transponder would release would either tell the good guy jocks there was a bad guy with old intelligence, or a good guy with an ambush plan. If they chose the former, they'd shoot to kill, and hopefully the aliens would fire on the same target too. That would give Steele a chance to get his shot on the intruder. If they chose the latter, his buddies should drop to tree-top to wait and see what the signal meant.

Working his way around scattered brush, Steele thought back to that one kid from Louisiana who must've dropped 30 or 40 pounds in boot camp. Every time the boot camp Private Steele noticed something other than his own discomfort, like trying to crank out fifty or a hundred pushups, he saw Majette. Majette always wanted to do things his own way. The DI's wanted Majette to do things the Marine Corps way. Majette wanted freedom; the DIs wanted control. Majette lost. When Majette lost, he was rewarded with 'up and overs,' a kind of physical activity that required pushing one's rifle all the way over one's head then down in front to the chest, then all the way up, and back down behind the head. Up and forward; up and back. Up and forward; up and back. Thousands of times a week. At the end of training, Majette had bulging traps, lats, delts, biceps and triceps. He could do nearly 40 pull-ups. And he was compliant. He was not damaged physically or mentally. And it's not that he was *beaten* as in subdued. He just looked at things differently. He was working his tail off for Marine Corps values. He just didn't realize it at the time.

Steele pondered this phenomenon. When you're doing something you don't really want to be doing, but don't have any real choice, you've gotta come up with some explanation in your head. Steele saw it with prisoners of war in another generation. Being taken prisoner...being in prison...is being on the receiving end of an external force. On threat of death or punishment, most people will comply. After a time though, some of them will begin to identify with their captors... the *Stockholm Syndrome*. Most, however, continue to seek freedom in some form. In order to graduate from boot camp, Majette let go of his old values – which weren't doing him any good where he was. He began to identify with the Marine Corps, embodied in his DI. Here was an overweight 18-year-old Cajun kid with no family, a smart-ass attitude, and in trouble with the courts as late as two or three weeks before shipping off to Parris Island, at least according to Majette. Three months later and he's promoted to private first class meritoriously and swears he's going to become a drill instructor as soon as he makes corporal. Figure that one.

Fully aware that none of the invaders had ever been taken prisoner, Steele shrugged off the concept of compliance or identification in this equation. Their values and our values just didn't seem like a good mix right from the start. They wanted to kill us and take our water. All of it. We didn't want them to take our water. Any of it. They wanted to kill us. We killed them. No sitting around the campfire singing "Kumbaya."

The alien fighter drifted in and out of sight in relation to Steele as he moved northwest, the intruder continuing southwest.

The last time Steele saw Majette he was a sergeant major. He'd stayed in the Corps while Steele was off in college and eventually ministering to a different audience. When

Steele ran into him years later, Majette still embodied the vision of a Marine. He was trim. His uniform was impeccable. Absolutely conscious they had been privates together in another time and place, Majette was far more gracious and comfortable with the situation than Steele, who remembered being a little nervous running into Majette now that he was back in the Corps. Majette's salutes were crisp. His demeanor was professional. And the word "Sir" was tendered in respect. The Corps lives inside Marines – like Majette. Like me. Couldn't get it out if we wanted. But it doesn't mean the Corps invades everything we do. Steele swept thoughts of Kathryn from his mind.

Thirty seconds to closure and Steele readied his position. He selected a stand of trees that offered good temporary cover and concealment, but with a clear shot to where his prey should be based on heading and speed. The plan was that the transponder would ping; the intruders would pick up the signal and go crazy, then start blasting away with their own variation on the laser theme. While they were distracted, Steele would pick his shot and take the intruders out of action, then cover his own six in case the jocks in the Mach M decided he should be a target. That was the plan anyway. Twenty seconds and counting.

Steele tried to shake Majette from his crowded mind.

"Gotta concentrate! Gotta focus!" But something was eating at him. What was Majette trying to tell him? Until Majette found religion – the DI's version – he was always looking for loopholes. Work-arounds. Contingencies. In the beginning, Majette was expert at getting out of doing things the Marine Corps way, and even better at avoiding punishment. For Majette, avoiding a punishment was the same as winning a reward. No pushups equals a prize for the day. Once the DI's caught on, however, Majette switched tactics to the fine art of developing contingencies. Anyplace else and he might have gotten away with it. In boot camp, recruits don't have a chance. DI's have seen it all. Eventually, of course, Majette discovered the rewards and the value in doing things the Marine Corps way. He was rewarded for doing things the Marine Corps way. But the lesson for Steele right now was, "I need a contingency!"

Steele steadied the laser, waiting for his transponder and the enemy reaction...prepared to release the alien crew of all of their Earthly burdens with a single pulse targeted on their muzzle flash. He watched the final seconds tick off....Three. Two. One. The transponder's electronic message went out in 360 degrees. Nothing.

He tipped the laser slightly on his right shoulder and peered past the range-finder sight, cautiously keeping the business end pointed in the right direction and his finger on the trigger.

For the first time in a long time, Captain Dave Steele was momentarily at a loss for a plan. Precious seconds – maybe a hundred - were left to make a decision. Maybe the transponder didn't transmit. Maybe the idiots didn't read it. Maybe they didn't have that channel open. Maybe they didn't know what it was. Maybe their computers recognized the signal as an outdated code and smelled a trap. Too many maybe's. "Geez it pisses me off when I lose control of a situation," Steele thought.

Nine: Anger

Tuesday, 27 November 2001
enron

I backed away from the small crowd standing in front of the wide screen, flat panel monitor suspended near the ceiling to head down to the locker room. Everyone in the building had access to a television somewhere – in office spaces, in the enron elevators, even in the locker rooms. We had been watching people dump stock for weeks. Sell-offs came in huge chunks, tens of thousands, hundreds of thousands of shares. Early on, back in September and October, much of that was probably insiders getting rid of whatever they could salvage. After Skilling announced his departure, stock headed south toward $30 a share. But some analysts continued to blindly rate enron as a 'buy,' and until almost the very end, there were probably some investors who thought the company could recover from $20 a share, or even $10...and bought in, waiting for the eventual return to the glory days of $80 or $90 a share or more. But it wasn't going to happen.

Talk of bankruptcy and the proposed $9 billion deal with Dynegy was all over the building. It's almost funny...we don't think about it, but the German word for 'bankruptcy' is 'bankrotten.' There was no way to escape...except to run.

Jackson and I stretched out in enron's fitness center. Ricky came by and asked if we wanted to run with him, but even if it weren't three days after a marathon, I would have politely passed on the opportunity. He's a rabbit. He runs the five-mile loop along the bayou in 30 minutes or less, and those days for me are gone. History.

I asked Jackson to take it easy on me. He did. We took off from the corner by the old Methodist church across from enron at what felt like a seven to seven and a half minute pace. The more relaxed pace allowed conversation. Jackson's favorite word that week was 'hubris.' The pride before the fall.

We didn't talk about 'if;' we talked about 'what.' What are you going to do in your next life? Jackson said he knew the VP would be telling us about lay-offs at tomorrow's staff meeting. I hadn't heard that for certain, but I didn't exactly have the inside track. We didn't know for sure it would be us, or our department.

After I showered and returned to my cubicle on the 14th floor, I pulled out my original paperwork from orientation and found my resume. Nobody I knew of had been doing anything productive for at least a couple of weeks. I did have one meeting earlier in November with a potential subcontractor interested in supporting a multimedia training program for the lighting retrofit contract with The Limited, and The Gap, but like the others, that too dissolved into empty hopes.

I didn't have an electronic copy of my resume at work, and there was nothing else to do except play solitaire on company time, on a company computer, so I retyped and updated my resume. I printed out five copies, then tracked down the retired military officers I knew in the building to continue my networking. Conversations were brief, polite. The humor in the occasional jokes, like a cup of coffee at a hockey game, grew cold quickly and lost its effectiveness. It reminded me of the mood at the funeral home the day my Mom's mother was buried, a month before my Mom.

Wednesday, 28 November
Interstate 45, inbound

"Who the hell's this?"

"Oh...Hello Roy. It's Dean and Rog'. Perhaps you've heard of our show – Dean and Rog' in the Morning?"

"Oh yes. Dean and Rog'. The only thing worth less than you two is a thousand shares of enron stock."

I switched the radio to NPR – National Public Radio. I don't know if the exchange between Dean and Rog' and their caller Roy ever happened that way...but I imagined it did, or should have. I was hoping NPR would have a war to cover somewhere, but the war was being fought in Houston and on Wall Street. I didn't want anymore. I hit the CD button. For another twenty minutes I could escape with the Beach Boys to Kokomo, over and over and over.

Premium parking spaces were available closer to the causeway from the MET parking garage this morning. Not a lot, but some. The first finger had been pulled out of the dike but the flood wouldn't start until Monday.

Staff meeting. No free lunch. No taco soup. Expect enron to file for bankruptcy next week, and probable layoffs as a result. No talk of earnings. No talk of contracts. No talk of probabilistic models or energy savings.

I walked out of the doctor's office and went to say good bye to a few dozen friends. We all had two days to live. Maybe three. enron had terminal cancer. We were going to be excised from the body of enron as if *we* were the cancerous cells. Nothing definite until next week, but we could read the mood. Some of us exchanged business cards and printed home phone numbers and e-mail addresses on the back. Some of us exchanged resumes.

I thought back to the last eight or nine months and how many resumes I had referred for friends and friends of friends. Forty? Fifty? Many of these were for enron's *hot jobs*, with referral bonuses of $5000. I could have used a couple of those. Four would have built me a swimming pool. Ten would have bought that Corvette. A year later – one of those would have covered a house payment, a truck payment, gas, electric, water and Ramen noodles. Priorities change.

When I got home, I rounded up five or six backpacks and huge gym bags and tossed them in the Ford. Then I tossed a T-bone on the grill, grabbed a beer and turned on Cartoon Network. I was pretty sure Bloomberg would not follow Sponge Bob Square Pants.

Thursday, 29 November

During the first week of Naval Intelligence Officer Basic training in Colorado, a year or two before the school moved to Virginia Beach in 1986, each of the 20 ensigns in my class started filling out the paperwork for a Special Background Investigation in order to eventually be granted a Top Secret clearance. The government wanted to know, among other things, every place I had ever lived. Even transient periods of 30 days. I wrote Mom and asked her to help out...I had never kept track of that kind of information. On top of the 22 addresses Mom mailed me, I added another 20 from 12 years in the Navy and Marine Corps. The house I moved into five months before enron filed for bankruptcy and discharged 4500 of us was now address number 49. I wasn't yet 50 years old. I knew how to pack and move, quickly and efficiently.

I packed.

Friday, 30 November

I also knew how to say good-bye, quickly and efficiently.

Never look back.

I carried boxes in two trips to my pickup, taking the 2nd floor walkway to the parking garage and avoiding the television cameras. I saw people I knew talking with reporters. I didn't want to be one of those people. I was conscious that if the world was watching, it stood to reason my next prospective employer was watching, and I was capable of letting a poor choice of words get out.

Anger builds. During my final 10 years in uniform, I had worked in military intelligence. I wasn't a grunt, a ground combat soldier. I was more familiar with psychological operations - PSYOP. I'd find another outlet. It wouldn't be until two or three weeks later that I would start to release that anger through the ex-enron chat rooms and writing letters. It wasn't just pinning the names "Osama Ken Layden, Jeff's Killing Enron, and Andy Fast-One," on the alleged perpetrators...on the former enron blogs, there were legitimate parallels. The two towers of Enron had been brought down by a force equal in power to the radical religious fundamentalism that shook the world less than three months earlier in New York, Washington, D.C., and in a field in Pennsylvania.

With profound respect to those close to the thousands killed by cowards in terrorist attacks, the impact of enron's implosion on the employees, retirees, families and investors seems incrementally less severe than losing lives. At least the living, who have lost millions in worthless enron (or Worldcom or Tyco or other) stock, are alive. If I'm alive, I can fight back. If I'm alive, I at least have the possibility of rebuilding a portion of my retirement, finding a job, rebuilding my life.

I consider again whether Lay, Skilling, Fastow and the others are guilty. That's up to the courts to decide. In a parallel military organization, Lay would have been the commanding general. In the parallel to a grand jury investigation, a Judge Advocate General (JAG) investigation would have been convened to determine if evidence warranted a court-martial. It would not have taken years to conduct the investigation. It would not have mattered how much money the 'general' had.

The events that took shape over years and led ultimately to enron's bankruptcy filing have rippled into the national and global economies, accelerating the dot-com bust and exacerbating the financial impact of September 11. It happened on Lay's watch. Skilling was second in command. These men were supposedly the leaders of this organization. Marine Corps Leadership traits come to mind:

- Integrity

- Decisiveness

- Judgment

- Dependability

- Bearing

- Courage

- Endurance

- Enthusiasm

- Initiative

- Justice

- Knowledge

- Tact

- Unselfishness

- Loyalty

The way I read it, those traits that *were* exhibited in a positive way (knowledge, enthusiasm, endurance) were exercised by some people for personal profit. Lacking in integrity, judgment, justice, unselfishness, loyalty, dependability, moral courage and decisiveness, people in leadership positions allowed *bankrotten* to start at least two to three years before the filing. The patient doesn't know he has cancer until after it's been festering and growing, sometimes for years. Spreading. Like greed.

When the new boss hands the new employee a coffee cup emblazoned with the company values of Respect, Integrity, Communication and Excellence and says, "Welcome to enron," the new employee expects Respect, Integrity, Communication and Excellence. There was a circus atmosphere at enron in August, 2000. Everyone was in a good mood. Everyone was happy. We had just been named Fortune's "Most Innovative" for an unprecedented fifth year and would ride into the Fortune top 10. People opened doors for strangers and made conversation in the elevators. And I had just walked in the door.

By late Autumn of 2001, there was no mistaking what the banner's new message meant. Enron wanted to take over the world. enron wanted even more power.

Monday, December 3

With one box left to carry out, I waited. On monster.com. There was a director-level job posting at the Texas Transportation Institute in College Station – affiliated with Texas A&M University. I started a cover letter and worked a bit on the resume until Steve came in.

"Department meeting in the 13th floor conference room at 11:00."

"Thanks, Steve."

I saved my cover letter and resume to a 3.5-inch disk and tossed the disk in the box with the rest of my personal things. I thought back to the process of conducting an inventory on a deceased Marine. It's the same as doing an inventory for a Marine who's gone AWOL. A senior non-commissioned officer retrieves the bolt cutters, usually in the custody of another, more senior Marine like the sergeant major. With a witness and assistant present, the senior NCO cuts the padlocks from a wall locker and a foot locker and the team inventories the personal effects of the missing person. Personal effects will be mailed to the survivors.

There's an element of anthropology in this brief service. Whether in combat or in a car accident while home on leave, when a Marine dies while on active duty, the unit to which the Marine is assigned will appoint someone to conduct the inventory. The Marine is not coming back. When a Marine goes AWOL, the locker is typically left untouched for 90 days. When the commanding officer determines it is time to decide on a case of desertion, the Marine's personal effects are inventoried. From the anthropologist's point of view, if the Marine has taken his uniforms and military ID card, he at least has the chance to have charges reduced to Absent Without Leave, which carries a less severe penalty than Desertion. Desertion in time of war can bring a death sentence. The Marine who takes his ID card can at least argue that he intended to return. The following meeting would guarantee my KIA status. I would not be coming back. More than 4000 would not be returning.

11:00

The Enron Energy Services President and his Director of Human Resources addressed the standing-room only crowd of about 200 people, many from my team in Fundamentals. Ten minutes. No jokes. Tough questions. Few answers. No response on severance pay.

"Clear the building by one o'clock. Take all your stuff. Some of you may be called back. enron will be in touch."

I wasn't deserting. I was taking my enron ID cards – my coffee cup and trinkets with enron logos. I expected to return. Denial lasts a long time.

But to enron I must be a dead non-person. I went back to "my" desk to finish the anthropology assignment. As I trudged out to the parking garage, with my final box of goodies, in advance of the one o'clock deadline, I noted common cultural themes and artifacts in the boxes other exroners were carrying: coffee cups, baseball caps, toys, rocks and trinkets imprinted with the company's values: Respect, Integrity, Communication and Excellence. R.I.C.E.

Ken Lay had graduated from Rice University.

Ten: First Principle 3 - Leadership

One might guess that the debate over what distinguishes "leadership" from "management" has been going on for centuries – certainly for all of the past 100 years of relatively modern business practices and resulting formalized education in *business administration* or *business management.* I won't pretend to be able to solve the riddle in this essay, but I do have some opinions.

As Pirsig's QUALITY pushes us out the door in search of the values and the tangible tools – the mind and matter of business – the Leader's role must step forward for scrutiny. In an anthropomorphic sense, when a car is ahead in the Indy 500 or a NASCAR race, we talk about the leader. The leader is in front. As such, the leader becomes a symbol, sets the pace, provides an example for others to follow.

When I arrived at the Marine Corps Recruit Depot, San Diego, in 1973, I was as young and apprehensive as any other 18-year-old. I didn't feel like 'the leader.' I did have some advantage in that during much of the Vietnam War, the percentage of high school graduates entering the Armed Forces was rather low, and I could actually read and write. (I had graduated from high school weeks before.) In truth, I was in or pretty close to the top 10 percent of my high school class. But the real secret weapon I wouldn't discover until the fourth or fifth day at San Diego, after all of the multiple choice examinations.

It was Saturday or Sunday afternoon, July 14th or 15th, and time for our "inventory physical fitness test," or IPFT. The general idea was for the drill instructors to get an initial assessment of each recruit's physical fitness as measured by a 3-mile run, pull-ups and sit-ups, evaluating upper- and lower-body strength and overall endurance. A perfect score was normed at 300 points, with pull-ups counting 5 points each for up to 20; sit-ups worth a point each to 60 – then 2 points each for the next 20 to equal another 100 points. For the 3-mile run, an 18-minute time is worth 100 points, with one point deducted for every 10 seconds – or 6 points a minute. Each of the three events has a minimum (like 3 pull-ups or a 28-minute run), and the scoring is adjusted for age.

Just like every PFT I would take over the coming 22 years, we did our sit-ups and pull-ups first, then had time to catch our breath and get a drink of water. When it was time to move to the starting line – alongside the fence separating MCRD San Diego from Lindbergh Field (San Diego International Airport), I looked down at the Marine Corps-issued flat-bottomed Keds basketball sneakers, and the broken rock surface of the running "track" and moaned. This was a far cry from the synthetic surfaces I ran on for track meets in high school, and I wasn't able to hang on to my Adidas running shoes that first week of boot camp. A drill instructor standing in the sand and broken seashells on the side of the track called out, "On your mark – Go!"

I finished that 3-mile run in 18 minutes and 10 seconds or so. By the time I graduated from boot camp, that pace would drop to 16:10 for 3 miles. The drill instructors – all fresh from tours in Vietnam – were looking for any sign of leadership for the five recruit leadership positions: the platoon guide and squad leaders for each of four squads. Out of a sea of scared, ugly teenagers with shaved heads, they picked me to be the platoon guide. I had come in first on that run by at least three minutes. They hauled me into the drill instructor "hut," and quizzed me.

"Do you have any friends out there?" they asked, signaling the squad bay, with 72 other recruits.

"Sir! Yes Sir!" I started to reply, preparing to explain that my buddy from Minnesota and I had signed up on this "buddy program" and...

"Bull shit! You don't have any friends, do you, prive?"

"Sir, the private, uh..."

"So you don't know if you have any friends? A leader can't have friends, lad. Got it?"

"Yes Sir!" I lied. I *didn't* get it then, but I had had

enough advice from both my Dad and my older brother (who had graduated as platoon honor man two years earlier) to play along and just do what the DI's tell you to do.

"Got any friends out there, lad?"

"Sir No Sir!"

"Good. You're the Platoon Guide until we say different. Got it? Now get your skinny ass out there and clean up that clusterfudge! MOVE!"

I did. Boot camp wasn't easy. But it wasn't hard either. I don't know if being "out in front" in a 3-mile run and having a high school diploma (only 50 percent of my platoon had graduated from high school) were legitimate reasons to identify me as the leader, the Platoon Guide. I never lost the post, and carried the platoon guidon all the way through graduation three months later. I graduated as the platoon honor man and was rewarded with the dress blue uniform. I was close to getting fired once, and accused of being too serious about it all on another occasion.

When our series (four platoons) headed off to Camp Pendleton, astride Interstate Highway 5 just north of San Diego, for field training and marksmanship training, three or four of the recruits had already been talking about going "over the hill." Literally. Camp Pendleton offers unlimited possibilities for a homesick recruit to disappear over hills, into a canyon, and show up on the highway with his thumb out, hitching for a ride back to South Dakota or New Mexico. The problem is getting civilian clothes and hiding the fact that you don't have any hair, in an era of wide ties, wide lapels, bell-bottom jeans and really long hair on both men and women. Civilians who turn in an AWOL GI can earn a cash reward from the government.

At first, I figured the DI's were always prepared for this kind of thing, but when Staff Sergeant Bnotz pulled me aside at the pistol range, I knew he had first-hand knowledge of something specific, "Keep an eye on Private Frick and Private Frack. They miss their mammas and might make a run for the interstate. Got it?"

"Sir yes sir. Got it, Sir."

Late morning that day, the DI's rested the platoon from "snapping in," or dry firing our .45 caliber pistols at the black targets painted on white 55-gallon drums in the center of a circle. The junior DI instructed me to herd the platoon over to the cinder block shack that served as a head, with 5 urinals and 5 toilets. The four squads of about 15 to 18 recruits each, entered one squad at a time. I stepped inside the hatch – the doorway – to keep an eye on things and make sure no one "forgot" to leave the building. Interstate-5 was within sight, down the hill, a mile or two away. As the final squad finished its duties in the head, Staff Sergeant Bnotz stepped through the hatch. I had been leaning against the wall in the most casual "back on the block" pose, but quickly "snapped to." I started to call, "attention on deck," but he put his finger to his lips, "Ssshhhh."

He waited patiently for the final recruit to leave, then whispered in that private's ear, "Tell Private Hughes he's got the conn.'

"Aye-aye SIR!" and the last private was gone.

Staff Sergeant Bnotz took about 5 steps and faced me. I had been standing at the position of attention since he had walked in the door, doing my best to not let him see me watching him. I'm told things have changed, and in fact, I later spent nearly three years at MCRD Parris Island working in public relations, where I observed some of the changes had taken place. But this was the 70s and Vietnam was still a reality. Staff Sergeant Bnotz faced me as his hand clamped around my throat. "We've gotten a bit lax, have we, Guide? Back on the block? We think we can just rest our slovenly civilian ass against any old brick shithouse when the drill instructor isn't watching, is that it?"

Every pause, every sentence, was punctuated with Bnotz' fist to my gut. I got the message, but maybe, at 18, I took the message too much to heart.

Two weeks later and my platoon had scored the highest number and percentage of expert riflemen at the rifle range. One of the Hughes brothers, my 4th squad leader, from Texas, had the highest score in all four platoons and earned a root beer at the chow hall that final day. As a result of "taking the range," we not only got a pennant on our guidon, but honors in the field exercise. What that meant was, going into combat training, our platoon would be the lone defender of one hill and the other three platoons would be arrayed on opposite hills, half a mile away on opposing sides of a canyon.

This was kind of fun. The DI's were a bit more relaxed, and I was theoretically the platoon commander (the "student platoon commander"). We had a "field problem" or exercise and the September weather in Southern California couldn't have made it any nicer. What a life. I'll be home in 3 and a half weeks. I moved from squad leader to squad leader, ensuring that each of them had supervised their teams to ensure every three-man fire team had properly dug their World War II-style foxholes according to the lessons we had learned back in San Diego.

As I returned to the CP – the Command Post – the horizon was scarlet to the West and most of the DI's were sitting on sandbags, laughing at someone's off-color jokes. Then I noticed my senior DI. He was grabbing his throat. Then he was pointing. What was he pointing at? All I saw were DI's and a couple of recruits.

Then I spotted it. One of the recruits was trying to pull MY flag from MY guidon. They were trying to capture the flag. The war would be over before it started!

I raced toward the offender, hurdled the sandbag wall and reached for the flag. Too late. He had it, and jumped the wall. I followed. He raced down the hill, toward third platoon's CP. Running down hill; we both took unnaturally long steps. I was taller by a few inches and finally caught the thief. I tackled him.

"Gimme the flag, dirtbag!"

He pulled off his 'cover,' the soft (starched) fabric cap Marines wear when they're in combat utility uniforms but not in combat, and glared at me, "I'm a drill instructor, boy. You *will* get your hands off me or you will be court-martialed."

Instantly I recognized this joker as one of the other platoon's DI's, dressed as a recruit. I refused to let go of the flag. "You can't take our flag. Sir."

"I'll court-martial your butt. GIMME THE DAMN FLAG!"

"This is NOT happening to ME," I thought to myself. I could easily be back in Fergus Falls, Minnesota, swimming, playing golf, working at the Holiday Inn trying to make some money for college, or going through some other rites of passage like other 18-year-old guys get to do. This could NOT be real. It would not have mattered if he had a gun to my head; all I wanted was the stupid flag. I had him in a one-armed headlock and my other hand on the flag. He had me in a headlock with his other hand grabbing the other end of the flag. It was a no-win situation. I gave in.

Drill Instructor Staff Sergeant Dirtbag marched me back to his platoon's CP. By now it was dark. I was 'invited' to lay prone in front of the platoon's senior DI, who called his guide and two squad leaders over to get information out of me. They pulled my jacket up to my shoulders and placed what was probably three or four rocks on the small of my back.

"These, lad, are heat tabs. You know – Sterno. The kind you cook your C-rations with. We're going to light one of these every minute unless you tell us where your platoon is dug in."

"Now what?" I thought. We had had that crap about POWs before we left San Diego, but this was ridiculous! I was in California! I figured the best bet was to give them false information and they'd let me go. I switched everything around and made up squad positions. I told them the command post, the CP, was being moved just as the sun was setting. What I didn't know, of course, was that my DI's, aware that I had evidently been captured, had moved the squads around anyway. To just about where I said they would be, but believed they weren't. As a POW – I sucked.

Then the other platoon's guide and one of the squad leaders marched me off in the direction of the company CP where they were supposed to turn me over to the captain as a POW. Stumbling along the ridge, out of sight of both the last platoon CP and the company headquarters, with my hands tied behind my back with one of my boot laces, I pushed one private into a pile of rocks on one side, and the second private over the cliff, then made a run for it, down the canyon. When I got to a gully, I slipped in, hid, opened my mouth wide and did my best to breathe silently. By the time these two were headed back to their CP for a search party, I had wriggled my hands out of the boot laces and was on the road back to my own headquarters, which by then had been overrun and captured.

The next morning, as I was nursing a black eye and picking cactus needles from several inconvenient places on my body, two of my drill instructors came over to escort me to the captain who was holding my flag.

"Did you tackle this drill instructor?" the captain asked, gesturing to the joker, who was smiling and now dressed as a DI with his Smoky-The-Bear campaign cover on his head."

"Sir yes sir."

"Why?"

"He stole our flag, sir."

"Do you realize that attacking a drill instructor is a court-martial offense?"

"Yes sir. But last night, he wasn't a drill instructor. He was dressed as a private." That's all I said. I looked the captain in the eye, equal to equal. I looked the drill instructor in the eye, equal to equal. The DI grinned. The captain didn't. By the ribbons the staff sergeant was wearing I could tell he had been to Vietnam at least once. The captain had not.

As the captain tossed me the flag, he said, "Take it easy, lad. It was only an exercise."

As I saluted and performed an about-face to return to my platoon, I replied, "Yes sir, but it could have been real."

The lessons are easy in retrospect: lead from the front; don't get complacent. But – don't take yourself too seriously either. When I go out for a training run, up to 13 miles on a Saturday morning while the traffic is light, I write "LASER," – that Captain Steele book – in my head. Thirteen miles is about 2 hours. When I'm teaching a class, I probably talk at about 150-200 words per minute. When I read, I can easily read comfortably at more than 800 words per minute. That would be 9600 words in two hours. But when I think as I run, my mind is racing too. I can't write or even record something while I'm running. When I run, I run. Captain Steele runs along. That phrase from the FMFM-1 comes back to me again:

> The Corps' style of warfare requires intelligent leaders with a penchant for boldness and initiative down to the lowest levels. Boldness is an essential moral trait in a leader, for it generates combat power beyond the physical means at hand. Initiative, the willingness to act on one's own judgment, is a prerequisite for boldness. These traits carried to excess can lead to rashness, but we must realize that errors by junior leaders stemming from over-boldness are a necessary part of learning. We must deal with such errors leniently; there must be no zero defects mentality.

I'd learned some hard lessons on initiative, decision-making and judgment along the way. As an observer, I'd seen the zero defects mentality at NASA. What I saw at NASA was an over-reliance on an ingrained culture of success, which had an impact on decisions. (We ROCK! We haven't had any significant problems so far...what could go wrong?)

Organizational culture is at least as powerful as laws, rules and policies in shaping decisions. Less than six months *before* the tragic loss of Columbia's crew, I made a courtesy call on the new director at Johnson Space Center, telling him I wished to do business on his campus. It was now almost a year into being de-employed by enron, and I was preparing to market a 2-day Leadership Skills workshop that I thought might fit with NASA's ongoing professional development program.

I didn't expect the new director at Johnson Space Center would or could just hand me business, but he did graciously forward my name to his Human Resources Director. We scheduled an appointment for late 2002. I made a presentation to the assembled team of some four or five HR and training managers, which eventually led, in January 2003, to scheduling a pilot workshop at JSC for July, 2003.

February 1st the Columbia crew was lost. I won't pretend I wasn't worried about losing my contract. I was close to bankruptcy and needed any business I could get. But I was also sensitive enough to not call or e-mail my contact for about six weeks as the Space community entered a period of mourning. But the seminar did go as scheduled, in July of 2003. In the class, we had a ringer, a senior manager. Although my understanding was that the workshop had been marketed to and would be attended by civil service personnel who were preparing to take on their first supervisory positions, one of my "students" was a veteran flight controller from Apollo days. An evaluator?

When I teach a class of adults, I do my best to provide analogies or examples that my students can relate to. Because I had worked as a contractor at JSC from 1997 until moving to enron in 2000, I had enough stories and examples to bring up in the various discussions. Inevitably, in a discussion on that "zero defects" mentality concept, the lore of Gene Kranz' "Failure is not an option" was certain to come up. It did. And the senior manager, who eventually identified himself as having worked in Mission Control during several Apollo missions, denied Kranz ever spoke those words.

How did the zero defects mentality get ingrained in the culture?

NASA was still in mourning. My mind went back to the fire on the NIMITZ in 1988:

I was in SUPPLOT – Supplementary Plot. As a Navy lieutenant at the time, one of my jobs while deployed to the waters off Korea and later in the Persian Gulf Theater was to stand a 12-hour watch at a top-secret post, monitoring the movement of ships and aircraft that might be a threat to the NIMITZ battle group. What was Top Secret about the post was how the intelligence information was derived. Standing watch, I was surrounded by computers, displays, specialized communications equipment, radios, telephones and printers. One of the monitors showed the flight line – the view you get when an aircraft takes off on one of the four the steam catapults.

In the middle of the Indian Ocean, shortly after Thanksgiving, and not long after midnight, something caught my eye in the flight deck monitor. I looked up. It was a flash of light. At first I thought it was some plane's navigations lights. I looked back to my intelligence display at the oil tankers and Russian, Pakistani and Indian naval ships in the area. Then there was movement on the flight deck display and I looked again. At the same time, General Quarters sounded.

If I had been anywhere else on the ship, I would have been called to man a General Quarters station at that point, and eventually joining a thousand other sailors and officers putting out the fire on the flight deck. But I was on watch and couldn't leave my post. My first thought was to call my roommate. I shared a two-man stateroom with another lieutenant:

"Rich! Wake up! There's a fire on the flight deck! Turn on the Monitor!" The TV in our stateroom had an optional channel so we could watch the flight line.

"Thanks Man!"

The next several hours were a blur, but I recall going to the flight deck with Rich and our buddy Dave the next morning after I got off watch, to look at the burned out hulks of several planes. Some were pushed off the carrier into a deep-water grave in the Indian Ocean; others would survive until we made port, to be craned off at Subic Bay in the Philippines on the way home. But the three lost crewmembers had mortal bodies and could not be replaced with spare parts and new paint.

As I recall, the court martial eventually determined that a young sailor in the cockpit of one of the A-7's, crowded onto the "pointy end" of the ship amongst 40-some other planes and helos, was performing routine maintenance. He was tired. He had been at sea for months. He missed his family. He had been through the same maintenance rituals time and time again. He was complacent.

In non-technical terms, he accidentally pulled the trigger, which should have been put on SAFE, on the 20MM canon in the A-7. By doctrine, aircraft deployed in a potentially hostile theater would be parked on the flight line with machine guns loaded – but with safety precautions. Rockets, bombs and missiles would be loaded and off-loaded before and after scheduled missions. Two to three rounds of 20MM cannon from the A-7 struck the 500-lb fuel tank of the A-6 parked perpendicular to the A-7. The tank exploded, releasing burning fuel, which quickly spread over the flight deck. One sailor was incinerated almost instantly. As the fire spread, the other fuel tank on the A-6 ignited, spreading more fuel and critically damaging other aircraft. Two more sailors were down. One died aboard the NIMTZ the next day; the third was flown first to Israel, then Germany for emergency lifesaving measures, but he too perished.

Complacency is not a legal defense, and the lad who pulled the trigger accidentally was punished. But it wasn't just the young sailor in the cockpit, performing perfunctory maintenance, who was punished – his leading chief or leading petty officer was also punished.

Complacency is following the rules, the procedures over and over and over and over – and forgetting *why* we're following the rules in the first place. Lack of focus.

I've mentioned the Marine Corps Leadership Traits; perhaps this is the right spot to surface the Leadership Principles:

- Be tactically and technically proficient.
- Know yourself; seek self-improvement.
- Keep your people informed.
- Employ your people and your team in accordance with their capabilities.
- Ensure every task is understood, supervised and accomplished.
- Train your people as a team.
- Make sound and timely decisions.
- Develop a sense of responsibility among your subordinates.
- Set the example.
- Know your team and look out for their welfare.
- Seek responsibility and accept it for all that you or your team do or leave undone.

I could probably write a hundred pages or more on what I think the obvious and not-so-obvious lessons are for each of these specific leadership traits and principles, but not only would that be sophomorically preachy, it would go well past what the 17- to 25-year-old Marines get when they learn Leadership Skills. enron's most senior former executives are both over 50. They can figure it out.

But this begs a response to the question: Are military standards of conduct truly higher than civilian? And if so, why? Until the so-called dot-com bust at the turn of the century, it was not unusual to read of corporate CEOs with paychecks, perks, stock options and bonuses "earning" hundreds of millions of dollars. On paper, a few of them were at a billion. For one year! As of 2004, some still were in the hundred million a year club. The CEO who is also president and/or chairman of the board for his or her corporation is in the driver's seat on a multitude of decisions, and while I will agree that the farther removed "the boss" is from day-to-day operations, the less they know about the specific details – the charismatic ones still set the pace.

Think Steve Jobs. A $100 billion corporation with a $100 million boss touches millions of people, from tens of thousands of employees and retirees, to stock holders and vendors, to customers and local citizens and beyond. I do *not* have a problem with CEOs making $10 million or $100 million a year in pay, bonuses and stock options – as long as they deliver in all ways, including ethics and leadership. I *do* have a problem with people who earn minimum wage and complain about wealthy people earning large incomes. Wealthy people do not *prevent* other people from earning whatever they want to earn, and most importantly – are *qualified* to earn. The lesson in this is: if it's important enough to complain about (your income), it's important enough to change.

In comparison, a general officer (admiral in the Navy) may also have personal responsibility for tens of thousands of men and women, tens of billions of dollars worth of equipment, and impact the lives of millions of people either at home or on foreign soil. The general's total compensation, in all forms, is less than $200,000 per year, about what a well-paid football player makes in the first half of a game. About what a well-paid CEO makes in less than a day.

Countless volumes have been written over the centuries about leadership. Many are good; some offer excellent lessons. It serves no purpose to try to repeat all of those lessons or distill them here, but I sense the need for a feeling of closure on what all of this means in terms of finding or creating the kind of company I would be proud to work for. And so, I look to a single example of Leadership, in a single volume.

First Principle 3 – Leadership – proceeds from QUALITY, and therefore is QUALITY Leadership. Whether I hire them or work for them, I want my leaders to demonstrate that they believe the Leader's role is a service role. The Leader works *for* the people on his or her team, and in that sense must be selfless. Like any other position in the organization, 'leader' is a temporary position; you can't take it with you even if you started the company and die on the job. And so, like bricklayer, programmer, administrative assistant, teacher, truck driver or analyst, 'leader' is a position, a role to play. Playing that role means responding to your customer's needs, not your needs. Leadership requires stewardship.

Sometimes a leader has to sacrifice for the sake of his or her team members. Does that mean they should live like paupers? No. That's obviously simplistic. People with significant responsibility should be able to *earn* a lot of money if the market supports it. But they should also be prepared to take responsibility for not only their own actions but also the actions of the people on their team, especially if they help create the corporate culture.

Sacrifice and service require a measure of humility. When my leaders are great, I need them to show it, not say it. When they make a mistake, I need them to come clean and not only say it, but show that they mean it.

If we expect to have team members perform as if they truly understand they are part of something bigger than themselves, then should not the Leader also be 'part of something bigger than himself?' <u>The Leader is not the corporation</u>. The buck may stop there, but consider for a moment the critical intersection of customer and customer service associate in any given retail trade. When you are buying a pair of blue jeans or new set of tires for your car, who is most important at the split second of that financial transaction – the CEO or the sales associate? The customer never sees the CEO. The sales associate is more of an ambassador for the company than the CEO every day of the week – where it matters – and earns $8 or $9 or $10 an hour. The CEO who brings in $100 million a year in salary, future retirement benefits, stock options and other perks, 'earns' <u>$50,000 an hour</u> on a 2080-hour year. Just something to think about.

The leader recognizes employees – team members – as customers. They were customers when we sold them on the company, the nano-second before we hired them. They're still customers.

I need to train my junior leaders to be forgiving. Expect much, teach a lot, work 'em hard, but be forgiving. That simple lesson in Marine Corps doctrine applies to all of us. There is no zero-defect mentality. We all make mistakes. But sadly, most of us are quick to jump on the poor soul whose most recent mistake makes this morning's gossip at the water cooler. That sucks and it's not fair.

In order to respond, as a team, to your customers' definition of quality products and services, the leader must be able to get around obstacles. I want 4X4 truck leaders! Rugged. Dependable. Flexible. Tireless. The leader's *job* is to ensure team members have all the resources they need to get their jobs done. You don't have to know how to do everyone's job – just be able to find the experts who *can* do every job. Resources include both mind and matter – in other words, knowledge, training, values and culture *in addition to* tools, time and finances. If there are innovations in your organization – they will come from all corners and NOT just from the "front office." You're not as smart as you think you are...meaning: you're not smarter than all of the people in your organization *combined*. (Think about that too.) Treating my team members with dignity and respect, helping *them* look good, will inspire loyalty and focus them on the value of responding to our customers' definition of QUALITY.

The leader, like everyone else, is guided in following the rules by the *values that created the rules*. When the rules don't make sense, or when the rules fall short of providing an answer to a difficult question, the leader makes a decision consistent with the values that created the rules. Like Captain Steele, the leader has to prepare for contingencies; we can't write enough rules to cover every accident, every incident, every difficult choice. And when plan A fails, the leader has to have the intellect and courage to craft a plan B, based on values, and the determination to follow through.

On top of all of these qualities, I want to teach my leaders how to respond to their team members' urgent desire for *inspiration*. If we go back to the list of Marine Corps Leadership Traits, "Inspiration" is not on the list. "Enthusiasm" comes close, but the employee in the cubicle next to you can be enthusiastic without inspiring others. Some of them can be so enthusiastic as to be annoying. We could make the case that *all* employees should have these leadership traits – integrity, knowledge, judgment, tact, and so on. But even if we are fortunate enough to assemble a team on which every member owns each of these 14 traits, there will always remain a number of team members who just want to do their job, practice their trade. They don't want to be leaders, but they desperately want competent leadership. They want challenging but realistic goals; they want someone to tell them *what* needs to be done next – but not how to do it. They want autonomy – to be treated like adults and have the freedom to grow, expand and innovate.

Communicating inspiration requires a leader who can communicate coherently. The message has to make sense; the message clarifies external incentives that respond to team members' internal motivation.

Which brings us back to the LASER: A LASER, light-amplification by stimulated emission of radiation, is: Intense. Focused. Coherent. One Wave Length. High-Energy Light.

That LIGHT is your vision and values. Your goal is Light Amplification by Stimulated EMPLOYEE Radiation. In a working LASER, an electrical charge excites atoms, causing electrons to move to a higher than normal energy level. Returning to a normal energy level, the electron releases energy as light – photons. Bouncing around inside a tube with mirrors on either end, these photons create an intense, coherent, single wavelength beam of light. As excited atoms bounce around - they excite other atoms, releasing more energy.

Your company is the LASER. Your message is the electrical charge. Your customer's needs for quality products and services are the FOCUS. Your employees are the HIGH-

ENERGY, excited photons. Your vision and values are the COHERENT, single wavelength beam of light. That SINGLE WAVELENGTH is your company, division or team's product or service. The level of INTENSITY depends on releasing the energy stored in your corporate culture.

Where's the model for this kind of leadership?

Jesus Christ is one model.

Does this mean I think the leaders I hire or the leaders I work for should be perfect? Of course not. But just as Pirsig says we can't define QUALITY – but we know it when we see it, it is likewise difficult to quantify Integrity, Decisiveness, Judgment, Dependability, Bearing, Courage, Endurance, Enthusiasm, Initiative, Justice, Knowledge, Tact, Unselfishness and Loyalty…but we generally know them when we see them. The same is true for the Marine Corps Leadership Principles, or anyone else's list of leadership qualities.

Responding to his twelve disciples' discussion about who among them was the greatest, Jesus replied, "If anyone wants to be first," He told them, "he will have to be last of all and serve everyone."[xvii]

So just as 2000 years of legal canon have laid the ground work for what a CORPORATION should be, well more than 2000 years of leadership and followership have laid the groundwork for what a LEADER should be. LEADERSHIP is its own metasystem, which proceeds from QUALITY. All past, present and future leaders are imitations of LEADER. Some get closer than others

What's the point? In the midst of scripture, in the midst of the story of creation, is the small detail that "God created mankind in his own image." It doesn't say "God created other gods equal to himself in every way." GOD doesn't expect us to be GOD, God or even god.

And you know what…I don't want a business leader who thinks he or she *is* a god.

Eleven: Laser Chapter 4

Quandary.

Steele relaxed his trigger finger and eased the laser down to rest on the butt plate. Peering through the midsummer leaves in the direction the alien fighter had been seconds ago, he was at once relieved, confused and more than slightly pissed off that there was nothing to shoot at. He sat.

Turning to the southwest, cautiously, he could no longer detect the Marine Mach M fighter either. There was no target and no one to warn. That meant he didn't have a ride home. The two-minute warning had come and gone. It was genuinely time for the players to get their asses back on the field.

"Where the heck is everyone?"

Nothing. The night was as quiet as it was dark. Minutes dissolved silently into the obsidian sky. Steele stood slowly and peered into the darkness once more, in both directions. No threat. No jocks. Four or five more lost minutes. Standing on the ridgeline, as if ready to scratch his head like any other hayseed, Steele muttered aloud, "What the hell's going on here?"

"Freeze!"

Steele froze. Just like in the movies. When someone's got the drop on you, you freeze first – negotiate second. Maybe. At least this incarnation of John Wayne spoke his kind of English.

"Put the laser on the deck and turn around!"

Steele grinned. More pure American English...Marine Corps style. If this wasn't a fellow Marine, it sure was a fine imitation by a good-hearted swabby. No one else in the universe would tell someone to put something on the *deck*. Not on purpose anyway. He turned slowly.

"Skipper!"

"Murdoch? What the hell are you doing here?

"I flew. What the hell are you doing here...Sir?"

"Uh, could you point that thing somewhere else? And how did you get this close to me without me hearing you? You missed your calling, son."

"Sorry, sir." Murdoch lowered the pistol. "Had to be safe."

"Flew what?"

"Sir? Oh. That...I took one of the Mach M's out of the maintenance bay back at Corpus Christi when it was obvious the squadron was in trouble. Figured I could help. I set her down about fifty meters south of you, sir. Pretty quiet, huh? Stealth mode...?"

"YOU were flying that 'M?' Haven't we had this talk before, Sergeant Murdoch? And how did you become such an expert at getting away with such illegal activities?" Steele asked with a grin. He recalled a slightly younger Corporal Murdoch working for him as a mechanic when Steele was a squadron maintenance officer. He had reprimanded Murdoch on more than one occasion for lofting the VSTOL fighters...flying them at anywhere from 10 or 20 feet off the deck to whatever he thought he could get away with. There was always some kind of justification. "Don't we have regulations about this kind of thing?"

"Have a little faith, skipper! I made it this far, didn't I? I'm a plane captain. I know every inch of this bird, sir. And besides, haven't you always told the maintenance division that rules and regulations just represent values? You want us to think on our feet? What value is there in a Marine in distress?" Murdoch insisted petulantly. "Anyway, I've got my flight line taxi ratings. I'm authorized to move this baby around the flight line, and I've been flying VSTOL sims in arcades since I was in 8th grade."

"Video games and flight line taxiing are a far cry from combat, lad. We'll deal with this later. The good thing is we've got a ride home. Your superior initiative and egregious lack of judgment may just save both of our asses. I'll probably have a hard time coming up with enough officers to court-martial you anyway." Steele reached for the laser's carry handle, glad that Murdoch had the good judgment to go well beyond the regulations.

Taking note of the bloody hole a few inches above Steele's heart, Murdoch offered, "I can get that, Skipper." Murdoch offered, reaching for the laser. "And sir...how did YOU get here? Where's your M? Where's the rest of the squadron?" The answers were obvious.

"No joy, lad." Steele's voice was hollow.

"Captain Purcell and Corporal Clancy? Corporal Walt...and Jamaica? Ramirez? Ashby?"

"All the gunners are gone, lad. Dead. Their pilots too. Everybody. CO...XO....There were just too many of those freakin' alien weirdoes." Corporal Walt had been Steele's gunner. As their eyes met, Steele started to realize the first pangs of guilt. He'd been too busy scratching for cover, then blasting space invaders, then mopping up, to consider what it really meant to be standing on the hill, in the clearing smoke of battle. Alone. With only the ghosts on the inside of his eyelids and the ringing in his ears.

He stopped. "Murdoch. Did you see the bad guy I was trying to ambush?" he pointed, "Over there? The one I was trying to keep from taking out your headlights?"

"Oh yeah! I was high, on look-down shoot-down and picked him up like 10 clicks back. He started to set down, then I got you on IR and set down in a clearing back there," Murdoch reported, jerking his thumb over his shoulder. "He must've been on look-down too. Probably picked up your IR too before he ever came close to getting my signature. If he'd seen me my guess is he would've rolled out to set up a shot."

Steele was impressed with the young Marine's knowledge, as well as his execution. So far. He'd have to see about getting the bureaucracy out of the way, purging Murdoch's record book, and getting him into OCS and some legitimate wings when this little global firefight wrapped up. IF it ever wrapped up.

"Did you read my transponder?"

"No, Sir."

"I wonder where that goof is now."

"My guess is he's looking for you, Skipper."

"On foot?"

"Well, uh, sure. If he was gonna shoot you from the sky, wouldn't he stay in the sky, sir?"

The lad had a point. So...one of the misbegotten was aiming to take yours truly as a POW, or try a little hand-to-hand combat. He might have tracked the transponder signal, and set down looking for a trophy. They must get some kind of brownie points for taking prisoners. Maybe it was a 4-light year pass. Maybe they got a vacation in a worm hole. "Okay Murdoch, listen up. We need a plan. Can you handle the laser cannon from the gunner's seat?"

Murdoch looked incredulously at the captain, as much as he thought he could away with, as he held up all five digits and started counting, "One – every Marine is a rifleman. Two – I wasn't just conceived in the back seat, Sir. I was raised there as a private and a PFC. I was a gunner before I transferred to Maintenance. Three – I've been shooting these things in the arcade since I was..."

"I know. Eighth grade. Enough already. Let's get moving; I'll feed you your dose of the Five Paragraph Order on the way. Get one step ahead of me and show me to valet parking, but don't move any faster than I'm going. It's an age thing."

Murdoch hefted the laser then looked at Steele's shoulder and quizzed the captain as they shoved off, "Sure you don't want me to take a look at that, Skipper?"

"I've got a dressing on it – No thanks! Move." As they trekked over the uneven countryside, Steele and Murdoch exchanged information freely until they had an agreed-upon FRAGO, a fragmentary picture of the Situation, their new Mission, how they would Execute that Mission, the Admin junk – like how they would communicate in case they were separated, and so on. Finally, Command and Control. Who's in charge under what circumstances. Steele had to consider the possibility of turning command over to the sergeant in case he became *really* incapacitated.

As they approached the clearing and Steele could scarcely begin to judge the outline of that beautiful fighter, he whispered abruptly, "Murdoch. Stop!"

Neither had expected uninvited guests. "What's up Skipper? We're almost there!" Murdoch's flying abilities were okay, but his field sense on the ground was a bit rusty.

In what seemed like slow motion, Steele reached for the laser slung over Murdoch's shoulder while the intruder poking around the cockpit on one of HIS United States Marine Corps Mach M fighters turned his weapon to respond to the unexpected sound of Murdoch's voice. In one liquid move, Steele stripped the cannon from Murdoch's shoulder, pushed Murdoch to the ground in defilade, flipped the switch and aimed the death machine at the unwelcome one.

"Jesus save us...."

Twelve: Shock
and the 4th First Principle: Faith

Monday, 3 December 2001

Jesus Christ, Disney's magic and the Marine Corps all have something in common. I won't save the punch line – it's FAITH. Belief. This may seem an irreverent package of comparisons, but we go through a singularly human processes when we encounter things that are unexplainable, whether spiritual faith, belief in Disney's magic, or the conviction that 'sending in the Marines' is the right thing to do.

Like most kids, I believed in Santa Claus. Now – as long as I've been writing the checks to cover the November and December credit card bills, I've *really* believed in Santa.

As a kid, I believed I was headed to another world on the moon rocket at Disneyland. And after three months and a day in uniform, where the men and women around me proudly claimed the title of 'providing 25 percent of the National Defense, with 7 percent of the budget and 9 percent of the manpower,' I too believed Marines could do anything. We use "belief" or "faith" in *generally* the same way with each of these experiences.

In August 2000, I believed ENRON really existed. They apparently believed in me too. (The tangible enron was depositing money in my bank account and telling me sexy stories about the metaphysical ENRON – so there was no reason *not* to believe in ENRON.) I hadn't interviewed for a job in 5 years and wanted to make a good impression. It was good enough – they offered a salary 20 percent over what I was then currently making. The day I walked in the door, ENRON made an impression on me too. It was the week enron and Blockbuster Video were announcing their landmark partnership. Blockbuster would provide on-demand entertainment and enron would provide the bandwidth to get that entertainment to the consumer. Beneath the enron-Blockbuster banner, a life-size Star Wars

Storm Trooper and Darth Vader graced the main lobby, with the fabled enron motorcycle. For the first six months, I was convinced the difference between the last job and this job was the difference between going to prom with my cousin – and winning the Powerball and a lifetime trip to the Virgin Islands on a 60-foot sloop with a crew of beautiful women and unlimited provisions.

Day one, enron's HR staff put on a new-hire orientation in a talk-show format. It was funny; it was fast; it was catered. Although I was one of the new employees, I couldn't help but also observe through my training manager eyes that they covered an enormous amount of critical, must-have knowledge in an enjoyable, informative single day. When I got to my desk the next morning, I had a lap-top computer with docking station, a note telling me to go the mobile phone carrier shops in the sub-basement and pick out a mobile phone with a calling plan that would suit my needs (at enron expense), and one of those really cool $1000 Aeron Chairs by Herman Miller. Oh – and my immediate supervisor, Justin, had left me a Nerf dart gun. A toy. His explanation: work should be fun.

I was impressed, especially with my boss and the members on my new team.

enron acquired the power to inspire belief in something less than 10 years, and they did it with money. It wasn't just us lowly training managers who benefited by moving to enron. In what was then a preview of the book *The Smartest Guys in the Room,* by FORTUNE's Bethany McLean and Peter Elkind,[xviii] Fortune Magazine reported:

> According to an analysis by Congress's Joint Committee on Taxation, in 1998, Enron's 200 most highly compensated employees took home a total of $193 million in salaries, bonuses, and various forms of stock. In 1999, that leapt to $402 million, and in 2000, they took home $1.4 billion. For their work in 2000 — the last full year before Enron went bankrupt — each of the top 200 employees made over $1 million; 26 executives made over $10 million. In 2001,

the year Enron went bankrupt, at least 15 employees made over $10 million.

It's not what constitutes *adequate, fair* or *appropriate* compensation; it's about how to get someone's attention, how to make an impression. It's about how to communicate, and at enron, where even a training manager could expect a 20% annual bonus on a six-figure salary, money communicated loudly. People who earn a LOT can afford to have some manners.

So – yes – my move to enron was largely a financial decision, and I won't apologize. It's part of history and I can't change it. I wouldn't if I could. I had become a single Dad the week before I started at enron, and at the time I had pretty much peaked at my NASA contractor job. I really liked the guys I worked with; I enjoyed being associated with NASA. But I needed a change, and I needed a bigger paycheck. Future prospects for my job specialty in the business I was in were unsettling, and I wasn't going to score a major salary increase without a promotion, in a company where promotions typically follow the funeral of your reporting senior who dies of old age. Three months earlier I had only heard fragments on the radio about a company called enron putting their name on a new baseball stadium for the Houston Astros. Six months earlier I had never even heard of enron.

Two years after enron's collapse, and a year after Lay stepped down as CEO, Jeff Skilling was indicted, led away in handcuffs. Lay and Skilling continued to claim there was nothing wrong with enron. The crash, they believed, in two-part harmony, was a classic *run on the bank,* brought on by a lack of faith in the value of enron's stock. Two weeks before enron filed for bankrotten protection, my boss, the young VP, had told us the same thing. All we had to do was go out and get those deals to help restore what was certainly a lack of faith.

Did I just say, "A lack of faith?"

As enron moved more and more into the distance, receding into history and off the front pages of the newspaper, I was stuck in the present. With a doctorate and an enron past, in a down Houston economy, I couldn't find a job. I couldn't see the future. One of the dead ends I followed, out of more than 400 job applications, was attending a meeting hosted by what turned out to be a subsidiary of Citibank, the folks who sell financial planning programs.

Once there, and the Citibank connection was revealed, I wanted to bolt, but out of respect to the 20-30 other desperate people looking for work, I sat through the entire presentation. When it was over, I brushed Citibank aside forever, following a debate with some guy who identified himself as a vice president of something.

I challenged this guy on Citibank's relationship to enron. He said he had no knowledge of that kind of thing, and he was probably right, but the discussion got into the reason enron, or Citibank, or any other commercial enterprise exists in the first place. His answer: to provide an attractive return to stock holders. He really, *really* believed this. He quickly became the john-the-baptist-ralph-nader advocate for creating wealth for stock holders.

Huh?

Now, I know a few MBA types out there think this is rather naïve, but I don't really give a crap what they believe on this particular topic. If I start a lemonade stand in response to a perceived market, and meet or exceed my customer's expectations for *quality products and services*, I expect to generate revenue. If I don't generate revenue, I get out of the business. If I stay in the business and manage my simple lemonade stand revenue wisely, I expect to take home a profit. Let's say I do. The more profit I take in, the more I grow. I expand. I decide to invite investors and I go public.

As my lemonade stand corporation goes public, why should my focus shift *from* my customers *to* my stockholders at my IPO? My original purpose was to meet customer expectations. The business was founded on faith in the

QUALITY of my products and services. Why, when going public, should faith's focus switch from QUALITY to share price?

Even a venture capitalist investing in an entrepreneurial start-up enterprise, and whose primary mission is to turn a profit from that start-up, is studying your business plan – looking to see if your scheme, your processes and products are going to delight customers better than the existing market.

If you have investors, they own part of the company. As part owners of the company, they should be focused on your customers' *faith* in the QUALITY of your products and services. If you continue to earn that faith, you should continue to generate revenue. If you manage your business revenue wisely, you should expect to take home a profit. Revenue and the potential residual profit are derivatives of QUALITY.

Did I just say derivatives? That's it! I found it! enron failed because they stopped selling QUALITY; they innovated the cobbled-together-pipeline-cum-energy company away from the *focus* on QUALITY as a way to generate faith in the company. They were selling derivatives of QUALITY. enron became a brokerage house for the derivatives of QUALITY, without actually *having* QUALITY.

I was two steps closer to getting past denial. But only one step closer to getting past anger. I needed a job. I didn't know it yet, but I was in the early stages of separation anxiety. The Grief Cycle. I was still in denial. Years from now, newspapers, magazines, television's financial pundits, motion pictures and books will have danced around the topic of denial in the minds of stockholders, major investors, Wall Street in general, the Securities and Exchange Commission in particular, policy makers and alleged culprits. Analysis of enron's meteoric rise, crash, and far-reaching crater will continue to generate fuel for MBA textbook prose for a generation, focusing in large part on accounting and business practices or ethics. Just as high school and college students of the 1990s read about Tammany Hall a hundred years earlier, students of the decade 2100-2110 will read about enron.

But one to two years later, analysis of denial in the minds of exiting employees will have been distilled into the concept of denying the probability of being laid off, or denial of the possibility of enron's wrongdoing.

It doesn't work that way.

It's more than two years later. Denial has long arms and the reach extends well into Anger, Shock, Fear, Frustration and Confusion. Denial is a catalyst for Stress.

The published research of Leon Festinger and Elliot Aronson (among others) defines the contemporary field of social psychology.[xix] By default, social psychology bleeds into organizational psychology, human motivation, and the dance between the mind of the employee and the culture of the corporation. One of the most interesting of the core concepts in social psychology is Cognitive Dissonance. This is that uncomfortable state in which your brain holds two cognitions, two competing realities: I'm cheating on my taxes; cheating is wrong. I'm driving over the speed limit; speeding is wrong. The doctor tells me I have cancer; this can't happen to me. I'm a good person; I've just been laid off. I'm making millions on this deal; there's nothing technically illegal about it.

Aronson and common sense suggest that the brain can't deal with the discomfort – the dissonance – so we justify one choice and deny the other. We minimize the bad on the bad side; we inflate the good on the good side. In combat, soldiers face the reality that killing is bad, but also that killing is part of war and thinking of the bad guys as "bad" guys eases the discomfort. Soldiers make war easier by dehumanizing the enemy, thus depersonalizing the art of killing people.

We can justify cheating on our taxes by accepting that "everyone does it," and the IRS and Federal Government are the big guys; we're the little guys and need a break. A hundred dollars or so won't make a big difference. We can justify driving over the speed limit because, again, everyone else is doing it. Getting to work on time is essential to taking care of my family. We can justify making millions illegally or unethically by realizing that lots of other people have good jobs as a result. That's the theory.

How do I justify (rationalize) getting laid off? How do I justify not finding a job in the first month? The second month? The 10th month? These two realities are engaged in hand-to-hand combat in my head when I crawl into bed at night, in my dreams, when I wake, while I'm paging through ten thousand jobs a day on the Internet. These two cognitions are posed as "I'm a success." and "I'm a failure." I didn't do anything wrong. I am a good person with a college education, a great work history, solid referrals. I'm unemployed.

I have to resolve this. Shock is a slap in the face, and denial is the first shock absorber. Shock is a surprise, like hitting a hole in the road or backing into a tree you didn't realize was there. Shock is when that someone special flushes the toilet while you're enjoying an already hot shower and the water temperature rises another 50 degrees. Shock is an earthquake in the middle of the night. Shock is the doctor telling you you've got a tumor. Shock sneaks up on you and stabs you in the back.

Shock is an instant.

By December 3, 2001, I wasn't shocked. I just didn't care. I didn't shave. I wore my Levi's 501 blue jeans and a T-shirt. Tony Lama cowboy boots. I got to work at 9:30. I didn't care. enron's RESPECT, INTEGRITY, COMMUNICATION and EXCELLENCE had already dissipated. Our division vice president toured the floor around 10 a.m. and told us where the meeting would be, at 11 a.m. By 12, I was gone, with one, last, small box. Everything else was already home. I wasn't shocked. It wasn't a surprise. I wasn't even in denial on December 3rd.... I didn't care. I was numb and I had the flu.

With a fever around 105, I drove home and found a bed. The next thing I remember it was Friday, December 7th. Pearl Harbor Day. I was driving into Houston for an unemployment seminar hosted by the Texas Workforce Commission. National Public Radio – NPR – undulated between stories of enron's crash and the beginnings of a war on terrorism. Body counts from the clean-up at Ground Zero in New York and the threat of biological warfare were headlines.

Weekly revelations from whistle-blowers, and 5th Amendment-mute or finger-pointing corporate officers would soon point to greed as the newest strain of anthrax to threaten the livelihoods and pension accounts of tens of thousands of Americans. With the backdrop of war and *bankrotten* corporations, 4500 former enron employees took their first steps into unemployment, many unemployed for the first time.

About four months earlier, in the wake of Skilling's departure, when Ken Lay had assembled the Houston masses in the ballroom of the Hyatt hotel, across the street from enron's 1400 Smith Street headquarters, and linked other enron employees by satellite, employees were offered the opportunity to send questions to the podium. I hadn't been at enron long enough to understand the details in questions about the gas-fired power plant in Dabhol, India, or the Azurix water deal. I wasn't tuned in to all of the internal politics at enron, and it probably wouldn't have mattered – I doubt I would have had enough information to formulate a decision to leave the company.

Enron's announcement that it was taking a charge of $1.1 Billion was not a shock like cold water in a hot shower. It was more like inviting 100 friends and neighbors to a big cookout in the back yard – and 23 people show up. Major disappointment. Some anger. Some frustration. But not shock because it takes a while for the realization to become reality. Besides, enron could weather this storm. Ken Lay said so.

But when Ken Lay was reading questions from the

assembled thousands and one of the questions was, "Are you on drugs?" *That's* when I was shocked. People aren't supposed to address the CEO of a major corporation with that kind of disrespect. The 60-something Lay with a broad, ready grin and Bob-Hope-ish nose looked like a kindly grandfather. We don't talk to grandpa that way.

It would be months before the soundness of the question would come clear. It was indeed a rational question. "What the heck are you doing with our company!" Some, maybe many, of the traders knew. The traders had the inside track.

Friday, December 7

At the end of a week of sleeping and staggering with the flu, there was a recording from enron on my home answering machine: "There will be employment seminars for laid-off employees at 9, 11, 1 and 3 at the George R. Brown Convention Center."

As the recording droned on with directions and information about parking, the final morsel was about a job fair at enron Field next week. I made it to my computer and dressed up my resume.

The Texas Employment Commission presentation was full of information, but it quickly became clear that even though enron itself was providing many resources to severed employees, overtly or covertly, it would be impractical for me to use those resources at downtown Houston locations. Gas prices were still relatively low at around $1.10 to $1.20 per gallon, but three round trips into Houston and I'd be filling up again with a ½-ton pickup truck.

As a segue into unemployment, the presentation was even amusing at times: "You mean if I make $25 mowing my neighbor's yard, I have to report it?"

"Of course."

"What about $10?"

"It's income."

Income is part of what keeps us working. Call it external, tangible rewards or extrinsic motivation. Either way, the paycheck is only symbolic, as we quickly convert it into house payments, car payments, consumer goods purchases and vacations. What we're really working for is internal rewards. Assuming our minimum financial needs are met, what we truly crave is intrinsic motivation. A pat on the back from the boss. Admiration from peers. Recognition, from our families, of our roles as breadwinners.

What we seek is Relevance.

Festinger's work, Aronson's work, and countless studies by other social psychologists in the decades since continually reaffirm that internal, intrinsic, intangible rewards – based on values – are longer-lasting and more effective motivators than financial – tangible – rewards.

What happens when greed steps in?

Two things. First, the guiding norms of society that keep most of us in check from day to day work well enough, until we get to the formalization of those norms as regulations or laws. Agencies, organizations, governments and even parents who emphasize the rules, laws, policies or generally accepted accounting practices, have set themselves a trap. The more we emphasize the law, the greater the chance the governed will try to find nuances, exclusions, exceptions and other ways around the law. Having fixated on the law, deviations from the strictest interpretations of a violation become justifiable – psychologically and perhaps even legally and ethically, as the phrase "even the appearance of unethical behavior..." is open to *interpretation*. Consider the language of the defense attorneys at Skilling's trial. Interpretation.

The second inextricably linked phenomenon is what behavioral psychologist B.F. Skinner called *non-contingent reinforcement*. The concept was visible during the welfare generations, when millions of Americans only had to be poor to stay on the dole. They didn't have to do anything. In other words, they were being paid far more than what their labors (nothing) were worth. One welfare generation bred the next. Because there was so much money to be made at enron, like million-dollar bonuses, with very little effort, enron had created a welfare class at the top, whose reinforcement (money and power) provided the *appearance* of positive peer recognition and positive self-esteem, and was contingent not upon QUALITY products and services but on profit – a false motivator.

Faced with the opportunity to make millions in an under-regulated energy market, or in risk differentials in broadband, water, wind energy or other arbitrage, a handful of people allegedly created a culture of doing the right thing. Not doing the right thing for the right reason. Just doing the right thing according to the prevailing culture – making money. Almost everybody bought in to this culture.

Almost.

Justification theory works for organizations as well as for people, as organizations (corporate officers) inflate the positive and minimize the negative in any controversial decision. Organizations have a personality, expressed in their culture, their expressions of social responsibility. That personality or culture is a semi-permeable membrane. If I were the Wizard of Ozmosis, I would have been able to break into the culture. But I wasn't. For one thing, at 45 I was too old by enron's unwritten standards. The fast movers were in their 20s and 30s. Secondly, I didn't have a math background, was not an energy trader, and so was not in the mainstream. As a training manager, I was playing the role of an extra. A non-essential cast member.

And so, non-essential, I collected information on the Texas Workforce Commission, instructions on filing for unemployment for the first time in my life, and headed home to my five-and-a-half-month-old house, newly constructed and first occupied in June. It was a middle-class home I could easily afford the day I started at enron. Months later, a few friends and relatives would ask why I didn't just sell the darn thing. I asked, "If you got laid off tomorrow, with no more than two weeks, perhaps a month of anticipation, would you sell your home tomorrow?"

"No."

"Would you put it on the market after a week?"

"I don't know."

"When *would* you decide to sell it?"

"I guess when it seemed obvious I wasn't going to find a job..."

"There's your answer." It never seemed obvious that I wasn't going to have enough to cover the house payments, utilities, truck, gas, groceries and so on. Besides, with new construction going up all around Houston, I couldn't sell the house for what I owed. But I found the faith, month after month. And that faith was answered in some of the strangest ways.

When my 5-year-old daughter asked why I was home, I told her enron was broken. She was sad, but supportive. She suggested I could get a new job, at a Toys R Us. They have discounts for employees.

There are 168 hours in a week. If I could have found four full-time jobs at 40 hours a week, making $10 an hour bagging groceries (not likely), it would have left me with an hour of sleep a day, one hour a week to play around with, and less than 80 percent of my enron income.

January, 2002

After the marathon in Mississippi, I started to pay much closer attention to my personal finances. I had started personalizing my new home, but mostly with paint. I put off the expense for sod in the back yard. The bigger ticket purchases could wait, like furniture for two of the bed rooms, the dining room and kitchen; wood floors; plantation-style shutters for the front windows; landscaping – the usual things new homeowners try to take care of on Pleasant Valley Sunday, with rows of houses all the same.

After the lay-off on December 3rd, with increased vigilance on the checkbook and credit cards, I hatched what would be a workable plan for Christmas to convince my daughter that everything was going to work out just fine. I had just cleared most of the hurdles that come with a new home, with a new refrigerator and washer-dryer combo – all before any of us had an inkling that enron was sinking. I had traded my '97 Chevy truck for a '99 Ford in September 2001. I didn't have a cash cushion. By juggling the $1200 monthly unemployment (for six months), the available credit in bank lines of credit and on credit cards, with my monthly military pension – which by itself covered about two-thirds of the house payment but nothing else – I could make it through December and January. By February 1st I had to have a job or I would be at that decision point, selling the house and filing bankruptcy.

January dissolved. The records I kept for the Texas Employment Commission show that I applied for 20 jobs between December 7th and January 28th. Pickings were slim, but every one of these seemed like a natural fit: executive director of a community college satellite campus, director of training, soft skills trainer, director for international e-learning, director for youth publications. I had a pending application in at the CIA. As a retired military intelligence officer, I had sent in a query within a month after 9/11, and two months before bankrotten. It would be months later that I would receive a form letter thanking me for my interest in the Clandestine Service Recruit Training Program, and learn that the CIA had been swamped by tens of thousands of resumes following 9/11.

There must've been an east wind blowing. My grandma used to say, "When the wind is in the west, the fishes bite the best; when the wind is in the east, the fishes bite the least. Heck, my "fishes" weren't even looking at the hook.

We cleared January with all bills paid on time, then angels started showing up. On Valentine's Day a dear friend offered a small loan. I was beginning to understand despair. Lots of things fell off the list of what used to seem routine – eating out at a restaurant, going to a movie, shaving, pickles, paper towels, steak, gas for the barbeque grill, buying anything at a store other than essentials like Ramen noodles, milk, eggs, bread, fruit. I recycled contact lenses that were supposed to be worn for a month, and kept two pair clean and serviceable for another two years. I used a gift card to get groceries for dinner with my daughter – chicken, hot dogs, real salads. I couldn't let her see me as a failure.

I did my best to stay engaged with real people even though I didn't have the gas money to get out, and checked the ex-enron message boards daily in the hope that networking might point me to an interview or a job.

February 25, 2002

Then came word that there might be some movement on the severance issue. A town hall meeting was planned for Monday, the 25th of February. The meeting was to be hosted by U.S. Representatives Shelia Jackson Lee and Kevin Brady, in cooperation with the AFL-CIO and the Rainbow-PUSH Coalition. Now I'll be honest; I've never had much time for unions. My very first paycheck, when I was 16, came from a union job. I bagged groceries and paid into the union dues. But through a lifetime in the military, unions just didn't have any meaning for me. I ain't fer 'em or agin' em, so they have a right to think they generally help workers and I have a right to think they generally inflate the cost of labor and therefore the cost of American goods and services. What I wanted was to hear interim CEO Steve Cooper at the town hall meeting tell us enron was going to pay severance. Described in the media as *embattled,* Ken Lay had stepped down in late January. I decided to spend the $5 in gas money and go.

I dressed for the occasion – jeans and a T-shirt. I hadn't shaved in nine days. I listened with disinterest through nearly an hour of self-referential soap boxing and I've done this and I've done that by politicians before we got to the issues. And then finally, Cooper, who had been at the dais the whole time, was prepared to respond to questions.

The more I listened the angrier I got. Cooper was a hired gun who had been brought in to disassemble and reconstruct the remnants of enron. He'd been successful at this kind of mission before, and in most of those cases restoring life to a corporation's corpse meant reducing costs. In the corporate boardrooms of the United States, cost translates directly to salaries. I wanted to get up right there and give this joker a piece of my mind, but I was nervous. What if I made an ass of myself? There were TV cameras. There were armed security officers. Many of my friends were there. I composed myself, then composed my comments.

Finally I got in line to ask a question. This was not like me. I don't carry banners at causes. I don't campaign for politicians. It turned out I would be the final voice asking Cooper about what he planned to do for ex-enron employees.

As I began my intro, at the request of the moderator, I introduced myself as a doctor of education, hired as a training manager 18 months before bankrotten. I told Mr. Cooper I expected enron would make good on its published corporate severance plan – a week's pay for every $10K in salary, plus a week's pay for each year or partial year of service, doubled if the employee doesn't sue the company for the separation. enron owed me more than $230,000 in severance alone (not counting my now-worthless stock options and the $20,000 bonus I was expecting in two months), a fraction of what some of my colleagues should have been getting. I told Mr. Cooper directly that I expected to have that check this week as I was running out of Ramen noodles at 15 cents a meal, that shave cream costs 90 cents a can at Wal-Mart and I wouldn't have the gas money to make it to any more of these staged media events.

Mr. Cooper responded that his hands were tied by the courts and bankruptcy law. We had been sent home December 3rd, officially laid off on December 5th and enron had filed for bankruptcy on December 1st. He just wasn't allowed to pay severance to employees who had been released *after* the bankruptcy. (How convenient.) Some of my fellow exroners had lost millions in the value of their retirement funds, 401K's and outright purchases of enron stock.

"You can't pay $50 million in severance to 4500 employees but you can pay $175 million in retention bonuses to a few hundred people?" I asked. I was shocked again. This son-of-a-CEO wasn't going to do anything for us.

"That's right." Cooper replied.

"Then, sir, I have a plan for you...for enron. Right now. Right here – hire all of us back." My fists were clenched and my muscles were twitching. "We'll be active employees. Calculate our severance. Pay it. Then we'll all quit and disappear with the cash and I promise you won't hear from at least me ever again."

Cooper's negative response was muffled by the applause. Before I left, I approached Mr. Cooper and told him I would be glad to offer workshops on leadership and ethics to the remaining senior managers at enron. No reply.

A week later, enron announced a $5 million relief fund that would pay out $1100 per laid-off employee. Once. I *know* I contributed to that decision. I had personified desperation. It was pennies on the dollar, but I'd take it. It would be the first check from enron since their check for my saved vacation cleared the bank in late December.

I could generate megawatts from the leftover testosterone brought on by Anger and Shock. (or is that adrenaline?) The truth was, I had just discovered a new endorphin – pistofferone.

Denial was gone. For now.

I was unemployed and enron wasn't going to pay severance. I wasn't going to find a job.

Thirteen: Laser Chapter 5

"Un-flippin-believable!"

"You okay Lad?"

"Sure, Skipper. Did I say 'unbelievable!'? Let me say it again. I've never seen anything like that!" Murdoch exhaled in awe of the alien's disintegration.

"Me neither, Murdoch. Me neither," Steele said, tapping the laser. "This thing wasn't designed as an anti-personnel weapon. Obviously."

The two Marines uneasily surveyed their surroundings from the firing position, fully expecting some sort of retaliation. As satisfied as they could be that the intruder had been on his, or its, own, Steele and Murdoch approached the Mach M and inspected the shreds of the alien scout, some of which were still floating to Earth like so many pieces of dandelion fluff.

"Keep an eye out."

"Roger that, sir...sure looks like this M is out of the game, captain."

"We'll see." Steele replied as he mounted the service step beneath the inboard jet of the rotational thrust-lifters. The area was covered in goo, a quickly hardening plastic of no-kidding alien origin.

"Probably some sort of polycyclic aromatic hydrocarbon."

"Oh gimme a break, captain. Sir. Could you say that again in plain English? And besides, I thought you was a preacher in your past life."

"It's an old Indian trick, Sergeant Murdoch. I read a lot. Just signs of life on Mars," Steele grinned as he picked with his K-bar at the substance pitting the canopy, and now eating into the fuselage and wing of the aircraft.

The alien form that apparently carried life had burst like a papier-mâché piñata. The snow-falling fragments were reconstituting in the gathering dew on the wing, canopy and starboard side of the fuselage and solidifying like melted crayons dripped onto a cold surface.

"These guys must be hydrocarbon based..."

"You're doing it again, Captain."

"Oh. We're carbon-based life forms. Didn't you ever watch Star Trek?"

"Way long before my time, Skipper."

"Me too. I watched the re-runs. Point is...they must have lots of hydrogen in them. We don't have so much free-standing hydrogen on Earth, but it's the most common element in the universe. Hydrogen combined with carbon, or hydrocarbons in various forms, make oil, gas, kerosene and a variety of petroleum-based things, including gas, diesel, plastics. Ya just gotta cook it right."

"Looks like we cooked it all right! Geez...So these guys are made out of plastic?"

"Well, some sort of oil or goo. And I would guess their blood runs liquid chlorine."

"Like bleach?"

"Like bleach. Cook hydrocarbons and you knock off hydrogen molecules. When you mix hydrogen and chlorine in the right balance, you get hydrochloric acid. It takes on a liquid form when it comes in contact with water, and heat speeds up the process. Hmm....Wonder why they want so much water."

Murdoch noted the rising tendrils of smoke as the corrosive beads continued their assault on the fighter. "Is all that true, Skipper...all that hydro-acid stuff?"

"Doesn't matter if it's good chemistry. It sounded good when I said it, and a theory is good until someone else comes up with a better one." Steele glanced over his shoulder, grinning, to see if Murdoch even cared about the chemistry, and by now had already determined that the cockpit was unsafe for human use. "I don't suppose Ma has any more back home like you?"

"Sir?"

"Any other NCOs back at Corpus who know how to fly and who have the stones to break the rules and might be headed our way?"

"I doubt it, skipper. Weren't many bodies back at the flight line, and not much left on the base but hangar queens. We took this jet out of mothballs and strapped her together with hundred-mile-an-hour tape."

Steele shrugged and hopped off the plane, motioning for Murdoch to step back further. "That stuff will eat through the wings and get into the fuel soon. There's no immediate danger with the JP-4 but we don't need to be walking around in jet fuel mud, either. Meanwhile, it looks like we're back to being pedestrians for the next hundred miles. That's about three to four days to Corpus Christi."

"But Skipper. What about old bleach blood here? His fighter is still out there somewhere. He ain't gonna need it soon."

"Good point, Murdoch." The thought had crossed Steele's mind too moments before, but he had passed on the idea thinking the controls, the navigation would probably be too – well, alien. "And you think we can get it flying?"

"Why not, Captain? Things fly. You know – weight, lift, drag...."

Fourteen: Fear

The thrust of my job search was about to change. I reviewed the past three months, trying to figure out what was wrong in my approach. On the one hand, it could have been a negative attitude. I'll accept that was a possibility – but I doubt it. Perhaps I had an elitist perspective that told me bagging groceries, selling cars or stocking shelves would be counter-productive. If I took any old job, I would not be engaged in finding the right job. But I would not believe I was one of those looking for *instant gratification*. I wasn't even looking for gratification – I just wanted a fair chance. I didn't believe any corporation owed me a job, and I didn't believe 'the system' owed me a job. I just wanted the chance to compete like anyone else. I retraced my steps to the first job fair.

Retreat to Tuesday, 11 December 2001
Job Fair – enron Field

It had been a candy store. The possibilities seemed endless. Several hundred opportunists had descended on the mezzanine level of the new baseball stadium that would quickly grow weary of its nascent association with enron. The business world had shaken off an initial stock market drop following the terrorist attacks of 9-11, with the Dow recovering back to well above 10,000 at year's end. In mid-December 2001, there seemed to be no hint of the coming gloom. The cherry pickers were in a hiring mood. They were the Haliburtons and Bechtels, IBMs and Shell Oils, Boeings and Goodyears. Hundreds of companies showed up, including the small and medium local enterprises. All looking for the best and brightest. We couldn't all be crooks, could we? Both the exroners and the hiring companies were browsing for candy. It was a level playing field. For now.

I had three versions of my resume, 50 of each, and left one appropriately tailored copy with each of scores of headhunters, hiring managers and human resources scouts from companies large and small. Done and armed with a collection of various companies' business cards, brochures and job descriptions, I headed home to plot my course.

Most appealing was the immediate opening for Dean of Education at some art school – a 3rd rate for-profit college, but it would be fun. I had the academic qualifications and the experience for the job title, and I had an abiding interest in art, even if it was mostly a hobby. Three years earlier I had taken a series of junior college courses in commercial art so I could learn Adobe Photoshop and Illustrator. At the time, I wanted to learn how to build websites and interactive training media, among other things. This looked like the ideal job. It would even be a reasonable drive.

By Christmas that possibility was impossible. They wanted someone with management experience in a for-profit college, like University of Phoenix or DeVry. In the midst of becoming very, very good friends with the monster.com search engine, and careerbuilder.com, sixfigurejobs.com, the Houston Chronicle, Management Recruiters International and who knows what else, Daughter and I set about making Christmas as normal as possible. With the first unemployment check on the way, Daughter and I headed to the local Christmas tree farm to select and cut down our own. The house filled with scents of evergreen and apple pie. I managed questions about why there were few presents under the tree, "Santa will probably be bringing most of your presents this year, little one. Remember – enron is broken and Daddy doesn't have a job. Santa has a fulltime job, right?" She took that at face value, and agreed that Santa could probably come up with more from his workshop than I could on unemployment.

Saturday, January 5, 2002
@ monster.com

Reinvent

When those old established brands come face to face with new products in their markets, they reinvent. The Corn Flakes and Volvos, Compaq computers and Washington

Mutual banks come out with "New and Improved" somethings on a regular basis. There's my strategy. I'll reinvent myself as a utility player. You want a dean of education? That's me. I'm new and improved. If there was one thing I could do – I could write. At least I thought I could. Without stretching the truth a bit, I had experience or education, or both, that I could write into qualifications for a variety of jobs. You want someone with experience in business development in aerospace? I've done it. Intelligence officer? No sweat. Training manager for a call center? A beauty products company? That's new but I can do it. A restaurant chain? I've eaten there – I can do customer-service-anything-training. A nuclear power plant? Training is training...I can do that too. Musical instrument repairman? Roofer? How about that director of leadership and organizational development position? Wanna read my dissertation? Hey! Over here! Look at me!

Please.

The journal says: "It would be nice to have a job. The finances are getting tight. I've made the payment on the truck, and water, and gas. I filled the tank in my truck and have $90 left to the end of the month. Haven't seen an unemployment check yet. Paid the credit union line of credit payment and can pull out $900. When the unemployment check comes, I can make January's house payment...I hope before the 15th so I don't have to pay the $60 late payment fee."

I allowed myself a Christmas present. I added $10 to the $50 check from Favorite Auntie and registered for the 2002 Houston Marathon, January 20th. Running was medicinal.

Monday, 21 January

Confidence? Ignorance? Stupidity? More denial? If there was anything in life that seemed normal or natural, in addition to my Sons' and Daughter's love and support, it was running. Everyone has their own reasons for why they enjoyed or detested life at enron. For me, much of enjoying enron was the camaraderie of the enron running club and enron picking up the tab for 20-plus races a year – the 5K, 10K and half-marathon variety with smaller entry fees – and up to four marathons each year. All of this from $35 annual enron Running Club dues. With more than 200 members wearing enron-logo shirts and shorts, and a huge *Crooked E* team flag at every race, enron got plenty of advertising mileage out of the runners.

Some runners run, in part, for the same reason gamblers gamble. When you put a quarter in the slot machine and win $100, psychology says you'll probably drop another quarter, expecting another win. There's a science to the percentage of wins in scratch-off tickets (about one win in 4.75) that keeps regulars coming back for more. For my first race as a member of the enron running club, I joined a caravan of cars at 5 a.m. in early October 2000, to trek to Huntsville, home of the State Prison, for a half-marathon and 5K. I didn't feel ready for the half-marathon, so registered for the 5K. I took home the gold in my age group, with a 19:20-something time. Now I was stuck in the club and would go back to my high school days, looking for success.

But 15 months later and I was paying my own way. There would be no enron-sponsored 5K, 10K or 20K races on my deficit budget. Favorite Auntie's $50 Christmas present was my entry fee to the 2002 marathon and a contribution to my sanity. She didn't have to tell me, but I knew she would want me to use the money for Christmas, not pay bills. Of course, if I did pay bills, or buy groceries, she would never know the difference. I needed a healthy body to keep a healthy mind.

My second Houston marathon was the chance to run a smarter race. Better training and better carbs. On the evening before the race, I pinned a cloth to the back of my shirt, with the notice: "EX-ENRON PhD WILL DESIGN AND MANAGE CORPORATE TRAINING PROGRAMS FOR FOOD (& $$$...)" with my phone number and the additional information: "SWM SEEKS SWF RUNNER, 30-45." It was worth a shot. Like the resumes, the final line got some comments, but no takers.

Weather was nearly perfect, if a little warm. I melted another six minutes off my time, with a 3:55 finish. Slower start. Steadier pace. No 7:30 miles for me this time. I started with the 8-minute crowd and hung on to an overall pace of around 8:55.

All of these runners wanted my job – my position in the marathon. Some were older and had been doing this marathon thing for decades. They kept their jobs. They finished ahead of me. Some were younger, and finished ahead of me too. On the sidelines – an endless sea of anonymous faces. None of them could help. The orange slices, candy and cheers are like words of encouragement, but the cheerleaders can't pick me up and carry me to the finish line.

At the finish, I spotted my daughter at the final corner and I ran over to kiss the little one on her forehead. I was aching. She was crying. She told her mommy it was "tears of happiness."

I looked back. Thousands trailed. Many were older, but many were also younger. Lots younger. I wasn't beat yet. I didn't fear the marathon, but there's no money in running – at least not for guys like me.

Tuesday, 5 February
Two months

One interview. Through a head-hunter, I was introduced to the president of a small training company looking for a soft skills trainer. Someone to go into refining and pipeline companies and tell funny stories, throw candy and koozies to the participants, and deliver top-quality training in leadership skills, communication strategies, sexual harassment, diversity and similar topics.

Busted. This time the career track at General Motors, NASA and enron shot me down. This very nice fellow was afraid my resume was too-much oriented to technical training. My plea was that my work in technical training was all an accident. I didn't mean to do it. It just turned out that way. One of the accidents of history. I called this guy off and on for two more years and he never *got it.*

I remembered a movie, probably made in the 1950s or early '60s. I think Paul Newman was in it. Maybe Steve McQueen. Whoever the main character was, he was in a logging family. There was an accident, and one of the other logger's legs got pinned beneath a log in the water. Newman – the brother? – didn't want to leave him to get help, but he couldn't move the log either. The river current shifted the logs and pulled the brother's body further and further under the water. Eventually, he was submerged, holding his breath. Newman was powerless. His brother could hear him, with his face inches below the surface of the clear, racing river. Both knew he was going to drown. Newman said something to lift his spirits, and both laughed. The doomed brother, out of reach of fresh air, let go his laugh and swallowed the river. I cried.

So I cleaned out the garage and prepared to laugh at the river of debt. I sold furniture and tools. I sold clothes. I sold dishes. A neighbor delivered a $200 gift certificate for a grocery store. That day, I had more than I needed. It's just that I had no idea how I was going to cover the house payment and everything else for February.

Sunday, 10 February

I wrote, "Good Morning, Lord. Every day I wake up and ask – what is it You want me to do? It's been 67 days since enron."

And so I asked myself, what *can* I do? Or – what else can I do? In addition to the lengthening list of job applications, I looked at teaching in public school for less than half of what I was earning at enron. Cypress-Fairbanks Independent School District had openings and all I had to do was take two courses, "Instructional Leadership" and "Teacher Evaluation." I suggested I could teach those courses. They were not impressed. And all I had to do was wait for June and come up with $250. I didn't have $25.

After I rolled pennies and dimes, and cashed in the cigar box full of copper-clad Sacajawea dollars Daughter didn't know I was saving for her, I paid the electric bill, thankfully deflated without the air conditioner running through Houston's cool winter months. Then I started making plans to sell the rest of what I could part with, put the rest in storage, and move to life in a tent. Believing the sales pitch in 1977, I had bought an acre and a half of Robertson County, about 10 miles north of Texas A&M University. The idea was, College Station and Bryan were going to grow, and the Highway 6 corridor to Waco, then Dallas, would fill with development. My $6500 investment in 1977 would be wise. It didn't turn out that way. More than 25 years later, Bryan is all-but forgotten; all the growth has been in College Station, and the growth corridor is now a four-lane highway between College Station and Houston.

Unrealized dreams or not, that acre and a half was mine. I'd finished paying for it long ago. It didn't matter that the neighbors to my undeveloped lot had four cars on cement blocks and 12 dogs in the yard. I already knew I couldn't sell the lot for what I paid for it, but I could sure live on it. And if I did sell the lot, and cleared four or five thousand dollars, I could stretch another month or two with the unemployment checks, but then I wouldn't have an empty lot.

Thursday, 14 February
Valentine's Day

Some guy called about the air compressor. Sold. Then I sold the engine hoist. I wasn't going to get around to buying and rebuilding that 1971 Barracuda for a while. And then Dear Friend sent me a Valentine with $500. Finally I knew what I feared – I was a charity case. How would I be able to spend time with Daughter if I didn't have a house with four walls and a door? I wasn't worried about losing things. I feared failure.

Driving back from taking Daughter to school, listening to the news on NPR, I thought about the black humor. In the announcer's list of sponsors: "...something-or-other

Foundation, dedicated to finding and fighting the causes of homelessness..." Give me a call, you idiots. I'll tell you about the causes of homelessness.

One of my exroner buddies asked me by e-mail how things were going. E-mail and the coalescing association of former employees' chat rooms were a life-line. While my fear of failure was tangible, it would be months before I realized a fear of loneliness. It wasn't that I had yet developed a lot of strong personal bonds with people at enron; I had only been there a year and a half. I had closer friends from my previous job, contracting at NASA, but I would not go back there looking for salaried work; with the move to the new home it was now 110-mile a day round trip to jobs around Johnson Space Center. Three to four hours a day commuting? No thanks. And they were losing contracts to United Space Alliance on a monthly basis anyway. But with no day-to-day contact with fellow employees, and a year into single life, I lay in bed at night trying to calculate what percentage of my four-bedroom house my body took up. Alone.

I told the ex-enron buddy that week-to-week was like some kind of extreme sport. Free-falling out of an airplane with a skateboard or something and not knowing where I was going to land. I developed a mental image of the F-117 Stealth "Fighter" – dubbed the "Wobbly Goblin" by Air Force pilots. The F-117 is storied to be unstable in flight, but therefore also very maneuverable and thus – a good bomber. That's how I felt. Unstable. Uncertain. But maneuverable. I can do anything I want...But what? I wasn't getting any traction in the job hunt.

The $500 Valentine and proceeds from the yard sale, compressor and engine hoist, with the next unemployment check and my pension...cleared the February hurdle. I had until March 15th, March 30th at the latest, to worry about the next house payment. Everything was current, and I now had $35 for groceries. That would be plenty for more than two weeks' worth of groceries. I shifted further into the ramen noodle diet. I could've made millions if I had written down the recipes. Dieters would have loved it. I could still run on ramen carbs, and shed another five pounds in February.

I talked with my brother this week. He knew I was leaving the door open for him to offer me a loan, but I wouldn't ask. I did my best to explain my 'situation' in unemotional terms, though the frustration certainly leaked through. But I wouldn't ask. And then his final comment, which would resonate through the coming weeks and months, "You're not unemployed; you've already retired once. You're self-employed...you're just not making much money at it right now."

Saturday, 16 February
The garage

Another 20 resumes and job applications out the door this week, and no new responses. I had to get away from the computer screen. The Justice Department's investigation into enron's accounting practices was five weeks old, and while the stock market had gasped, the DOW was on the way back up. Wasn't it? This should be a great time to move back in to corporate America. But today I didn't care. Most days I was up by 4:30 a.m., had run five miles, showered, cruised through more than 10,000 job postings in search of maybe two, maybe eight or ten new possibilities each day, and had sent electronic cover letters and resumes to each of these, all by noon. Jobs were available in California, Massachusetts, Florida, Indiana, New York, Minnesota and all over the Middle East and the Former Soviet Union. They turned their backs on me...fine! This weekend I'll turn my back on them.

Cabin fever. On pinball and solitaire, I had the highest score in the house. Of course, I was the only person in the house, until Daughter came home. I had to get away from the computer, so I turned to the garage. The subdivision was starting to take shape. New home construction north, south and across the street offered unlimited supplies of scrap lumber, and I needed shelves in the garage. I already had a huge supply of deck screws from projects at the last house.

Midway through the project, I had to take a break. With 25-foot steel tape measure in hand, I drove five miles to the nearest Chevy dealer, parked my truck and strode over to the magnetic red 2002 Corvette convertible. Placing the tape on the ground beneath the front license plate, I extended it about 18-20 feet, then locked it and set the case on the deck. As I walked around to the back of the car, the ubiquitous salesman showed up with a quizzical look.

"Are we buying a 'Vette today?" he inquired politely.

"No-sir," I replied as I pushed the tape back to the edge of the rear bumper and walked back around to the front of the car to make adjustments and check my measurements.

With hands on hips and one alligator-skin-cowboy boot toe tapping, the fellow looked like a cowboy principal catching a couple of errant high school seniors contemplating a graffiti crime or something. I was waiting for him to scratch his head when I let him off, "I'm building shelves in my garage. The truck fits on one side...I need to make sure I leave enough room for the virtual 'Vette on the other.

He was nodding before I even finished explaining.

On the way home, I thought about this odd freedom to drive down to a car dealer any time I wanted without checking out with my boss, without being restricted to real car shopping on Saturdays. It didn't matter that a 'Vette, or any other new car for that matter, was so unrealistically removed from my current situation. I could do anything I wanted, any time I wanted. And so I did. I continued to wake at 4:30, study the job postings through two cups of coffee, run 5 to 10 miles and shower, then write and send cover letters and resumes and make job queries by phone, and be done by 10 a.m., 11 at the latest. I exhausted every possible job opportunity every day of the week.

But then I had another 12 hours to fill. I had to do something productive and I knew it. I started writing, but kept hitting dead ends. I started trying to learn Microsoft Front Page and other similar programs so I could build a web site, but didn't have enough of the fundamentals to get off first base. I finished the shelves in the garage and started rearranging scores of partially empty paint cans on the new shelves.

I had thought my painting duties in the new home were done. The formal living room was bright white and waiting for a white piano some day. The dining room was scarlet and waiting for a dining room table, chairs and buffet some day. Daughter's Wizard of Oz room was complete, and the master suite could wait until I could buy a bed and dressers. I was in no hurry to do any more painting.

Sunday, 17 February
A Lutheran Church

"Good morning," Pastor Ebullient began. "Today, we're continuing with the Apostle Paul's letter to the Romans, in Chapter 12, on his admonitions to the new Roman Christians on how they should conduct themselves in the creation of new churches. Beginning in verse 5, Paul writes:

> We have many parts in one body, and these parts all don't do the same thing. In the same way, many as we are, we are one body in Christ and individually parts of another. We have gifts according to what His grace gives us. If you can speak God's word, do it according to the faith. If you can teach, teach. If you can encourage, encourage. If you share, be generous. If you manage anything, do it eagerly. If you help people in need, do it cheerfully.[xx]

Hmmm...

I left the room with a swarm of ideas and walked to collect my daughter from her Sunday School class. As I walked and she skipped to the chapel, I asked, as I usually do, "So, what did you learn in Sunday School today?"

"I learned a new rule," she offered as she stooped long enough to collect a winter blossom.

"What's the rule?"

"You're s'posed to wake up every morning and look in the mirror..." she began.

I interrupted, "Before I have a cup of coffee?"

"Yup."

"But I'd be too scared to look in the mirror before I have a cup of coffee. I'm getting too old and ugly," I teased.

"No silly Daddy. You're s'posed to look in the mirror and smile," she insisted.

"Why?"

"Because then you'll ask yourself what you have to smile about, and when *I* look in the mirror, I'll be happy about YOU!" she explained matter-of-factly as she handed me the flower and skipped off to the chapel.

If you can encourage, encourage. I was getting the same kind of encouragement from Son One and Son Two by telephone from the East Coast, but as their local representative, Daughter put a special face on it.

I knew what I had to do. Then I remembered another Sunday School lesson from decades before:

A mountaineer was ascending the face of a treacherous peak, bringing up the rear in a party of five climbers, all linked by ropes and D-rings...carabiners. As they neared the summit, the rope snapped, releasing the fifth climber into freefall and headed for certain death.

Instantly the climber shouted out his prayer. "God! God! Can you hear me? If you're out there...SAVE MEEeeeeeeee...," he called out as he sped toward terminal velocity and his voice dopplered to the top of the mountain.

A branch shot out from the face of the cliff and snagged the doomed mountaineer. Somewhat bruised from the collision but thankful to be alive, the climber quickly wrapped both arms around the branch, and responded,

"Thanks God! Thank you SO much."

As the climber surveyed the situation, a strong, confident, disembodied voice spoke, "Did you get what you asked for?"

"Yes, God. Yes! Thank you!"

"Do you truly believe?"

"Oh yes, God. I believe. I really, truly believe!"

"Good. Then let go of the branch."

The answer was clear. If I was going to survive I would have to start my own business. With no money. Letting go of the branch meant I would have to put everything in God's hands. To get control I would have to release control. I wasn't an engineer but I could teach. I wasn't a heart surgeon, but I could manage. I wasn't an architect, but I could encourage. The little hope I had held on to so far had been the wish for severance from enron and the want ads, and those experiences had gone wanting.

I prayed, "What do YOU want me to do?"

"What do you *like* to do?"

"I like to teach. I like to paint. I like to write."

"Well...what are you waiting for?"

February 25th I filed a dba for Laser Consulting. I could round up $11 for that. I had a computer and a telephone. I had some ideas. That was the same night I attended that Town Hall meeting featuring Cooper and the Texas State Representatives, confirming that any hope for a just severance from enron was gone. Faith in the financial lifeline was futile. Belief that I would find a job through monster, careerbuilder.com, or 6-figure jobs seemed like a dead end. I could continue networking with little investment in time, and keep my job search active – I had all the time in the world. But I had to do more.

Driving home from the Town Hall meeting, I went through the trade-off studies in my mind: could I operate a business from a tent on an empty lot north of College Station? Probably not. Could I hang on to the house if I sold more stuff – had another yard sale? Possibly. If I had to make a decision, would I sell the refrigerator or washer and dryer? Turn off the phone or the electricity? What goes first, the old dining room set or the old living room furniture? The TV or the stove? People live without these things all over the world. I'd seen it in the Philippines, in Korea, Thailand. If I had just the shell of a house left when it was over, damn it all – I was still going to have a home.

I was tired, and close to my own neighborhood... my own home. I didn't want to think about emptying the house. Then, as if it had been choreographed, I hit the radio button for distraction. The local public radio station lit up the LED display. It was late; NPR and Marketplace had long since been replaced by a Schubert symphony. I pushed the button for the Oldies station, 107.5. Janis Joplin was "busted flat in Baton Rouge, waitin' for a train, feelin' nearly faded...' as her jeans." Freedom's just another word for nothin' left to lose.

I drove on through the night as Janis wailed the blues, stoned and near the end of her creative, desperate, innovative musical career. Barbara Streisand couldn't sing this song. Madonna couldn't. Olivia Newton John couldn't. Britney Spears couldn't. To sing the blues, you had to live the blues. Janis Joplin had the blues in her blood.

Fifteen: First Principle - Freedom

An unsolvable problem was flashing its lights at me, honking its horn and trying to get me to pull over. I had the same kind of dilemma Pirsig had faced. It was the puzzle police. For a time, my mind was under arrest, locked in an illogical loop.

On the one hand, I was searching for the American dream – a house, a red pickup truck, a job with a salary that would give me the freedom to do anything or buy anything I wanted. Financial independence. Freedom. Down the road I could imagine a red Corvette to keep the pickup company, a sailboat, a swimming pool, an aquarium in my office, a piano that I wouldn't be able to play but that my neighbors would admire and perhaps even envy. What could better define freedom than to have all these things, to have tons of cash in the bank?

On the other hand, if I accepted at face value the notion that *freedom's just another word for nothin' left to lose,* and I could imagine selling every*thing* in my home just to hang on to the house itself, and then two, three, six or some unknown number of months later admitting defeat and selling the house anyway – I'd be left with nothing. Nothing left to lose. Freedom.

These weren't just different versions of FREEDOM; they were totally contradictory. One of them had to be false.

Freedom is supposed to be a good thing, right? How could having nothing be a good thing? enron had given us our freedom, but it turned out to be a scary ride to the bottom. Worry about the bills, worry about the lack of dental insurance. Worry about whether there will be any food at the end of the week. The race to the bottom seemed like the *low-quality* option, but I didn't seem to *have* an option.

I considered the race to the top: 12- to 16-hour days under the control of corporate authority, creating wealth for someone else, three hours a day in Houston traffic...It didn't take long to see some of the major flaws in this version of freedom.

I looked back at the no-job, no-money version of freedom. Total freedom to turn any direction I wanted, any time I wanted. All I needed was air, water and minimal amounts of food. Air is free. The water bill was about $21 a month. Where was I going to get the food?

It was nearly midnight when I pulled in the driveway. Before I hit the rack that night, I turned to Matthew 6, starting at verse 25. Jesus taught the people:

"So I tell you, don't worry about what you'll eat or drink to keep alive or what you'll wear on your bodies. Isn't life more than food, and the body more important than clothes? Look at the birds in the air. They don't sow or cut grain or gather anything in barns; but your Father in heaven feeds them. Aren't you worth more than they? Can any of you by worrying add anything to your life? And why worry about clothes. See how the flowers grow in the field, and learn from them. They don't work and they don't spin. Yet, I tell you, even Solomon in all his glory didn't dress like one of these. If that's how God dresses the grass in the field, which lives today and tomorrow is thrown into a stove, how much more certainly will he put clothes on you – you who trust him so little? Don't worry, then, and say, "What are we going to eat?" or, "What are we going to drink?" or, "What are we going to wear?" The people of the world run after all these things. Your Father in heaven knows you need them all. Seek first God's kingdom and righteousness, and all these things will be given to you, too. So, don't worry about tomorrow. Tomorrow will take care of itself. Each day has enough trouble of its own.[xxi]

I hit the rack, scared, taking up a tiny percentage of a house I could no longer afford.

"So, God... You mean, if I give up everything, I win?"

"That's what I've been trying to tell you. The more *things* you have – the more you have to lose. That ain't freedom."

"What's it gonna cost me?"

"Trust me. I'll take it from here."

It wasn't a puzzle any longer. Freedom founded on wealth was a false derivative of Quality. I had fallen into the same trap as enron, and when we were kicked out, I was trying to force myself back in to the corporate solution. There certainly must be a company, an organization out there somewhere that exemplified the goals and values I was looking for, but for now, I would be less willing to jump at the first opportunity. While I kept my options open, I would focus on what I *wanted* to do, on my terms. In fact, if I could help other organizations find that kind of quality...if I could help them be successful, then I would be successful.

'Freedom's just another word for nothin' left to lose' was the punch line. It was the point. The song was *Me and Bobby McGee*, a Kris Kristofferson song that echoed his own decision to pursue an unlikely career. In September 2003, *Nashville Scene's* Michael McCall tells the story of Kristofferson's career, as he was preparing to return to Nashville to receive the Spirit of America Award from the Americana Music Association and the First Amendment Center. In 1964, Kristofferson had been

> ...an army captain and a veteran of the elite Airborne Rangers who had trained as a parachute jumper and helicopter pilot. He was a Rhodes Scholar, a graduate of Oxford University and an authority on the English romantic poets, especially William Blake. He was a Golden Gloves boxer who had lettered in football and soccer in college. He'd married his beautiful high-school sweetheart. He had two healthy, bright kids. And, just after turning 29 years old, he'd been appointed the esteemed post of literature professor at the United States Military Academy at West Point. Then he threw all of it away. The week he

was to assume his new job, he informed the military and his family that he had decided to move to Nashville to become a country songwriter.[xxii]

Kristofferson hung on to his dream through the second half of the 60s, with a single credit that failed to make the top 100. His wife left him. After a series of dead-end jobs to make ends meet while hustling music, Kristofferson landed back in Nashville. He tells McCall that his brother traveled to Nashville to confront him: "When are you going to do something you can *do?*"

Kristofferson had talent. He had vision. He had sweat. He had faith.

I could beat fear with faith. Deny ENRON ever existed. It's a distant memory. Release the anger. Get over it. Recover from the shock. Freedom – nothin' left to lose – is a Quality event.

The next day, I started work on a real business plan for Laser Consulting. I promised to give every one of my employees freedom...freedom to create, to innovate, to synthesize, to wear whatever they wanted to work. But to have faith that their labors were worthwhile, they would need a vision to work toward. They would need direction. They would need focus.

This would be an easy message to get out...but convincing my employees was another matter. I was the only employee. But I was still working for free.

Sixteen: Laser Chapter 6

Retrieving the transponder as he and Murdoch shoved off toward the last good position on the alien craft, Steele tossed the handheld device to the sergeant, "Here you go, Murdoch. See if there's anything up on the net. We're still in receive mode, got it?"

"Got it, Skipper."

"If we don't hit pay dirt on the bad guy's plane, it'll eventually make sense to start pinging the net once or twice a day...see if anybody out there is receiving."

"Roger that, Captain."

Twenty minutes later, Murdoch's azimuth on the war bird proved accurate enough. An Invader fighter/attack air-breather, unattended and ripe for the taking. As they made their way over the final ridge and down to the strange-looking metallic bird, Steele thought back to flight school. He couldn't wait to get his tail in a cockpit and his hands on the stick. He grinned to think that the first thing the training squadron C.O. had said was, "Don't forget: Every Marine is a rifleman." What a disappointing but accurate truism. "That multi-million-dollar piece of hardware on the apron out there is on loan. Pay attention. Fly right. Get your wings. Screw up and we take the little airplanes away and send you back to a ditch with a platoon of grunts."

Fate delivered Steele to a ditch anyway, with a rifle and a platoon of grunts, even though he still wore the wings. Surrounded by endless miles of sand, hills, and a few million poor, underfed, restless non-combatants in a far-away country still reeling from decades under yet one more self-important dictator with terrorist tendencies, Steele was in the squadron that drew the short straw – sitting on a flight line in a desert.

The adversary: air forces from three neighboring countries intent on imposing their versions of tribal democracy. A rifle company from 3rd Battalion, 4th Marine

Regiment rode shotgun as a ground force to the expeditionary unit.

When the rocket and mortar attacks fell inside the perimeter and ten thousand natives overran the flight line, Steele was sure he had already seen his last day in a cockpit. Suddenly the non-combatants had decided the Americans should go home. No warning. Self-organizing systems with social media? Flash Mob? Bad memes? Coming out of that death dance alive was only part of the reason for the first career change.

Kathryn was the other. She needed someone to rely on, closer to home than 10,000 miles, and home more often than six months out of every twenty-four. Out of seven billion souls on the planet, how did they pick her for a hostage? He knew his "why me?" wasn't going to get her back, and if the troopers from the far side of the galaxy had picked on someone else, they would be saying, "Why me?" instead.

When the aliens showed up most of the globe's petty squabbles got put on the sidelines. That doesn't mean two hundred different countries, with different cultures, instantly started playing nice and working well together. Most were intent on self-defense, circling their own wagons. Steele put his primary calling, the ministry, temporarily on the sidelines in favor of another calling, and jumped on the wagon headed back to active duty, like millions of others. Kathryn's abduction was witnessed by hundreds and made the headlines in seconds.

Now it was personal.

As he cautiously stepped up to the Invader aircraft, Murdoch asked, "Whatchya thinking, Skipper? You been pretty quiet..."

"Working on a creative way to get into the bad guy's HQ."

"Huh?"

"Don't worry. You don't have to ride along. We can

worry about that later. Now, let's take a look at what Galaxy Motors has been rolling off the assembly line."

Murdoch kept the laser canon on 'ready,' keeping an eye on the breaking dawn and surrounding terrain as the captain climbed into the open cockpit.

"Hop into my new '58 Chevy, Sergeant Murdoch," Steele called down. "There's room for two up here."

Murdoch safed the weapon and climbed up the ladder into the starboard seat.

"Heck, Skipper. There's no labels on any of these switches. No English. No nothing."

"What did you expect... they would build these things for export?" Steele put Murdoch to work, "You're qualified in a cockpit...see if you can identify comm and nav systems. I'll see if I can find power and weapons. Whatever you do, BE careful!"

"Geez, Skipper, you don't have to tell *me* that," Murdoch grunted, happy to be getting his first real test pilot lesson. Steele and Murdoch gingerly flipped switches, one at a time, looking for indicators on the dashboard to show signs of life. Murdoch discovered the first. "Hey Captain, heads up," he said as he looked joyfully at the HUD, projecting the top half of a green spider web on the interior of the front windscreen.

Steele's heart jumped a beat, thinking for a moment that Sergeant Murdoch was delivering a warning, but the tone of his voice wasn't consistent with the words.

"Good job! We've got internal batteries, Steele replied as he eased the joystick aft. Now all I've got to do....is...Got it!"

"What?" Murdoch asked as the plane started humming with a deep-throated vibration.

"You'll see."

"See what? What's going on, Captain?"

"Look over the side."

Murdoch complied. "Uh, Skipper...I think you found power." They were hovering silently ten feet off the deck.

Steele shut down the alien fighter and quickly climbed out of the cockpit as the craft settled its skids into the sand. "I've got to check this out. Come on!"

"What?"

"I want to see what this thing runs on, and I bet it ain't gas."

Murdoch followed. "What difference does it make? If it runs, it runs. Let's fly this thing the heck outta here."

Releasing panels from the port-side belly of the fuselage, Steele responded, "Because, if it is what I think it is, the way this thing powers up will have a significant impact on flight dynamics. Not just mom and pop thrust, or pitch, yaw and roll, but stopping, acceleration, thrust-to-weight, the touch of the stick and everything else."

"Oh." Murdoch was not confused. He'd had plenty of ground school. None of the jargon was at all alien. He just wanted to get back to some friendly, familiar territory, like Corpus Christi.

"Bingo!"

"Now what?" Murdock asked, peering into the belly of the fighter.

"Check this out. Looks like a magnifying glass."

"But I can't see through it, Skipper. What is it?"

"I told you – I think it's *like* a magnifying glass. Get back up there and pull back on the stick."

"Got it." Murdoch clambered into the cockpit and

complied. As he pulled back on the joystick, gently, the craft lifted inches off the deck, then one, two, three feet."

"That's it! Shut 'er down!" Steele called out.

Murdoch hopped out of the plane and rejoined the captain under the fighter. "What the heck is it, Captain?"

"Take a look," Steele urged. "Think about it like this," he said, "For the past hundred and fifty years or more, and especially since the Wright Brothers, we've been fighting gravity rather than working with it. We've been pushing against the gravity that holds us to Earth, rather than reaching out to the gravity pulling us to the stars. Gravity is everywhere in the universe. Mass is everywhere in the universe. Even that rickety old space station gets a tiny tug from Jupiter and Saturn, away from Earth's gravity."

"How much do you weigh, Sergeant Murdoch?"

"Sir? About 150 pounds. Why?"

"But it's really more like 151 pounds – 150 pulled toward the center of the Earth and 1 pound being pulled away from the Earth by the Moon, and the Sun, Jupiter and Saturn and the rest of the mass of the universe."

"That's crazy. Sir."

"No. It isn't crazy. We've known it all along; we just never knew what to do with it on Earth. Astronauts deal with it in space all the time. You know how a magnifying glass focuses the sun's rays into a point, how it can get hot, even start a fire?"

"Sure. So...?"

"I figure this alien contraption gathers gravity – even distant gravity – and focuses it. Gravity is a form of energy, like energy from the Sun. Like our jammers use electromagnetic energy. Gravity, magnetism and electricity are all related. The more focused it is, the easier it is for these alien dudes to counter the effects of Earth's gravity. All they have to worry about in our atmosphere is drag. If they're on the top end of this, they probably figured out how to drink Earth's own gravity, focus the energy, reverse the field and use it to push against the rest of the mass."

"That's nuts, Skipper. Where do you get this stuff?"

"I've got a muse. Hop in. Let's give this baby a test drive."

Seventeen: Frustration. Confusion. Stress.

Daughter has gradually moved on from making Pooh and meta-Pooh in the sand box, and as the normal course of events for a 7-year-old has recently started delivering Girl Scout cookies for her Brownie troop. Some of the girls think it's not fair that she lives in two subdivisions and has two families. She sold more than 200 boxes of those troublemaking cookies. (If no one is watching (and no one ever is), I will down a box of Thin Mints with my two cups of morning coffee.)

It's carbs.

(I run.)

Selling cookies, it turns out, is a lot more fun than delivering them. As we set out for our fifth trip through the neighborhood, hopefully to find at home some of the people who were not home earlier in the week, it took some urging to get Daughter moving toward the doors and doorbells. As the public service television commercial urges, I suggested she "Verb to the door and verb the doorbell. Verb on the door and don't forget to verb your customers."

"Daaaa...........ad. 'Stand' is a verb." (I was actually looking for an action verb.)

Smarty pants. But I'm a patient guy, and gently coaxed her on to finish what she had started. I thought wistfully of the days of Winnie the Pooh in the sand box, but realistically had resigned myself to this one growing up too. Long ago. She was a second chance, and chances are ethereal. They come; they disappear. I was still patiently focused on making the most of this chance, and worked on it like a teacher, a mentor. I'm no stranger to work, and I want her to value work too.

I believe Eternal Salvation, Eternal Freedom, is free – Grace through Faith – but I've never believed human, earthly *freedom* was free. I spent 22 years in uniform contributing my very small part to American freedom. Over 40-some years,

I *have* bagged groceries, sold popcorn, cleaned toilets, roofed houses, picked berries, installed linoleum, unloaded steel and dug fence post holes for miles. I was more than willing to put the effort into creating a business.

Daughter's advantage in selling cookies was in the breadth of her network. Mom has home-based businesses and family members across the country; I have a home-based business and other family members in different parts of the country. Just checking in with the network isn't a guarantee that someone will buy cookies, but you can't find out if your product or service responds to your potential customers' desire for *quality* unless you contact them.

Checking in with *my* network, for a Leadership Seminar, means tracking down relatives, friends, former Marines, Aggies (those beloved graduates of Texas A&M University) and past business associates, by phone, e-mail or in person. I find it tedious, tracking down and targeting prospects. With a laser range-finder, the operator sends out a low-powered beam of light; the time it takes for the reflected beam to return indicates the distance to a target. At the speed of light, the process is accurate and essentially instantaneous. Job-hunting is neither.

With telephone and e-mail, the experience is more like radar. Sometimes the targets are operating in stealth mode. They know the calls are coming and they don't want to respond with bad news, "Sorry. No jobs at our location. We're actually looking at laying off." Sometimes the signal gets jammed (Mr. Johnson will return your call tomorrow...but he never does), or the field shows false targets. The bad guys want you to waste your time shooting at false targets.

Time is a bad guy; frustration, confusion and stress are bad guys. On a radar screen, good targets can hide *in the grass*, meaning the legitimate signals are indistinguishable from the radar noise sent out by the jammers, and appear as green static on the radar screen. But if the arsenal is full of inexpensive ammunition, like resumes and cover letters, why not take a shot at everything?

March through September, 2002

Hanging on to hope at this stage was a function of prayer, patience, minimal financial resources and any lead on a job or contract...*any* job or contract where the work was honest. Prayer and patience are internal; someone else had to conjure up the contract even if I put the thought in his head. But when it came time to juggling finances, I could have beat even enron on the end results.

During this time of too-good-to-be-true interest rates, I was receiving daily come-ons in the mail, like most people up and down the street. I usually tossed them, figuring no one would refinance my home given my current situation. Besides, I didn't think I had 'owned' the home long enough. Then one day in March, one of these post cards caught my attention. I called the toll-free number. It turned out there is a "VA Streamline" option that does not require an appraisal, a credit check, or proof of employment. If you don't offer the information – they don't ask.

By the time it was over, I had refinanced my home at a lower interest rate and was preparing to skip two house payments. I also received a check for the excess escrow. The $1100 check from Enron's so-called relief fund arrived in March, and many of us called the Texas Employment Commission to find out if we had to report that as income. If we did – it would cancel about three weeks of unemployment benefits.

The Commission's response was music. We didn't have to report it as income, so I was another $1100 closer to making it all the way to the first weeks of May. Skipping two house payments and receiving the extra checks allowed me to keep all of the other accounts paid on time. With that burden lifted, I turned my attention to the network, and scored again. My friend and mentor still working on a NASA contract referred me to another independent consultant and trainer who had a new course to market. If I could sell it, I'd get a commission. If I taught it, I'd get a check on contract. Two of us showed up to discuss the project.

From March through September, we spent countless hours on the phone, on hundreds and hundreds of e-mail messages, and occasional office presentations to plant managers and training managers in the chemical manufacturing plants around Houston. By June we had booked a demonstration course, about half full. The principals who owned the course were kind enough to pay a contract fee for two days of teaching, but in the long run, 2002 was not a good year to be selling training to industry. Training is one of those things that gets cut first when the economy is tight.

All in all this was a positive experience. The guys I worked with are superior, and I learned useful nuts and bolts about the petrochemical industry. But it was frustrating. For the time spent on a dead end, I was rewarded with knowledge and good friends, which are invaluable.

Neither is edible, however.

Being able to market this course from my home office meant I still had the opportunity to scan the job search engines and maintain other networking connections. In April, I responded to a job posting looking for someone qualified to lead a training department. It turned out to be a venture capitalist who was considering starting a training company. But through two meetings in April and May, I discovered the banker's real goal was to find someone who had done this before.

Potential is a good thing, a track record of success is better. This was another dead end, but the experience forced me to complete the work on a business plan for a training company.

Hey – that's what I'm doing! Building a training company. Duh. I compared where I was to the ideal described on paper for the venture capital guy. That ideal and my reality (the meta-training company and my paper simulation) were miles apart. I was still using an old computer with dial-up internet access, on a desk in my daughter's bedroom. I had no scanner, fax or copier; no web site and only a personal e-mail address. I had created business cards on my home computer, but they delivered the message "home-made." I would soon disconnect the land-line telephone voluntarily and rely on just a mobile number. As a training company I didn't even have a course to market. I would look for the opportunity to change all of this.

As school let out, June, July and August offered endless opportunities to spend time with Daughter, now 5 ½, often going to our version of 'the hundred acre wood' in search of Winnie the Pooh-bear tracks. At the start of her summer vacation, we released Turbo, the box turtle we had brought back from the woods in April. Daughter said the words, "Turbo deserves her freedom."

Turbo had become our icon for survival. At some point in Turbo's turbulent past, it had apparently survived an encounter with another animal, lost an eye and recovered from a smashed shell that grew in crazy angles along the rear quarter. Daughter was *too* excited the day we found it. All thoughts of finding Pooh, Piglet or Tigger vanished in favor of going home to the internet to discover how to care for a box turtle.

As a muse, Daughter filled my head with ideas for stories that children would appreciate. We would lie on a blanket in the driveway in the late evenings, watching clouds disappear to the East as the temperature finally moved south from daytime highs around 100. With her birthday approaching in September, I asked, "What do you want for your birthday?"

"Just you."

After checking the job postings, making hundreds of phone calls and sending out the marketing e-mails each week, I turned to filling the time with painting. Daughter was in day care some days, at her mother's other days. I didn't have enough to do in an 18-hour day. In one spare bedroom, reserved for Son One and his wife, I escaped frustration and the forces of gravity at the same time. After clearing the room and covering the floor with drop cloths, I marked off the long walls with pencil in 2.5-inch vertical panels, drew the circumference of the moon from floor to ceiling on the back wall, and a 20-inch Earth on the near wall. Finished, I have a full moon on a flat black wall that fades in shades of black, black-blue, blue-black, to blue-white, to white...in 69 panels on both walls. It's my studio – 250,000 miles from the full moon on the north wall to the Earth on the south wall.

I moved on to the next spare room, reserved for future visits by Son Two and his family. The bottom became ocean, the top sky blue. I painted a hundred tropical fish on the walls, and with Daughter's help, added some dolphins. A play room for the little one, in a home that was increasingly ridiculous for me to own. The 26 weeks of unemployment ran out in June.

In the hallway to the still-empty 'home theater,' also known as the Texas basement (the bonus room over the garage), images of Indiana Jones started to take shape, then the album cover from American Graffiti, and the faces of some of my favorite entertainers: Bugs Bunny, Olivia Newton John, John Wayne, Marilyn Monroe, Elvis, and others. Day after day – when I found myself engaged in less-than-productive business, I painted. And I painted. And I painted. I scored a few jobs painting murals, but I wasn't making much money at it.

Throughout the summer of 2002, I continued to work on marketing the course my colleagues described as industry essential. It was, and still is. It's a superior program, but it wasn't the right time. No sales. I limped along financially month to month, with a gift from Career Recovery Resources, Inc. one month, a loan from Dear Friend another month that covered the house and truck payments, another loan from another friend in another month. In the midst of all this I had invitations for media interviews with The Financial Times of London, Market Place – which airs at the end of All Things Considered on National Public Radio – and USA Today, all looking for perspectives on the Enron experience. I did each interview, looking for some opportunity to market my own interests. No apologies there; I'm sure they knew that, especially considering the circumstances.

I finally figured out in 2004 that reporters must keep a database of likely voices and their phone numbers or e-mail addresses, when ABC News called the week enron CFO Andy Fastow, and his wife, were apparently close to a plea bargain. The 2002 and 2003 interviewers were interested in the curiosity of an enron exile and retired Marine Corps intelligence officer with a doctorate in education, who was trying to make a living as a painter of murals. I had tried to get a plug in for my training and consulting business. The option to send my comments to Peter Jennings in January 2004 seemed like circus, and past experience suggested I wasn't going to get a phone call out of it, asking me to interview for a job. It's not that I felt *I* would be exploited...but the Fastows. If it were a choice, I would much rather have unemployment with Ramen for breakfast and dinner than what the Fastows would be facing, headed off to tandem prison sentences with children at home. I passed on that interview.

In September 2002, the break I had waited for finally surfaced. Sort of. A buddy of mine who is well-placed in the aerospace industry had discovered that I was still looking for work. "Why didn't you tell me so?" he asked. "I'll see if I can get you connected with the right folks in Houston."

Again – this appeared to be *THE* opportunity, and I had the qualifications, but my buddy was not the hiring manager. He did everything a friend could do or should do, it just wasn't his job to assign. Eventually I sent resumes and applications in on six or seven jobs on the project he told me about, but the final decision to invite an interview rested with someone else. The hiring manager was the son of a notable astronaut, and that hiring manager, an engineer, was only interested in hiring engineers.

In the end, I was confused and disappointed. I didn't have the opportunity to even find out why I wasn't called for at least an interview, but suspect that in this environment – if you're not an engineer, you're not. You're just *not.* You don't exist.

That painstaking process led to the eve of October, and I was at the decision point again. I could make one more house payment and cover all of the other bills, but four weeks later would have $5000 in obligations and $1100 in available cash. Four weeks more and that would multiply to $10,000 in debt but $2200 in available cash.

Stress.

Thumbing through a growing stack of business cards, many from days in aerospace, business contacts in the petrochemical industry and various job fairs, I came across a card from one of the University of Phoenix administrators. The Houston-based campus was growing, and trumpeted frequently in local radio advertising. Those who can teach, teach. It would not have been practical to return to my last adjunct teaching assignment on the far side of Houston. The round trip was 100 miles. But the University of Phoenix campus was in reach, about 15 miles from home, and was now advertising for instructors. I started the application process, with an eye on teaching undergraduate courses in organizational psychology, human motivation and team-building skills for managers.

I know some people don't accept this concept of a cause-effect relationship when it comes to prayer, but when I look back it's like I drove through a sea of telephone poles in an 18-wheeler with my eyes closed and never scratched the paint. It certainly wasn't luck; I never put faith in luck. After the unemployment ran out, the mailbox delivered a check for $5000 from a loan company. Because I had been making payments on all of my debts, my credit score had not yet taken any hits. "This is not an application," the letter read. "If you want the loan, sign the check and deposit it in your checking account." When I went in to sign the papers a few days later, they offered me a credit card. I accepted it, and took cash out of the cash side and bought groceries out of the purchases side. Then I got another loan offer – $1200, pre-approved. No-kidding pre-approved. I was cognizant of the interest rates, but knew if I made a single score on any given contract, I could pay all of them off in seconds. When I received yet another offer, for a zero-percent-interest credit card, I took that too, and paid off other accounts with high interest rates. The experience didn't seem far removed from 'playing' the stock market. Is it an investment, or a gamble? Through all of this, I had been able to not only make regular payments on the usual monthly obligations but my life insurance and lines of credit as well. I drew cash out when I could, driving toward the day I would replace loans with income.

I'm gonna make it to Christmas. I'm gonna make it to Christmas.

I finally had a temporary surplus and could buy professionally printed business cards to replace the homemade ones. I could get cable-based high-speed internet access. I could pay the fees to own a domain name and stand up a web site. By now, my American Express card had long-since considered itself an orphan. If I couldn't pay the bill, I tried to avoid putting a charge on the account. When I was a few days late, American Express was gracious and encouraging. The Gold Card got used to sitting dormant in the junk drawer. Then I received the Fall edition of the American Express Rewards program catalog, and out of curiosity, took a look. I had earned points in my past life, using American Express, that I was totally unaware of. I had enough points to order a color printer-fax-scanner-copier outfit that would suit my needs and wouldn't cost me a dime. In real life, it would cost about $400. This was a dream and I was off and running. Walking. Well – 'stand' is a verb. What was I going to do? I had had a business name since February, but didn't really have anything to sell. No lemonade.

Honestly, it was not deep introspection. I already I knew what I would do when I would have the freedom to work at it and the minimum financial resources to market it. I had told Mr. Cooper that I would be back with courses on Leadership and Ethics for the senior staff at the incredible shrinking enron. I wrote to the Marine Corps at Quantico, Virginia, to the command that could respond to my question on intellectual property rights for Marine Corps leadership training materials. The reply: it's a government document, so it's public domain. Their request: give the Marine Corps credit and do it justice.

At any given point between March and September 2002, it was absolutely clear that a check in the bank was only fuel. Job satisfaction was the red pickup truck I wanted to ride in. I was determined to brush aside *frustration* with determination. I focused on eliminating *confusion* with clearer focus on my goals. I put all the *stress* in God's hands. It didn't matter that I couldn't see around corners, didn't know what the next month or two would bring.

The unknown became an adventure.

Eighteen: First Principle - Goals as Values

Start your *own* business!

Driving toward downtown Houston to deliver yet another sales presentation, past the wooded expanse surrounding Compaq, later Hewlett-Packard's, sprawling campus, I had the opportunity to witness a different sort of presentation, absurdly disembodied from the cars, trucks, glass towers and asphalt that created my temporary and quickly changing space. A quarter-mile ahead of my position in 65-mile-an-hour traffic, a 12-point buck leapt over the concrete barrier separating the south feeder road from the state highway and eight lanes of traffic. The display was over in seconds, and I don't recall a single car or truck with brake lights on. Other drivers must have been as astonished as I was.

This magnificent creature never stopped, never looked back, as it bounded through southbound traffic, over the next set of concrete barriers, across four more lanes of north-bound traffic, and into the woods beyond. Should I not say, that deer was goal-oriented?

It wasn't that simple. Everything's a metaphor. CORPORATION is a metasystem; every aspiring 'corporation' is a subsystem, a metaphor, an imitation or representation of what 'CORPORATION' could be. Every organization, every marriage, every process, every employee is a hypothesis to be tested through trial and error. Theoretically perfect is the goal, hypotheses are test runs. The *theory* exists first (quality); *hypotheses* seek to explain what we've observed.

That buck sprinting across the highway came as close to perfect in a test run as I'd ever seen. It's never as simple as WHY did the buck cross the road? (...to get to the other side). We don't ask *why* enough. Why did the buck need to be on the other side? Actually, it's a *how-why* process. We dissect QUALITY into qualities by asking *how;* we reconstruct and justify behavior by asking *why*. Lack of commitment to, or even a clear rationale for *why* leaves employees going through the motions on *what,* and they lose focus on *how.* They are disengaged.

Among the hundreds of articles on 'employee engagement' since 2001, Kowalski succinctly labels engagement as "the degree to which individuals are personally committed to helping an organization by doing a better job than required to hold the job."[xxiii]

Like the rest of us, the buck crossing the highway is focused on survival; getting to the other side is only one step in the process. The lack of purpose in a career can make work nothing more than survival, particularly in an age of lay-offs, huge bankruptcies and mergers. A netscape.com news clip offers additional perspective:

> Fully 71 percent of U.S. workers are slackers. They aren't doing their jobs. That's the astonishing word from a Gallup poll that used more politically correct terminology than "slackers." Nearly three-quarters of us are "not engaged" in our jobs. Gallup's Curt Coffman, who is also a co-author of "First, Break All the Rules: What the World's Greatest Managers Do Differently," told Denver Post reporter Al Lewis that at best, these folks are clock-watchers and break-takers. At worst, they mock their bosses and undermine the companies where they work. What causes employees to become disengaged? Primarily, it's having to perform useless tasks. The Denver Post got this confession from a slacker who worked at Hewlett-Packard in Denver and was recently laid off due to the merger with Compaq. Not surprisingly, he wouldn't give his name. "I started working 6 1/2-hour days, and I had no problem taking two-hour lunches," he revealed. "I was basically coasting for the last six months. I knew what was coming. So why would I kill myself on the project I was working on?"[xxiv]

The article does not suggest that employees *choose* to do useless tasks; it reads "having to do useless tasks." How did those useless tasks get there? What are the leaders doing? Coffman says "the bottom performing 20 percent of many large organizations should just be fired – including managers." One might add that if there are managers performing useless tasks, not only should they be fired, but their managers as well. That buck crossing the road, intent on survival, is not performing any useless tasks. Considering that snapshot in time, the buck had speed, strength and agility. Accuracy and courage were a must, as were decisiveness and determination. But the entire process sprang from motivation as surely as the buck sprang from the tree line. If we don't proceed *from* the motivation, and move on, we risk the certainty of living the aphorism – so far deep in alligators that we lose sight of the original goal to drain the swamp. Useless tasks are alligators. Getting rid of them requires mating values to goals, assigning purpose to tasks. When we get to the other side of the interstate – the buck doesn't stop here.

I already know that financial independence is not a goal, but a *result* of achieving my goal of job satisfaction. Real survival is job satisfaction, whether I'm working for someone else or running my own business. For now, the prospect of running my own business runs parallel to the satisfaction of coming in 4th in my age group in a marathon. A distant third is working my tail off to create personal wealth for some corporate executive. But the close second is the notion of helping an organization focus on the goal of customer satisfaction, and looking back to find out that our success has indeed created wealth for the organization. When it comes to running my own show, like running a marathon, no one put me on the street at 5 a.m. to train, no one yelled in my ear to the 5-mile point, or 10- or 15-mile point. How do I get this ethos into the thinking patterns of my employees? How do I find a corporation that fits this pattern?

"How" is the starting point, emerging from a goal. If we go back to Pirsig's *quality,* take the time to fully understand a customer's view of quality, and then embrace our customer's vision as our own, we're headed in the right direction. But customers aren't shopping for "a quality." They want a quality "something" in the form of a product or service. That's our ultimate goal, but not the only goal. Finishing the marathon is *the* goal, but the first step is a goal too. The first mile is a goal. A better time than last year is a goal. Finishing without pain in the knees and hip sockets is a goal.

Understanding *quality* as the primary goal, and *qualities* or attributes as supporting goals, we start from the paired observations that we can perform in a given market and there are customers with needs in this market. The customer has already answered the first question: "What do you need?" with the response, "A quality home," for example.

We start asking questions: How will you use this home? How many people are in your family? How old are they? Does anyone in the family have special needs? What are your entertainment needs? Your telephone and computer needs? Do you have pets? Will you plan a swimming pool? How much time will you spend gardening? Do you require privacy or prefer an open backyard relationship with neighbors? How will you use your kitchen? We may ask hundreds of such questions for something as involved and complex as a home or a car, perhaps fewer questions for a toy, game, frozen food or electric drill. Eventually, the price of a finished product or service is almost always a discriminator...one of the qualities.

Exhausting this line of questioning may seem obvious, but who really does it? Mass produced commodities (simulations of the *ideal*) aim to please "the average consumer" in a given market. Would that minivan be less expensive without 24 cup-holders, or do you just put 24 cup-holders in all of your minivans because a survey of 1127 households has determined that 24 is the ideal number? Getting a feel for what the customer is truly looking for is the art of "architexture," akin to Pirsig's *quality is just what you like.* It just feels right. To the *customer.*

Armed with the in-depth understanding of what the customer's needs are, we proceed through a logical, deductive process, asking *how:* How do we deliver a four-bedroom house with a two-car garage? How do we deliver a back yard big enough for three kids, a dog and a swimming pool? The process proceeds *from* Quality *through* qualities and sends us to answers that may be called Operations, Departments, Divisions or Directorates: A land development operation, a framing operation, an appliances operation, interior design, electrical, plumbing, roofing, flooring and painting operations.

With an eye constantly on Quality, the next set of questions deconstructs each operation: How do we deliver quality flooring? Quality appliances, paint, wall coverings? Each of these delivers a subset that may be called a System. The process proceeds from quality systems to quality processes, to quality tasks. All we've done the entire time is ask "*how?*"

Go back and check your math. Ask "*why?*" Every individual task should trace logically back through processes, to systems, to operations to a *quality finished product or service*. In the development of military tactics, individual tactical operations (tasks) should be derivatives of a larger operational goal, which is a subset of an overarching strategy, and that strategy a derivative of the "commander's intent." If this process seems so obviously unnecessary as to appear inane, what IS preventing your organization from meeting its goals for quality in the finished product, or cost to produce, time to deliver, accuracy or any of dozens or hundreds of other criteria? Useless tasks? Outmoded processes? Inefficient operations? The wrong tools? How about lack of communication? Overlapping egos and someone's desire to "get ahead?" The wrong people?

Tasks – those verbs people *do* on the job – include not only the steps taken to create a finished product, but the squabbles between directors over resources, the time a manager takes to counsel an employee, telephone calls or e-mails to track down missing parts, negotiating with your own legal department to get a contract on paper in a reasonable amount of time. Each of these unnecessary or wasteful "tasks" blurs the focus on goals and hinders organizational performance.

Finding the organization intent on moving from company to COMPANY, repairing an existing organization, or building my own from scratch all have the same requirement: Consider every operation, system, process, task or employee as a hypothesis to be tested through trial and error. In a scientific sense, I want to prove my hypotheses on the way to creating a theoretically "perfect" organization. To do this, I wear a surgeon's mask.

Occam's razor

Creating, finding or repairing an organization requires some potentially difficult choices, which process to keep, which to discard. Which tasks to perform, which to discard. Which employees to keep, which to discard. Which benefit plan to keep, and so on. Enter Occam's razor. The Principia Cybernetica project explains:

> The principle states that one should not make more assumptions than the minimum needed. This principle is often called the principle of parsimony. It underlies all scientific modeling and theory building. It admonishes us to choose from a set of otherwise equivalent models of a given phenomenon the simplest one. In any given model, Occam's razor helps us to "shave off" those concepts, variables or constructs that are not really needed to explain the phenomenon. By doing that, developing the model will become much easier, and there is less chance of introducing inconsistencies, ambiguities and redundancies.[xxv]

Many organizations do this already, on the operational side of business. We see it in concepts like Lean Manufacturing. While working as a training manager in Detroit in the mid-90s, I had the opportunity to watch General Motors technicians disassemble three or four vehicles from various (other) manufacturers to learn more efficient processes and assemblies, en route to the concept of Design for Manufacturability, and later, Design for Reparability. Lean manufacturing won't save GM from its culture, but it's a start. Bit by bit, generation after generation, manufacturing in many industrial sectors has continued to improve to the point at which most redundancies and inconsistencies have been identified and eliminated. In some cases, people are redundant. Robotics replace people at LEGO; automated scanners replace human clerks at the grocery store check-out counter.

But it's a long journey from corporation (your company) to CORPORATION (theoretically ideal); team to TEAM. Why are we still missing our goals? I think...my *hypothesis* is...by the time we convert QUALITY into goals, most goals have become purely objective. The subjective side, the values, often disappear. Many (most?) organizations do not understand, and therefore do not deal with the "human domain." It's too complex; to opaque; too "squishy." Instead, we measure and report on number sold, total dollar value sold, size, shape, ratio, stock price. The *qualities* are only quantities.

There are exceptions, of course. Many organizations concentrate on safety as a value; it's ingrained in the culture. Nuclear power generation and some petrochemical manufacturers are good examples. Many companies in the pharmaceuticals industry not only emphasize the culture of *Good Manufacturing Practices (GMP),* focusing on purity, consistency and quality, but demonstrate that emphasis throughout their culture. Eli Lilly's core values are a good example: **Respect for people** includes their concern for the interests of all of the people worldwide who touch – or are touched by – their company: customers, employees, shareholders, partners and communities. **Integrity** embraces the very highest standards of honesty, ethical behavior and exemplary moral character. **Excellence** is reflected in Lilly's continuous search for new ways to improve the performance of their business in order to become the best at what they deliver.

There are other great companies that nurture their cultures as well, but it seems after the excitement died down in the 1980s, following *In Search of Excellence*[xxvi] and

Corporate Cultures[xxvii] and a few good knock-offs, most organizations treated the concept of actually having a corporate culture like a novelty, another too-hard-to-do, touchy-feely flavor of the decade. Guess what – if you don't consciously create it, an *organizational culture will develop on its own.* It's always there. It develops on the job site, at the water cooler, in the performance appraisal process, at the coffee pot and in the parking lot. It's embedded in what we say and the stories we tell, in the tasks and processes we complete, and in the tools we use, clothes we wear, flags we wave and any other symbol that has meaning and carries value.

If I'm hiring, I look for clues to a candidate's real motivations, and watch for reactions when we discuss external incentives. Ideally, incentives should be mirror images of motivations. In simple terms, I'm looking at an employee's values. If I describe a work environment that offers job satisfaction, the astute candidate will recognize the incentives. If the candidate seeks primarily financial incentives in response to financial motivations, I'll recognize it. But financial rewards are like eating at a Chinese restaurant – 20 minutes later and you're hungry again. I've seen countless examples of employees who grow attached to their bonuses, as if they are entitlements. Angst develops when the efficient, effective workers see the slackers get the same bonus.

There's a Maslow's Hierarchy kind of explanation for this that suggests when humans meet their basic needs – air, food, water, shelter – they move on to conquer the next needs in the hierarchy. Where we get stuck is in one-upmanshipping the 'things bring esteem from peers' or the 'wealth creates positive self-esteem' routine. Instead of winning praise from peers, we win envy, inciting competition for more toys, bigger homes, more expensive cars. We sacrifice freedom to chase down things.

Apart from a spiritual sense of *peace* is the Maslovian sense of self-actualization. It's job satisfaction. It's success. It's doing what I want to do, when and where I want to do it, and feeling fulfilled and rewarded in the pursuit. But not everyone wants to own their own business; many are satisfied to leave the headaches to someone else and clock in to a career five days a week. There's nothing wrong with that, as long as the experience meets *all* of my needs.

If I'm looking for *the* organization to work for, I look at the culture. Let me restate that...I *scrutinize* the culture, analyzing the organization's values. Looking at the culture from the outside, all I get is a view of the storefront window, the façade. I must inspect the structure of that culture, brick by brick. If the cornerstone does not have QUALITY written all over it, I'm gone. So far, my foundation, or First Principles, include Quality, Quality Survival Ethics, Quality Leadership, Quality Faith and Quality Freedom, and Quality Goals. Because this is becoming a potentially complex web of concepts, I offer another metaphor to help understand the concept of corporate cultures and how we communicate goals:

The Edifice Complex

In 1990, I defended my dissertation, *The Edifice Complex: A Study of the Causes and Effects of Conflict Between Generations of Marines, and of Cultural Changes in the United States Marine Corps.* I found far more than I was originally looking for. I started the original work on this project in 1980, about 5 years after the last Marines left Vietnam and I was starting work on my master's thesis. The Marine Corps and the other armed services were going through significant cultural changes, including the move to an all-volunteer force. Among other lofty goals, the Commandant of the Marine Corps set higher educational standards for enlisted Marines, with an eye on enlisting all high school graduates. Since the early 1980s, the Marine Corps has consistently enlisted between 95 and 100 percent of its goals.

Among other things, I became interested in the psychology of shaping behavior. What was it about the Corps that attracted young men and women to the Corps in the first place – a significantly different culture than the typical high school? And how does the Marine Corps so profoundly impact the core values of the majority of Marines – values that last a lifetime? I had dozens of questions; I interviewed hundreds of Marines, following the disciplines of anthropology and ethnographic analysis.

As a scientific tool in the social sciences, ethnography yields *emerging theory*. Any given theory, with supporting empirical evidence, is as good as the next one, until someone comes along with a better explanation for observable phenomena. I wasn't content to show up for work, do my job, and head back to the barracks. I saw the Corps, the Marines, and the culture of the Corps, as separate chunks of information that needed an explanation. My emerging theory took the form of The Edifice Complex.

The title combines two illustrative meanings. The first meaning alludes to the Oedipus Complex of Freudian psychology. As the original story goes, Oedipus' parents gave him to a shepherd to be left to die in the wilderness so that the prophesy of his fate would not come true. (The Oracle of Apollo at Delphi had prophesied that Oedipus would kill his father and marry his mother.) The shepherd instead gave Oedipus to a herdsman, who gave the boy to his master, King Polybus of Corinth. When Oedipus was grown, fighting with the Corinthian army, and unaware of his true parents' identities, he killed his father in battle, and not long thereafter, won the hand of Jocasta (his mother) in marriage by solving the riddle of the Sphynx at the gates of Thebes. (Schwab, 1946, 230-245)

In the Freudian sense, according to Webster's Seventh New Collegiate Dictionary (1972, p. 585), the Oedipus complex is defined as "the positive libidinal feelings that a child develops toward the parent of the opposite sex and when unresolved are conceived as a source of adult personality disorder," or in rough terms, the child falling in love with the parent. The analogy in the title of this study borrows from both myth and Freud: *The Edifice Complex* is defined by younger generations of Marines *falling in love with* (even as they modify) the mystique of the Corps' military culture, and metaphorically and unknowingly *killing* the old Corps' culture (thus the older generations of Marines). This phenomenon evolves as the younger generation becomes larger in numbers than the next older generation, and brings with it symbols, values and beliefs carried from their civilian culture. The process continues through each generation.

The second meaning of *The Edifice Complex* explains another possible cause of cultural conflict – evolution, thus change, in the belief systems and values of the Marine Corps. The *edifice* of *The Edifice Complex* represents two structures: The formal structure of laws and regulations governing the Marine Corps, some of which are imposed on the Corps by Congress or presidential decree, and some of which are created internally by Marine Corps policy makers to govern the Corps, and: The formal structure of belief systems and values, created by the historical evolution of the organization's folklore and imposed on Marines through formal training in the Corps' history. Considering the structure as building blocks arranged like a maze, with the blocks representing formal symbols, values, rituals, beliefs, stories and myths, even rules and regulations, one can see a maze which each Marine must negotiate through his career, however brief. That maze is the *complex* in the title, and parallels the widely accepted concept of the rites of passage. There are many rites of passage – boot camp, officer candidate school, combat, reenlistment, retirement, etc.

Now it's 15 years later and The Edifice Complex reemerges hauntingly. The Columbia Accident Investigation specifically cited management culture as a root cause for both the Columbia and the Challenger tragedies. NASA will recover, when NASA's culture focuses every single employee on a single goal, a single mission: You're an astronaut? Your mission is Safety of Human Space Flight. You're a training developer? Your mission is Safety of Human Space Flight. And you over there – you mow the lawn at Johnson Space Center? Your mission is Safety of Human Space Flight. You're a Senior Engineer? Safety of Human Space Flight is more important than your ego or reputation, or making that junior engineer pay for embarrassing you at a staff meeting.

Suddenly everything comes into focus. Every operation is a *quality* operation that proceeds from QUALITY. Every system in a given operation is a *quality* system that proceeds from a *quality* operation. Every subordinate process and task is part of something greater than itself and all trace their roots back to QUALITY. Departments and directorates no longer need to compete because they're focused on the same, single goal. Occam's razor shaves off the unwritten law that junior engineers should not question senior engineers because that aspect of the culture, through trial and error, has proved to be a poor hypothesis, an unsuitable explanation for Quality manifested as Safety of Human Space Flight. That aspect of the culture is not a survival ethic contributing to the immortality of the NASA organization (or Safety of Human Spaceflight).

The corporate culture must be constructed by hand, one stone at a time. Tossing a bunch of rocks, etched with enron's proclamations of Respect, Integrity, Communication and Excellence, in a pile for the employees to ogle serves no purpose. The edifice, the structure of symbols, rituals and stories that make up the culture, grow out of the things we do, the language we use and the cultural artifacts around us. Symbols, rituals and stories – "tribal myths" – have meaning, values. Shared values form the glue, the bond, matrix or *complex* that holds all of these symbols, rituals and stories together.

Every organization is unique. If we tell stories about share price, share price becomes a value. If we tell stories about meeting or exceeding customer expectations, customer service becomes a value. If the company banner says enron will become the world's best company, the focus is on internal values. Instead of focusing on customer service, departments focus on being the best department. Vice presidents compete to be the best vice president. Directors and managers do their best to get *inducted* into the next "higher" level of management. Individuals fight over who gets the best performance appraisal. But if the company banner says "This company's products and services delight customers better than any other company's," the focus shifts and the change is astounding. Not only does everyone have the same goal, but succession planning for leadership positions becomes child's play. Succession planning is now *deductive*, starting from QUALITY. The customer defines *quality* as "X," and Manager Johnson has responded to that definition of quality as evidenced by results in *observable, measurable revenue*. They are *NOT* the same. Rewarding Manager Johnson for delighting customers will send one signal; rewarding Manager Johnson for meeting sales quotas will send an entirely different message.

Commit this to memory.

Using q*uality* instead of money to generate thrust could have rescued enron. Using integrity instead of money to reduce drag on innovation and competition can rescue any commercial enterprise. Focusing on quality serves the same function as Occam's Razor. Replace any symbol, ritual or myth that is inconsistent with superior performance with a culture that *does* contribute to superior performance. That kind of focus reduces confusion and frustration because core values become real, shared values.

Culture, in goals as values, is the *pitch, yaw* and *roll* of an organization.

It's all about attitude.

Nineteen: Laser Chapter 7

"Skipper. We got chatter on the net."

"Friend or foe?"

"Can't tell yet. Sounds like gobbledygook. Probably one of theirs. It's close to our freqs, but I can't tell for certain."

"Keep an eye on it, Murdoch," Captain Steele replied, turning to the final pre-flight task. Weapons check. "The bad guys might be wondering where Mr. Mean-green-chlorine-machine is."

While Sergeant Murdoch scanned the electromagnetic horizon, Steele toyed with the weapons systems, incinerating a couple of trees and vaporizing a pile of rocks. "Ok, I'm set. We've got a pulse laser in the visible spectrum and a directed energy weapon...not lots different than a Mach M. We've got a payload to deliver. What've you got?"

Murdoch looked up from the scanner, "I'd say foe. Northeast, out of Houston. Let me get a fix, Captain."

"Worth investigating?"

"Just a sec, Skipper...triangulates on Smith Street, downtown."

"Then let's suit up. Looks like an adventure to me."

As Steele stepped down the ladder to secure the power plant access panels, Murdoch placed the receiver on the pilot's seat, then turned to fit their own laser canon into the tiny cargo bay behind the pilot and co-pilot seats. Suddenly the handheld transmitter-receiver crackled to life, "Daddy.... Kathryn. Can you..."

Heart pumping, Murdoch lurched to respond. Before he could reach the handheld, Steele was running up the ladder, "Stop! Don't answer! We can't transmit!"

Twenty: Creativity. Skepticism.

October – December, 2002
The next race

Sometimes Houston weather sneaks up on Christmas gently, gradually shedding the blistering 98s and 99s of August for 80s in September, 70s in October and 60s in November. Other years deliver postcard weather on Labor Day and rainy days in the mid-40s a week or two later. In 2002, October 5th offered 88 degrees and no shortage of humidity. A broken toe had kept me off the road for a month, and the next Houston Marathon was only three months away. I ran out the door, in search of a new 13-mile course, desperately seeking to make up for lost time.

Exercising my mind with diversions, before settling in on Captain Steele, I had the flash of an old science fiction story. Like many in my generation, time travel stories caught my adolescent attention in the 1960s. Bradbury, Heinlein, Asimov and others delivered an endless library of time travel, aliens and strange planets. The genre offered escape well into my 20s, and I even made a stab at writing some science fiction short stories. Like other projects, writing science fiction was exploration, but I had to concentrate on a real job to put food on the table. So like most in my generation, I grew up. Until enron, everything was fact; everything predictable. Now it was chaos. Enron was historical fiction, now that the final check had arrived (more than two hundred thousand less than my severance could have been). All that remained were open roads and future. Many of the science fiction movies had memorable visual scenes, but few science fiction *books* left memorable lines that could stick for more than 30 years. Heinlein's *Time Enough for Love* was one of these:

> "A human being should be able to change a diaper, plan an invasion, butcher a hog, conn a ship, design a building, write a sonnet, balance accounts, build a wall, set a bone, comfort the dying, take orders, give orders, cooperate, act alone, solve equations, analyze a new problem, pitch manure, program a computer,

cook a tasty meal, fight efficiently, die gallantly. Specialization is for insects."xxviii

The only thing left on this list was to die gallantly; I'd done everything else. Guaranteeing the opportunity to die gallantly would take more than a little creativity, which in itself offers endless potholes and dead ends. Endless freedom spawns endless creativity, but screams for situational awareness. I can fly my stealth fighter anywhere I want; I have unlimited maneuverability. Common sense tells me to keep my eyes open. Starting a new business, I'm on the lookout for danger as well as opportunity. Fighter pilots summarize the concept in a tiny package – the OODA loop. Observe; Orient; Decide; Act. The lesson for business is: the quicker you can *get inside your opponent's OODA loop,* the quicker you are to market with the best solution. Combat is a series of OODA loops. Observe more comprehensively; Orient more accurately; Decide with more confidence; pull the trigger – ACT – with predictability...and do it all faster than the next guy.

Traffic on this 13-mile route was unpredictable. Running on city streets offers the worst of both evils – broken glass, uneven turf, mud or cracked sidewalks off the street, or drivers who seem to aim for runners and punish them for trying to share the road. Dodging potholes, bumpers and boulevard sprinklers, I kept to the pavement. It was solid. I started crafting my first workshop: Leadership Skills for Managers. This would serve as a foundation for commodity courses, pre-packaged seminars that I believed I could market in industry.

With the Marine Corps' 14 leadership traits and 11 leadership principles as a starting point, my first goal was re-writing the Marine Corps curriculum. Some, but not many, of the front-line supervisors I would address would be able to relate to the purely military examples in the original text. This turned out to be fairly straightforward, with both positive and negative lessons from years at General Motors, NASA and enron. The next step was to filter leadership, as told by the Marine Corps, through organizational psychology, but in civilian terms. Leaders lead people. Leadership may be a lonely occupation, but it's still about relationships with other people, setting examples for people, getting the most out of people.

Mile after mile, week after week, I wrote. First in my head, on the highway; then at the computer, chained to my desk after a shower. Justification theory resurfaced. I'm trying to give managers a clear picture of how people rationalize the decisions they make. As I head for the six-and-a-half-mile turn, I'm telling myself this runner's high is the reason I run. I can do this all day. Sure I'm tired, but it's a good tired. I'm supposed to be tired – and if I'm not, I'm not working hard enough. I check my watch and it's 48 minutes. Seven-and-a-half-minute miles. I'm justified and rationalized. An hour later, as I cross the bridge with two miles to go, I stop running. I'm walking fast, but walking fast isn't running. Now I'm not just tired. I'm beat. I'm dissatisfied that I didn't focus on just finishing. My first thoughts are that it's hot. It's humid. I didn't have a good breakfast. It's just as easy to rationalize the negative as the positive.

More miles and more weeks later and I added exercises on Quality, Freedom and Control, Customer Focus, Delegation, Planning and more, all designed to put leadership concepts into context. As the workshop fell into place, I turned my attention to building a first web site, starting with the painting business, *Renaissance Man*. I toyed with "Y'alls Walls" and "Beau's Art," but the two votes I got on those ideas were both humorously negative. I still had 18 hours a day to fill most days of the week, and if I could snag a job painting murals, I'd take the work. Painting was cathartic, and like running, offered a mental vacuum. My mind's got to do something while my feet are running, so I write. My mind's got to do something while my hand is painting, so I compose in my mind.

I tracked down college students who were starting their own business, building web sites, hoping to get a reasonable rate. But $3000? Give me a break! I designed the *Renaissance Man* site in PowerPoint and sent it to Dear Friend's son – one of those high school guys who knows more computer stuff than the teachers. I bought a domain name; I located a web host. Dear Friend's son imported the PowerPoint draft into an html program, and uploaded it to my first web site. I was in business. Taking two days off to deliver hundreds of business cards to sales agents at new subdivisions around Houston, I was anticipating more work than I could handle. With *Renaissance Man* up and running, I returned to Laser Consulting.

This time I wanted to build the site on my own. I didn't want to just own it; I needed to understand how it went together so I could update it later. *Renaissance Man* was a static site by comparison – pictures of murals and my portraits in oils. Dear Friend, who designs multimedia training for a living, gave me an afternoon tutorial in html. By the end of November, the core was done. But I didn't want to be Houston's Best Consulting and Training Company; I wanted to be The World's Best Company. I started translating my manifesto into French, Spanish and German. It wouldn't be perfect, but it was worth a shot.

This was daughter's year to spend Thanksgiving with her mom and step-dad. Each family had open doors at Thanksgiving and Christmas on alternating years, and I was glad for the invitation to join them for turkey dinner this year. But while I was dreaming about creating The World's Best Company, I was living in another world. I felt more solidarity with the homeless people than the World's Best Company people. I drove to the George R. Brown Convention Center in Houston to see if I could lend a hand, feeding the homeless a Thanksgiving dinner. I wasn't going to take great pride in contributing this year, and I wouldn't feel guilty either if I didn't do it the next. It wasn't a talisman to ward off homelessness – just something I had to do, like telling them to hang on to hope without actually saying the words. I washed pots and cleaned counter tops in the Convention Center's cavernous galley. Then I swept the floor as thousands stood in line to get a free meal. Four times in 12 months I had been at the edge of filing for bankruptcy and losing my home. Did we have the same kind of hope? What if I ended up in this line next year?

I started having second thoughts. I hadn't been actively searching for a job in at least two months, and I had just spent close to $800 getting set up in business. What if my "commodity courses" didn't sell? I wasn't visualizing the book *Zen and the Art of Motorcycle Maintenance* while I swept floors, but I did realize I had the freedom to come and go as I pleased. I owned quality, even if it seemed on loan. Most of these people had the same freedom (maneuverability) that I had – unemployment. But they seemed trapped. I didn't feel trapped. I had never felt completely trapped. There were days I didn't know which way to turn, but never trapped. I knew there was an end to despair. What was it?

Sure, I had faith that God would ensure my basic needs would be met, but I had to take an active role in this thing too. Now I was facing what I didn't want to become. Suddenly I felt privileged. It wasn't power or pedigree. I had a home. When I built that home, the foundation was laid on a job that grew out of my opportunity to go to college. Many of these people didn't have homes and most didn't have half the education I had; many never had the opportunity to even try. It was neither fair nor unfair. It just was. When I started college, I didn't take a seat from anyone. I paid my way on the GI Bill, but it was still a privilege. I was committed to doing something worthwhile with what I learned. enron had dissolved my opportunity to follow through on that commitment, and 400 job applications for positions I was well-qualified for had come up zeroes.

enron's power elite were privileged too. Handsome pedigrees in that bunch. enron's most senior officers lobbied for relaxed controls in the energy industry, and won. Freedom leads to innovation and competition, which should be good for consumers. Sounds good on paper. By 2001, it was difficult to impossible for most other companies to compete on enron's level. Success became a money tree; money spawned power. Power is a privilege, but corporations are not democracies, so the source of that power does not at first blush seem to come from the people. Democracies derive power from the people:

We hold these truths to be self-evident: that all men are created equal; that they are endowed by their Creator with certain unalienable rights; that among these are life, liberty, and the pursuit of happiness; that to secure these rights, governments are instituted among men, deriving their just powers from the consent of the governed...[xxix]

There's that word again – derive. **Power is a derivative**. But a corporation is not a democracy; does the concept still apply? Why not? When I buy a new pickup truck, I buy it based on trust in its *truck-ness,* that it will do what trucks promise to do. When I enter a business arrangement, I seek faith in my client's willingness to pay a fair price for a seminar, or a portrait or mural; I look for *customer-ness.* As I struggle to maintain a quality relationship with God, I base my hope on faith. So when I accept a job offer from enron, I look for ENRONness...and it proved to not be there.

How an organization treats its employees is a *derivative* of the employees' view of a quality work environment – including the freedom to buy or sell shares that represent their savings accounts and retirement plans. Enron's employees contributed to the power of the elite by their own sweat and basked in the success, feeling a shared sense, derivatives, of that power. Until the corporation froze 401Ks months before the company filed for bankruptcy protection.

Harboring millions in enron stock, those 401K's shrank to microscopic fractions of their previous worth, while corporate executives shed stock in a frenzy. Power can be derived from wealth; power can be derived from knowledge. One does not guarantee the other. Power may also derive from *quality*. Again, corporations are not democracies, but the people working in an American corporation, believing and trusting in the foundations of freedom in their own country, might be expected to think that as the 'governed' in their workplace... their consent provides the basis for the just powers of the government – the corporation. This is obviously not the case. Too often, the concepts of governing and governed, consent, freedom, power, all rotate in orbit around stockholders.

Throughout 2000 and 2001, enron's corporate officers assured the body of employees, retirees, stockholders and anyone else who would listen, that enron was financially sound. Denying enron employees access to their 401K plans, heavily weighted in stock value, in the Fall of 2001 was a fraud. Filing *bankrotten* on December 1st and laying off thousands on December 5th to avoid paying severance was a fraud. A hand-wringing Congress responded with the Sarbanes-Oxley Act of 2002:[xxx]

> ... to restore public confidence in the financial market and to reduce the likelihood of future crisis by ensuring that the public receives more information about possible corporate fraud. To encourage reporting of alleged corporate wrongdoing, the Act expressly provides protection for employees of publicly traded companies who "blow the whistle" on their employer.

Sarbanes-Oxley provides protection *after the fact* for employees who blow the whistle, but it's another law, an act, a rule. Is this supposed to stand as a deterrent to corporate officers? Like a speed limit sign on the Gulf Freeway? The speed limit only works if you get caught.

What if a lack of regulation, too much freedom, became a bad thing? Too much freedom and I was off trying to start a business while monster.com was sitting idle. I wasn't headed in the direction of Pirsig's question: "But suppose you *do* just what you like? Does that mean you're going to go out and shoot heroin, rob banks and rape old ladies?" But I also had never started a business before. I was skeptical about Pirsig's model. It was like an unfinished equation on the chalkboard, crying for a solution.

Friday, December 5, 2002

I celebrated with all of my employees. Me. It was a small party, but I had a lot to be thankful for – a year in the house after enron's implosion, with Daughter still close by my side. It would be more than a year before I would get my annual report from the Social Security Administration. Total taxable income for the year was less than $12,000. I had paid more than twice that in federal taxes the year before. My house payments for 2002 *would have* added up to more than $20,000.

A week after the ex-enron anniversary celebration, I started the paperwork to refinance my home once again, at a still lower interest rate. This time I would be able to time it so that I skipped three house payments, recover escrow and gain an additional refund. In 10 months I had reduced the necessary outgo on my monthly mortgage for the year by nearly $10,000 and gained an additional $5,000 in refunds through refinancing. Just my mortgage and truck payments for the year would total more than $14,000 after skipping five house payments through two sessions of refinancing the home.

I was living in deficit, like the federal government. This couldn't continue. It wouldn't continue, and there was work left to do.

As I put the finishing touches on the Laser Consulting web site during December, I started marketing the Leadership Skills course. I already had the telephone pitch down, but what I really needed was a professional web site from which to launch e-mails, business-to-business. The original site wasn't ideal, but it was the best I could do on a restricted budget. By mid-month, I was up and running. This time – really, really running.

The phone rang. "I've got Geeks."

"Excuse me?"

"I've got geeks. They need soft skills training."

I *SCORED!* Nicer-than-she-had-to-be Rebecca had browsed through my e-mail invitation and then visited my web site. One page in the original version asked the question, "Got Geeks? Need Soft Skills?" The rationale was along the lines of: "We all know some people who are better than others at public speaking, coaching or solving human problems. And some people are more comfortable solving technical problems – with machines, or numbers, networks, lines of code or processes."

Within days I was at the plant where Rebecca worked in human resources, discussing the prospect of using their conference room to host the pilot for Leadership Skills for Managers. My first student guide was done and I had a solid handle on exactly how the pilot would run – exercises, games, writing assignments and discussions. She felt it was worth a shot, and agreed the registration fee was attractive. Rebecca would register four additional team members, three free in exchange for use of the facility, and I had my first paying customers.

Now it was time to teach.

Twenty-One: First Principle - Sweat

With Rebecca's company as a starting point, and her permission, I could now go to other companies and invite them to make the same wise choice. My target was a class of 20. Twenty paid seats would cover a month of obligations. Or hey – with 20 paid seats, $6000, I could buy 75,000 shares of enron stock at 8 cents a share. Maybe it would be the same 75,000 shares Mr. Lay had received in August 2000 valued at close to $7 million.

I continued working my contact list, describing how my client's quest for quality was the seed for my leadership seminar. Meanwhile, my number had also come up with the University of Phoenix. I'd completed the preliminary training in September and October, and had been waiting for an opening. After Christmas, I'd be back in the classroom at last. It had been two years since serving as an adjunct professor at University of Houston – Clear Lake.

December 23

Like all 6-year-olds, Daughter couldn't wait two more days. With neighborhood kids out of school, we filled the time making Christmas ornaments. I filled a huge bowl with flour, added warm water, and let the kids make dough, trying to keep flour from invading clothes, hair, eyes, noses, ears and the floor. It was a lost cause, but they're all washable. Everyone had the chance to make at least 6 Christmas cookie-shaped figures, which baked into three-dimensional ornaments in about 15 minutes. Then we painted. Then we cleaned up. Then we talked about whose ornament was prettiest. Then we watched a movie. I didn't think the day would ever end.

Christmas Eve is just about the right time for the first day of Fall in Houston. If we're lucky, the first day of summer will be the day after the marathon in mid January. I think Winter was on the 6th of January, followed by Spring starting on the 7th. The weather was changing. As the other kids headed home, the first rain started pelting the windows on the northwest side of the house. Daughter and I retreated to the family room, dinner and a movie.

By the time Daughter was exhausted enough to carry to bed, the rain was mixed with hail. Thunder echoed through the neighborhood and frequent lightning overpowered the outdoor Christmas lights. Some of the neighborhood's snowmen, Wise Men and Santas were blowing down the street.

"Daddy, I'm a little bit worried about that lightning. It seems kinda close."

"Nothing to worry about, Little One," I told her confidently. "It's close to 10 o'clock. You need to get some sleep so you can spend time with Mommy tomorrow." She accepted that and turned to the nighttime shadows. I returned to the family room to exercise my rights as a grownup, and watch the cartoons *I* wanted to watch. Dissatisfied with the choices two nights before Christmas, I too hit the rack, and retired upstairs around 10:30.

As I lay in bed, mentally reviewing a thousand different images from the past week, months, year... something CRASHED into the house. On *my* side of the house. In seconds, Daughter was in my bed, "What was that, Daddy? I'm scared!"

"I don't know. It sounded like maybe a car crashed into the house or something." That didn't seem to make sense; there was no cross street. A car would have to be way out of control to hit the house. "I'll go take a look. You stay here."

"No way! I'm going with you."

And so she did. As we descended the stairs, I could hear the wind in the house. At the bottom of the stairs I flipped on the lights, first to the foyer, then to the living room. Then I could see it – a tree branch had crashed through a dining room window. Wind had blown down the 40-foot tall pine from its perch alongside the driveway. The window was smashed, broken glass covered the floor, and rain was flooding the carpet. All I could do until morning was board up the window and try to keep the rain out. I'd have to do this from the outside.

After retrieving a sheet of plywood, some plastic trash bags and duct tape, I left Daughter to watch from the inside while I went to inspect the damage on the outside. The fence was smashed and the gate swung wildly with nothing to close to. Beyond the fence, the tree had landed on the air conditioning unit that would service the upstairs during the summer. A single branch, no more than two inches in diameter, had scraped along the side of the house until it reached the window. Half of the panes shattered into the dining room. The patch worked well enough, and eventually I got Daughter calmed down enough to fall asleep. I followed, exhausted.

Christmas Eve

After dropping daughter off at her Mom's house, I went back to work. The Lord was looking out for us. The tree could have hit my truck or either of my neighbor's two cars. It could have smashed into either home. Instead, the tree had apparently first hit the edge of the roof on my home, leaving branches dangling from the eaves. Following the east-west line of the house, only the fence and A/C unit were in the way.

We were blessed – no one was hurt. We were blessed again – an A/C unit would cost close to $2000 and I didn't have it to spend. I'd kept my insurance premiums low with a higher deductible. As a result, I'd only have to run one A/C unit this summer. What's a little sweat? By July, Daughter and I were sleeping on sleeping bags on the floor downstairs. All of the bedrooms were upstairs.

A second tree had blown over in the back yard, so I started there with my chain saw. Bonus! The top half of the tree that had fallen over the fence did *not* land in the neighbor's new swimming pool. This was going to be the best Christmas ever! I cut the trees into pieces and cleaned up the mess, then got myself cleaned up and drove over to share Christmas Eve delicacies with Daughter and her mom's family, just as Santa showed up to pay a personal visit to a wide-eyed 6-year-old. This kind of thrill was off her Richter Scale.

All the way to candlelight church services, Daughter was trying to explain how Santa probably had helpers and in most countries Santa was originally a religious figure like Pere Noel or Saint Nicholas not a commercial figure and he was probably a symbolic messenger from God representing the gift of Baby Jesus which is why we got in the habit of buying gifts for the people we really and truly loved and did we think she would get that new bike for Christmas or not because some of the other kids were expecting bikes this year and they thought they had been good enough and she had been good too.

What she didn't know then, and I don't have the heart to tell her yet, is that Santa is a manifestation of the corporate world's modern performance appraisal. Hold that bonus over your employee's heads and measure the sweat as you get closer and closer to bonus time. Good works, not faith and values, get nice employees to bonus heaven. What are we rewarding?

January 1, 2003
University of Phoenix, Houston Campus

"Welcome to Psych 320, Human Motivation. Tell me, what motivates you to be here on New Year's Day?"

Student after student replied with unsurprising answers: To get a pay raise, to finish what I started 15 years ago, to be able to get out of the job I'm currently in, to set an example for my kids, to be able to start my own business. University of Phoenix is a second chance for some students, many of whom had to pass on the opportunity for college after high school because of the financial realities. Others got started on college years earlier, then got distracted by children, or divorce, or marriage. Like other accelerated degree options, it's incredibly convenient, allowing students to attend class one night a week, per course, and usually complete a bachelor's degree in around two to two-and-a-half years, depending on how much head start they have. The best part about adult students is that most of them are internally motivated and they're either paying the bill, or holding a job in a company that offers tuition assistance – so they still have a stake in their own success.

Somewhere in the five-week semester on Human Motivation, we always have the opportunity to at least briefly discuss how people acquire the attitudes that help shape motivation. There are textbook answers in Educational Psychology, Organizational Psychology's cousin, and then I have a model, synthesized from thousands of pages of textbooks, journals and classroom notes, thousands of hours in the classroom as student and professor, and thousands of hours training for the next race.

The Saline Solution

This model starts from the intuitive observation, clarified and expanded upon by theorists, that humans learn in three domains: cognitive, affective-emotional, and physical or motor skills. We learn math and English; music appreciation and ethics; baseball and brain surgery. Each discipline has an observable hierarchy. Every child who will become a rocket scientist first learns 1+1 = 2, on the way to algebra, trigonometry, calculus and beyond; every child who will become a playwright first learns words, then the alphabet, on the way to sentences, paragraphs, stories; character, setting, plot and denouement.

The discipline of educational psychology provides a lexicon for those who conduct research in the science of learning. As Curie, Faraday, Fermi, Hume, Planck and others provided a language for the so-called hard sciences, Benjamin Bloom and others have fashioned a theoretical taxonomy for each of the three learning domains.[xxxi] Like all theories, it's just as good as the next until someone else comes along with a better explanation.

From fundamental to complex, that hierarchy in the Cognitive Domain starts at *KNOWLEDGE,* and progresses through *COMPREHENSION, APPLICATION* and *ANALYSIS,* to *SYNTHESIS* and *EVALUATION.* Each level builds on the previous level, as in the progression from arithmetic to physics. Each level has a range of reasonable outcomes that a student should be able to demonstrate as a result of learning. Examples are:

- Knowledge – write, identify, state, define, select
- Comprehension – confirm, explain, predict, compare
- Application – repair, construct, produce, make, modify
- Analysis – research, categorize, disassemble, compare
- Synthesis – invent, formulate, plan, design, solve, create
- Evaluation – assess, judge, critique, summarize, recommend

We might expect junior employees to perform at the Knowledge through Application levels; we don't usually expect them to *invent* solutions for complex problems. Senior managers, however, should have mastery in the fundamentals *and* be able to Analyze, Synthesize and Evaluate. Bloom and others have likewise labeled taxonomies for the affective-emotional and physical/motor-skill domains.

Using this framework as a starting point, I offer the hypothesis-analogy (from lasers) that energy is required to move from one state to the next in any of the three domains, like the energy required to push electrons from one orbit to the next, higher-energy orbit, in order to coax them to join the photons as light emitted from a laser. An example would be the progression from Knowing the name for a guitar and the names for each of six strings, to the Understanding of how to form chords based on the relationships between strings, to the ability to reproduce a simple song (Application). Working on my musical career, I might, with some effort, graduate to the Analysis of various guitar-playing techniques, and eventually composing – Synthesizing – my own music. As an accomplished musical elder statesman, I am now well-qualified to serve as a judge in musical competitions, select music for a motion picture, or conduct an orchestra – Evaluating the harmonious efforts of scores of performers. I had started on guitar strings...long ago.

The energy, effort or exertion expended by a performer in any discipline can be said to produce perspiration. Sweat. The more I practice, the more I sweat. The more miles I run each week, the less it hurts when the marathon comes 'round. Or as one favorite Marine Corps maxim explains: "The more you sweat in peace, the less you bleed in war." At the far end of any worthwhile activity – music, surgery, writing, war, engineering, high school, building a business – is Quality. On the road from quality is sweat.

Although the sweat from physical work is only slightly more real than the analogous sweat from mental activity, or the practice required to hone social skills, they're all essentially the same. Results take time and effort. Effort can be uncomfortable, and it's easy to rationalize the decision *not* to go out for a 5-mile run today. And tomorrow. And the next day. Soon I'm a blob and start paying attention to television commercials for miracle weight-loss pills and patches. The next thing I know, I'm wearing the patch, watching TV, eating and sleeping my way to the Boston Marathon.

That's what enron did.

There's a reason 12- or 15-year-old Scotch whiskey costs more than Boone's Farm strawberry wine. There's a reason the hand-built luxury car costs more than the die-cast imitations, or a Stradivarius commands millions and catalogs offer cheap imitations for a few hundred dollars. enron was a cheap imitation of *the world's best company*, a cubic zirconium in a chrome setting. Living with a set of principles that insists on quality as a starting point is hard work.

Quality takes time. Patience. Sure, we all want to be first to market with the latest innovation, but if we're going to have to recall the product because of mechanical defects – what sense does it make? Every reporter wants to get the breaking news story on the wire first, but if the facts are plagiarized or wrong, where's the scoop?

What of the mental and physical sweat produced by thousands of employees, including enron's executive officers? Like the quest for the elusive perpetual motion machine, in which no energy is lost, no energy is wasted, enron aspired to become the perfect company with zero entropy. Indictment after indictment, it seems enron's executives were wearing the patch, popping the get-rich-quick pills. The energy required to move "company" to COMPANY includes not only physical and mental sweat, but ethical sweat as well. Moral courage is required to operate a business according to those core values, day-in, day-out. Sacrificing revenue in order to treat customers, employees, retirees and vendors with respect is a hard pill, but it's also a worthwhile investment in loyalty. More ethical pushups – stronger ethical muscles.

Different occupations require different muscles, different skills, different kinds of work. It may be obvious why female Olympians in gymnastics are young, but not so obvious why top marathoners are not. The average female gymnast competing for Olympic gold is often a teenager. In contrast, the average age of the top 10 male finishers in the 2004 Houston Marathon was 32. One of these was 42. I'll never be a top marathoner, yet my time in that same race was faster than all but three of the 12- to15-year-old males and more than half of the young men 16 to 19. I was 48. Gymnastics and marathons both require stamina, but different kinds of stamina

Running a global corporation is an ultra marathon requiring ethical stamina and maturity. The guilty verdict on Martha Stewart on the sale of her ImClone stock, the ouster of Michael Eisner from his role as Chairman of Disney's board of directors, and the parade of worldcoms, tycos and others has to suggest that people are weary of the immaturity of bullies on the playground who demand to be first in line, grab all the toys and blame others when something goes wrong. Leading a team from company to COMPANY requires adult leadership, grown-ups willing to sweat it out with the troops, physically, mentally *and* ethically. It turns out that sweat and tears are both salty water, and now that Mr. Skilling has been indicted, one wonders if others may be sweating, or if rich people just pay someone else to sweat for them until the verdict comes in.

Twenty-Two: Laser Chapter 8

Faced with the possibility – probability – that Kathryn was still alive was almost too much to accept. Steele fought tears. Waiting for nightfall was anguish, but after stealing a few hours of sleep, Steele and Murdoch filled the afternoon developing what seemed to be a reasonable plan of action. Returning to Corpus Christi was out of the question. In the first place, Murdoch was certain there were no airworthy fighters back at the base. All qualified flight crews were deployed with the 4th Wing. To make matters worse, Steele and Murdoch had just hijacked an alien fighter, so both visual and radar signature would precede them to the tower, long before they might have a chance to explain. Even with air crews deployed, ground support troops would be in high alert, with access to not only individual weapons but both long-range laser canon and short-range anti-aircraft guns and surface-to-air missiles fed by data from phased-array radar sites around the base.

Considering the lonely option the best option, Steele could rationalize this by the mission as well. They only had to make a pick-up for one dinner date. Kathryn.

Parking the out-of-this-world fighter in a deserted barn south of Houston was like pushing himself away from the table at a good meal. He just couldn't get enough. Nothing he'd ever flown was anything like this bird. Once the fighter was out of sight, Murdoch offered to stand watch while Steele, exhausted, took the first real rest he'd had in 36 hours.

Captain Dave Steele dreamed.

Twenty-Three: Acceptance. Impatience. Hope.

January – August 2003

"Daddy. Wake up...wake up."

"Whaaaaaa........t?" I mumbled, with face planted in pillow.

"I'm gonna ride my bike today! Without training wheels! Come on! Come on! Let's go!"

"I'll think about it if you quit jumping on me. Can't you see I'm sleeping. And it's still dark outside. What time is it?"

"Five. I got the milk out but you gotta reach the cereal."

Sure enough, Daughter was dressed for bike riding: jeans, socks and shoes, shirt and sweater, pony tail and a helmet. "I think the helmet could wait until after breakfast," I suggested.

"Oh, it's okay. It won't get in the way."

As we finished breakfast and Saturday morning chores, Daughter explained that almost all of the other 6- and 7-year-olds – and there were plenty of them in the neighborhood – already knew how to ride a bike without training wheels. There was even a 4-and-a-half-year-old who had taken to the sport like a natural. "Some of the kids laugh at me, so I gotta learn so they'll let me play with them."

"I see. And if you can ride without training wheels, but you're not as fast as they are, will that matter?"

"I'll be the fastest!"

"Hmm..."

Daughter sometimes had a difficult time not being first. Some of that is normal for kids anyway, but even more so for a first-born, or a child raised as an only child.

Daughter's brothers are 20 years older, so she is in effect an "only."

By now it was barely light enough to head for the deserted street. This would benefit Daughter's lessons; with all of the neighbor kids certainly still in bed at 7 a.m. there would be no spectators. The strategy for this session had started with the counterintuitive recommendation from Jerry, one of my old team members in Michigan, who suggested lowering the seat and removing the pedals. This would allow Daughter's feet to reach the pavement and effectively run down the street, seated on the bike. She could lift her feet at will and start working on balance. The next step would be to raise the training wheels just enough so the bike could tip and require some balance, but not far enough as to allow a capsize.

We started with this approach, eventually getting to the point at which Daughter could master about 10 to 15 feet with her legs extended and toes pointing forward. Every foot farther was a success and met with praise and applause. Yet the technique was not meant to lead to instant success. Daughter grew frustrated with her inability to balance and steer the bike for more than a few feet, and eventually retired to the all-American routine of Saturday morning cartoons until it was time to play with her friends in any activity that didn't involve bicycles.

Over the course of three Saturday mornings, Daughter's practice led to more and more confidence. By the third week, the training wheels were gone completely. The day she knew it was *the* day, I posted her at the top of the driveway. The seat was still lowered, the pedals and training wheels were off. With a small decline, she could coast down the driveway into the street, where I was waiting to catch her.

"Ladies and gentlemen," I announced to the empty street, "Today is the world championship bicycle competition, featuring the world-famous Daughter!"

"What do I get if I make it to the street?" she asked.

"Eighty points, maybe a hundred."

"That's it?"

"Okay... how about 800 points. A thousand if it's perfect?"

"That's more like it."

"Ready?"

"Ready."

With her face set in stoic determination, Daughter launched. In under five seconds, she had covered 30 feet, double the past week's performance.

"Ladies and gentleman... the new record. Daughter wins 1000 points!"

"Yeah! Let's do it again."

And we did. Each time she pushed off, I would back farther into the street, eventually turning and moving up the street, five feet, ten or more so she would now have to control the bike in a turn. With every success, I awarded her another 500 or 700 or 1000 points and praised the trial run. By the time she could coast 100 feet or more to the community mailboxes, she was ready. As daughter watched apprehensively, I reattached the pedals to the bike and had her positioned back at the top of the driveway.

"Keep your feet up. When you're ready, start pedaling. Got it?"

"Got it."

"On your mark. Get set. GO!" Daughter glided into the street, turned toward the mailboxes, put her feet on the pedals and went into action. I ran ahead to monitor her progress. As I caught up and jogged alongside, I said, "Look at you. You're a bike rider!" Daughter radiated.

Joy. Joy. Joy. What independence.

Delivering quality instruction in organizational psychology, leading to that first check from the University of Phoenix was my first step toward independence; getting the first Leadership seminar booked for the end of January would be the next. Finally, I was truly self-employed. Just a few years earlier, before enron, the entire corporation I worked for as a NASA contractor was going through 6 Sigma indoctrination. Ten people were selected for the first phase of 6 Sigma Black Belt training. I was one of those, and looked forward to contributing to anything that might energize my business unit. I was also interested in observing the consultants sent in to shepherd our internal team, with the eye of an organizational psychologist, even though my primary goal, like the other team members, was collecting and analyzing information that was supposed to help our company improve performance.

Observing one of these consultants in particular, I recognized I could do exactly what this guy was doing. He was a contractor, an independent consultant. I knew independents could make $200 thousand, even $300 thousand or more a year, but what was pushing or pulling me was not the potential income. This was something I would do on subsistence wages if I could find it.

"Ken, I've been watching you and the other consultants for the past two weeks or so. I can do what you guys are doing...how about tossing me some subcontract work and let me shadow you for a while. I think this is what I want to do in my next life."

"Sure," he said. "When you quit this job and can support yourself on your own, give me a call."

"You want me to walk away from an $80K salary, willingly? Just like that? But I can do what you do *now*."

"You probably can. You're sharp, but if I toss you a bone, how are you going to find the next one? I don't make a living finding work for guys like you. The operative word in Independent Consultant, my friend, is *Independent*."

Gosh that sounds like *Freedom.* I didn't see any possible way to walk away from the job, and as it turned out, the enron offer was less than six months away. As long as I had a salary, I thought I was in control. When enron gave me that freedom, it was not my choice. Then the realities of the job market suggested I was stuck with it. I lost control.

Teaching and banking one seminar's income allowed me to gain control of a flat spin in January. Running the 2003 Houston Marathon was cathartic emotionally, but painful physically. I would have to find a way to get from 16 miles to the finish without debilitating pain in my hips, knees and feet. The mental stamina was there but the 47-year-old body wasn't. Finishing was acceptable; finishing 15 or 20 minutes slower than the year before was not.

During the last of 2002 and the first few months of 2003, as United Nations Resolutions failed to extract the desired responses from Iraq, and the U.S. moved toward a war footing, the Marine Corps sent out a recall notice, inviting retired officers and senior enlisted Marines to apply to return to active duty. The recall suggested that the Corps was primarily interested in those retired 5 years or less. When I called the officer monitor at Headquarters, Marine Corps, I left a message with my rank, name, home phone number and the information that I had only been retired 4 years, 1,445 days. They never called back for some reason.

Throughout the coming six months, I would deliver six more Leadership workshops. Sometimes I seated a dozen or more participants; other times I had an audience of five or six. With these workshops going about once every four weeks, I had almost endless free time. Time to write; time to paint; time to develop new courses; time to market my stuff. This was the way it was supposed to be. I had exhausted unemployment. No more training wheels. There was no turning back. The only thing that might dissuade me from pursuing self-employment with all my energy would be a job offer in my field. But everything would have to work – the people, the boss, the company, the mission, the company's focus on customers, and most importantly, my job.

I asked for, and received, honest feedback from my workshop participants. From production managers in the petrochemical industry and engineers in aerospace, to civil servants anticipating their first leadership roles at Johnson Space Center, end-of-course evaluations were my real paycheck. Positive feedback overwhelmed constructive criticism about 9 to 1. As with any other course I had ever taught, I drank in the positive comments as confirmation on what I was doing right, but took special pains to learn from my mistakes. Skepticism and Cynicism are genetically identical. If as an employee I ever thought my boss (me) was just going through the motions to draw a paycheck, it would have been easy to become cynical. But I was predisposed to be Skeptical.

With an eye on Hope, one success led to another, like my daughter rolling down the driveway without training wheels for the first time. Skepticism faded as I felt both the acceptance of my seminar participants, and my own acceptance of this alien lifestyle. I still didn't have enough to do.

When America lost the Columbia crew the first of February 2003, I felt helpless, as I'm sure many others did. I offered appropriate condolences to friends who still worked closely with NASA. There's no denying that I was concerned about the impact on my workshop, scheduled for July. I'm sure the Boeings, Lockheeds, Raytheons and United Space Alliances were equally concerned on their scale about the future of business in the space arena as well. As I waited a respectful several weeks before checking in on the July seminar contract, I turned to other business development pursuits.

Old Bananas

One new business prospect showed up in the response from an HR manager who declined the opportunity to book the Leadership Skills workshop, "We don't have anyone for leadership training, but I do need to get Diversity training done for the year. Do you have a Diversity Workshop?"

"When do you need it?" I inquired.

"April. We would do half of the plant in one session, about 35 people, and the other half two weeks later. How would that work for you?"

Longer sentences are good sentences while the wheels are turning in my head. I wouldn't say "No." I would just start calculating on my computer and scratching out some numbers on a legal pad, while I talked on the phone, how long it would take me to develop a course. I based my estimate on 25 to 40 hours of development time for each hour of unique training. Four hours of training might take me 100 to 160 hours of development time. An April delivery would give me at least six weeks to build a course that would suit her company's needs.

"Sure, I have a half-day Diversity workshop, built on a game show format. When might I be able to swing by your office to discuss the demographics at your plant?"

Next thing I knew I was in the Diversity training business. By the time Trixie and I met, I had formulated a framework for the content of a workshop and devised a draft game show format to suit our needs. Creating the content for a three-hour course should take about 75 to 90 hours for a skilled curriculum developer, assuming a subject matter expert is available. But to *become* the subject matter expert and develop the course would require a bit more homework. I would rely on my strengths in organizational psychology and human motivation to present *a view* on diversity in the workplace. I don't know that there is *a correct view* on the topic other than the esoterica of rights and fairness. After meeting with Trixie, it turned out this was not an event to change a culture. The plant was in good shape; this would be one of those *reminders* that a team might need once every two or three years – to keep things running smoothly. That's all she asked for – refresher training.

Becoming the subject matter expert, or expert enough to be credible and able to respond to my client's needs, more than doubled the time it would normally take to develop a course. However, at the end of a month, I had the package. Now all I had to do was build a game show. I needed to get away from the computer anyway.

Home Depot: A round, 36-inch fiberboard table top and a bag of wooden pegs; 24 feet of 2X2 in 8-foot lengths; a 7/16-inch bolt with nuts and washers; and a couple of nylon sleeves with an internal diameter of 7/16 inch.

Academy Sports: A skateboard wheel and a set of bearings. Three days in the garage and I had a "wheel of fortune" game board that could spin freely on a skateboard wheel at the center, and labels for *Anglo, Hispanic, African-American;* and *Male, Female;* and *$175,000/year, $60,000/year, $25,000/year;* as well as other categories that people tend to use to determine differences amongst themselves.

The workshop played out exactly as planned: The first step was to point out that people do indeed discriminate. We have discriminating tastes in vehicles – some drive Ford trucks and some drive Chevy trucks. Some drink Coke; some drink Pepsi. The trick is to plant the reminder that some discrimination is healthy and necessary, and some is destructive, especially in a work environment.

As I had filtered Leadership through various principles from Organizational Psychology, I would project Diversity through the lenses of Freedom and Control, Logic, Quality, Risk and Values. I provided the audience with numbers: 1, 2 or 3, and assembled the first individual contestants from each of the three teams at the stage for a round of questions. Like on the TV game show *Jeopardy,* I would pose an answer; the first person with a good question would signal by tapping a "push-on/push-off" light. Questions were either ranked from 1 to 10 or True-False, and included such concepts as: "True or False: French people make good wine." (faulty logic/stereotype: *some* French people make good wine.) Or: True or False: Schools need to do something about bullies on the playground. (Freedom and Control. Adults will recognize this as a truism, but it sets the stage for discussion on bullies at work).

A good answer would allow the contestant to pick up a game piece from the wheel. In the end, the first team that had assembled a gender, ethnic group identity, age, income, educational level and marital status was the winner. We ended up with a "Single, Hispanic, 24-year-old female with a college degree, earning $175,000 a year" as the winning team, with more than 50 percent Anglo, middle-age males on the team "sharing" that identity.

The winning team won $100 to split or go to lunch, and was charged to prepare a response to the then-pending legislation on the University of Michigan's Affirmative Action program, from the perspective of their new, collective cultural identity. Second place team members won $50 to split, and worked with the third place team to craft a rebuttal to the winning team's anticipated comments on Affirmative Action. The last place team...they got old bananas. I had placed a fresh bunch in the freezer the night before, and by game time they were black. Most of us, with discriminating tastes, will pass on old bananas in the grocery store.

In general, the project was a success. We repeated the game show two weeks later, with some improvements recommended from the first event's participants. Debate was lively and responsible during both sessions, with populations of men and women of five primary ethnic groups, ranging from close to 20 to near 60 years old. In the end, however, I doubted the efficacy of a Middle-Aged, White-Angle-Saxon, Heterosexual, Protestant, Republican Male delivering future workshops on Diversity. I had to be realistic. Even if I could offer far more than theory, I would inevitably have workshop participants who would doubt my ability to relate to the concept of being discriminated against. Most of these petrochemical plant training managers or HR managers were told to think in terms of "cultural diversity" anyway, and not cognitive diversity – which should be the end goal. I returned to what I knew best, impatient for a bigger score training in leadership.

Twenty-Four: First Principle - Focus

Pirsig's *Zen and the Art of Motorcycle Maintenance* still had a dangling proposition. Pirsig's equation, still unfinished and hogging my mental chalkboard, seemed to suggest that pure Quality required total Freedom, total absence of rules or restrictions. If true, that prompts the question: what do the rules restrict me *from?* Pirsig's students had found themselves entangled in rules as they attempted to create *quality* papers for their instructor. I drafted the concept into the analogous production of consumer goods and commodities, suggesting that companies need freedom to innovate in order to advance and remain competitive. Non-profit organizations and government agencies need freedom to continuously seek ways to meet the needs of their clients. Educational institutions require freedom to expand knowledge.

In a sterile application, this seemed to make sense. So why couldn't a company innovate its way to a 3-wheeled car? Well...there actually are 3-wheeled cars. What if they went further and produced a 2-wheeled car? Most people would obviously intuit the result as something belonging to the class of motorcycles. Does everything with 2-wheels have to be a motorcycle? No...bicycles are a different class or category of land vehicles with two wheels. And now we're nowhere close to the definition of a car. To define is to limit, and to limit is to restrict freedom. If I build something with 4 wheels, three vertical surfaces and a flat horizontal surface made out of marble, I might have a desk with wheels but certainly not a car. Where does a car end and a desk begin? What has the quality of being a car in contrast to something that has the quality of being a desk?

It now seems I need enough rules to impose order, but just enough order to create an end result that fits in a class of products and services, employees, tools, systems or anythings. I need just enough order to define desirable performance on the job or socially acceptable behavior. But is that definition descriptive or proscriptive?

Pirsig's theorem is intuitively invalid without another factor in the equation. I win. But that doesn't mean Pirsig loses. I still need him around. Disproof of the theorem lies in Pirsig's attempt to teach writing, which by definition is not guitar playing or swimming. If pure quality exists, it exists in God, but absent a human appreciation of quality, quality just *is*, as Pirsig says. Quality just is. So what? People don't drive for miles to see quality. People don't save for years to buy quality. We appreciate quality manifest in some thing, some event, or as Pirsig noted, some experience. But winning isn't enough; now I need to either try to complete the philosopher's work logically, like divide it by 19, X or *pi*, or come up with a new equation. I'm not sure there exists a possibility for a unified field theory in organizational psychology.

I'm back to the chalkboard with a hypothesis, uncertain that it can factor into Pirsig's equation: Something, or someone, must impose order on the creation of a thing or event that manifests quality, like training wheels, or running alongside my daughter as she learns to ride her bicycle. Even if *quality* is the first step on Dorothy's trek down the Yellow Brick Road to the Land of Oz in search of the Wizard, Dorothy must first know that the Yellow Brick Road is the right path to follow. A-ha! Glinda the Good Witch of the North told her. Glinda showed her the way. She imposed order on Dorothy's quest, but did not hold Dorothy's hand on her travels. Dorothy was internally motivated to get back to Kansas and since the 1939 motion picture, has always had the self-discipline to follow the Yellow Brick Road to the Wizard of Oz, the one man who could help her achieve her goal. Glinda merely got Dorothy focused. In the real world, there is... well, the world: "In the beginning God created the heavens and the earth."xxxii

Most people, at least in the western world, are probably familiar with this passage, whether they accept it or not. The first chapter of Genesis describes how God imposed order on chaos, creating day and night, water and dry land, plants and animals. But as we read further, there is an answer to Pirsig's dilemma:

And God created man in His image, in His image he created them; he created them male and female. And God blessed them. "Have children," God told them, "and become many and fill the earth and control it; and rule over the fish in the sea, the birds in the air, and every living thing that moves on the earth.[xxxiii]

The answer is – God instructed mankind to impose order on his surroundings, to name the animals and plants. It is not at all a quantum leap forward to realize that we now have everything from Species-Genus-Order-Class-Phylum-Kingdom for animals to labels for flavors of quarks in the strange land of sub-atomic physics. But we also have the world according to the creators of Sesame Street, and Sponge Bob Square Pants. Curious species, that mankind. I want to impose order on the enrons, on the process of creating the best company in the world.

Somewhere between these two extremes, between the brief make-believe world of Dorothy and the endless universe, is the day-to-day challenge to make good use of God's command for humans to impose order on the world around us. In the Marine Corps, that good witch who imposes order on things is the Sergeant Major, or at least a good non-commissioned officer.

Sarge

During 2001, the History Channel ran the two-hour program "SARGE!" which tells the story of America's non-commissioned officers (NCOs)[xxxiv]. Through interviews and replays from newsreels and movies covering most of the 20th century, The History Channel defines and describes a unique culture that is truly only well-understood by those who have lived the existence of an NCO, and perhaps to some extent by those officers who have learned to rely on them.

In order to fix the position of the military NCO metaphor for the non-military community, it will help to understand the contractual – or business – difference between professional enlisted men and women who become non-commissioned officers, and those who are commissioned officers. In the civilian, business sense of the word, enlisted soldiers, sailors, airmen and Marines are on contract. When they enlist, they sign a contract for a period of time typically ranging from two to six years. At the end of their obligated military service, they are free to walk away from the military with no further commitment. This can happen at any point in their careers following a combined initial obligation to active duty and reserve military forces of six to eight years. So it is possible for an enlisted Marine, for example, to complete an initial four-year contract, and a second six-year enlistment and leave the Corps after 10 years with no remaining obligation.

Commissioned officers, on the other hand, are appointed by and serve "at the pleasure of" the President of the United States, and are confirmed in their appointments by the "advice and consent" of the Senate. There are subtleties of difference between reserve officers and active duty officers, but the significant point is that if they desire to leave the military, officers are required to resign their commissions. However, once commissioned, always commissioned – and an officer can theoretically always be called back to active duty.

Non-commissioned officers – starting at the rank of corporal in the Army and Marine Corps, sergeant or senior airman in the Air Force, and 3rd class petty officer in the Navy – may be promoted to that non-commissioned officer grade with as little as two years in uniform, sometimes even less. Enlisting as young as 17, that means they could be noncommissioned officers as young as 19 or 20. Men and women in the military take on leadership responsibilities before they become NCOs, as individuals are singled out for leadership roles starting in boot camp or basic training, in schools following boot camp, and so on.

The business world doesn't really have NCOs. Sure, there are "exempt" and "non-exempt" employees, and most of us understand the main difference: you can work a non-exempt employee to death as long as you pay overtime;

exempt employees can be worked to death with no hope of overtime pay because their salaries are supposed to be substantial enough to compensate for 49-hour weeks that sometimes become 90-hour weeks. There are blue-collar and white-collar workers, but that isn't the same either. And there are employees, typically directors, vice presidents and presidents, who sign real executive contracts and have specific terms of commitment to a corporation, but these distinctions still are not the same as officer-NCO differences.

The important lessons we can take from the treatment on SARGE! include the various missions of the NCO, and the description of *what* an NCO is. In these, we can see the parallel in our business world – and where the civilian leaders in an "NCO" role are both lacking in performance and in need of training.

Based on a variety of on-screen interviews with former NCOs, and voice-over narration during the film, an NCO's mission is "to train, to pass on knowledge, to discipline, to serve as a role model, to build teams, to ensure the welfare of the soldiers." They are responsible for "teaching, caring, and mentoring."

One NCO noted that the role of "the sergeant"[xxxv] during war is "getting people to do things that go against human nature. We need to convince them they are doing something bigger, more important than they are individually." Those things that go against human nature include both sides of combat – getting into the situation where someone is trying to kill you, and being in the situation where your job is to kill other people.

The video emphasizes that the NCO, as the "backbone of the armed forces," is in a position of authority, and serves as "the bridge between the officers who lead and the privates who follow." What defines the NCO, the mark of an NCO, is the answer to the question posed in the video: "Would I go to war with that guy?" One might think about that in the context of corporate executives who line their own pockets. Would I go into business combat with that guy?

What distills out of these concepts are the abilities of the NCO...ability to lead and be left in charge without supervision, and ability to teach and train junior troops so that they can operate independently. As the non-commissioned officers, past and recently present, observed in the video SARGE! their job is to equip troops to succeed without them..."to train soldiers to do what they're supposed to do without [us] being there: "If we've done that, we've done our job."

Aside from the occasional mentor in civilian industry – the one who is not in fear of losing his job to a junior employee, and is willing to train the up-and-coming junior troops – the "civilian NCO" is non-existent. Increasingly over the past generation, the concept of performing within a calling, of doing something larger than one's self, has eroded in an atmosphere of job cuts, mergers and acquisitions, lay-offs, and executive gluttony.

All of this could easily have been about VISION, and sharing the vision, but vision and focus are not the same. Any company can declare a vision. A person with color-blindness has vision, but it is imperfect. A person with astigmatism has vision, but that too is imperfect. It is possible to see and not understand what we are seeing, like the posters that enjoyed some popularity in the early 1990s. As we walked past the kiosk in the shopping mall, these posters looked like a jumble of colorful patterns that made no sense.

Publishers offered books about the phenomenon, with dozens of sample "out of focus" prints to entertain the reader. Instructions on how to bring the hidden image into focus suggest:

> All you need to "see" the 3D illusion...are your two eyes and some patience! To discover your MAGIC EYE, focus your eyes as if you were looking at a far away object; this is called "diverging your eyes." One easy way to do this is to hold the [picture] *against your nose* and *very, very slowly*, pull the book away from your face.[xxxvi]

For the commercial enterprise, what this counter-intuition means is that profit can only be realized by focusing on quality. The temptation is strong to look directly at the picture, the profit, even after we know the trick. Some guide must be responsible for bringing the organizational vision into focus and keeping it there.

The obvious answer seems to point back to Leader, and that's already been discussed. The earlier introduction to Leader, however, presented Leader in form. This is about Leader in function. Proceeding from Quality, quality yields both form and function. Just as a Quality event must have qualities (a form and a function) to actually be an event, Quality Leaders must have qualities – characteristics in form and function – to be quality leaders. Character constitutes the form.

Among the countless *functions* that define a leader, and specifically that function directed at getting team members focused, is the ability to influence. How that translates into practice is easily understood by the arts and sciences of *propaganda*. People tend to view the word *propaganda* in a negative light. Propaganda is what the bad guys do. We're nice people; we're just delivering a public service announcement – strategic communications. Propaganda by definition is:

> a set of methods employed by an organized group that wants to bring about the active or passive participation in its actions of a mass of individuals psychologically unified[xxxvii]

Advertising is one form of propaganda. Nations and political leaders engage in propaganda. We can understand some, but not all, elements of education and religion through a better understanding of propaganda. And, we can better understand how to bring about the active (or passive) participation of that mass of employees in the actions of our organization, the company, if only we better understood how to get them psychologically unified. Without focus, they are not.

Conformity

What we're looking for is conformity to a way of doing business. Aronson and other social psychologists have given us a taxonomy for this concept of *conformity* on three levels: *Compliance, Identification* and *Internalization.*[xxxviii] Starting in the 1990s, when the Internal Revenue Service began its push toward the goal of becoming a kinder, gentler government agency, the focus was on conformity to a new norm for customer service. As car manufacturers in the United States struggle to compete with European and Japanese automakers, the focus is on conformity to higher standards of quality in various categories (like durability, maintenance costs, reliability, resale value and so on). There are countless examples. The psychology of getting a team of people to conform suggests that we can get just about anybody to do anything if we beat them hard enough. This worked well enough building the pyramids, or when navies once used conscripted sailors. This form of conformity is termed *compliance,* and is still very much alive...just more subtle (most of the time).

Compliance relies on external pressure. This could be the drill instructor (a non-commissioned officer) screaming in the private's ear to get him to do something he doesn't think he can do, like negotiating the obstacle course. Or it could be the pushy car salesman who just wants you to step inside the showroom so he can get some more information. When relentless pressure produces a result, particularly a result contrary to the actor's beliefs or attitudes, *cognitive dissonance* is likely. As discussed, cognitive dissonance is an uncomfortable competition between two cognitions, which needs to be resolved: "I didn't think I could make it over the wall – but I did." I can levy the blame on the external influence, the drill instructor, or I can eventually believe I had it in me all the time. At the car dealership, I can blame the pushy salesman for getting me to reveal my phone number and home address, or I can ultimately believe I am smart for trading in my old bucket of bolts. Assuming external pressure continues, once one contrary step is taken, more are likely to follow.

Aronson and others describe *identification* as an external influence, but with a different kind of pressure. The emphasis is on imitation. Aronson refers to this as "the-good-old-Uncle-Charlie phenomenon," which says in essence that because I admire Uncle Charlie, I ascribe to his belief systems; I imitate him. The desire is to be like the model. The drill instructor who sets an example in not only posture and bearing but language and beliefs becomes Uncle Charlie. Every recruit who adequately imitates that model adopts the message as his own. This is why the Marine Corps intensely scrutinizes applications for drill instructor school, and attrition from the school is significantly higher than from other Marine Corps schools. Although recruits tend to regard their drill instructors as anything *but* "good old Uncle Charlie," especially during the demanding early weeks of boot camp, most Marines will acknowledge even decades after the experience that their drill instructors were the critical catalyst in their transition from boy to man, civilian to Marine. The Corps has less than three months to laminate a new culture over the recruit's existing beliefs, and extinguish behaviors that fail to define a Marine (smoking or chewing gum while in uniform, hands in the pockets while in uniform, saying "yeah" instead of "yes sir").

In the final stage of conformity, *internalization,* we see the actor separating the values from external pressure or influence. Rather than a desire to be like Uncle Charlie or my drill instructor, I can justify my actions because they are consistent with my own beliefs. I will have adopted those beliefs as my own. That phrase "Once a Marine – Always a Marine" means exactly the same as "you can take the Marine out of the Corps but you can't take the Corps out of the Marine." As Marines internalize the Corps' values, they *become* the organization. The organization's values are manifest in Marines, past and present.

Running parallel to Aronson's model, Perrow describes three orders of control. In "Stories which control the organization," Wilkins briefly describes what Perrow[xxxix] calls "First-order," "Second-order," and "Third-order" controls:

First-order control refers to direct supervision or control by direct orders (or rules). Second-order controls are more remote controls deriving from an assembly line layout, or from "programs," or "standard operating procedures" (March and Simon, 1958). Third-order controls are found in the assumptions or definitions of the situation which are taken as "givens" by organizational participants.

Organizational stories that have become scripts provide the same kind of cognitive "satisficing" device that a standard operating procedure does and are therefore like second-order controls. The decision maker has only to place an incoming problem into the framework of a well-known story about how such a problem was handled to decide what should be done. Of course, the difference between scriptal stories and standard operating procedures is that the story is an informally transmitted, and perhaps subjectively interpreted, event from the organization's history rather than a formally prescribed procedure or rule.

Third order controls are even more subtle and perhaps therefore less well understood. Perrow defines this type of control as control over decision premises (Simon, 1945). This is the type of control Durkheim, Malinowksi, Clar, Selznick and others refer to when they suggest that narratives as myths, legends and sagas are often viewed by participants as concrete instances of abstract values or implicit assumptions. An example of this form of control comes from a personnel manager in a company I studied. He told me of an experience he had while working in the Far East. He and the plant manager were confronted one day with an emergency decision and had been unable to contact headquarters in the U.S. for instructions. They sat down together and asked themselves: "Well, what would the company president do?" What occurred to them was a shared perspective which the personnel manager derived from a story the president had once told him. This rather implicit perspective made the decision clear to these men and they later found that top management agreed completely with their conclusions.[xl]

Values guide behavior in both *3rd Order Controls* and *Internalization.* Immediate results are almost always possible at the 1st order level, or compliance level, particularly when external pressure (enforcement) is present. But the business community, like the narrator in the video SARGE!, wants a team of people who will do what they're supposed to do even when no one is watching, which goes all the way back to stopping for the stop sign even with no cop in sight. Achieving this level of performance requires focus on organizational values. Moving a mass of people from compliant behavior enforced by rules and direct supervision (discipline) to behavior guided by internalized values (self-discipline) requires that we first get their attention. Few corporations have anything resembling a "boot camp" environment, although Xerox and IBM (for example) have historically demonstrated success in building Xerox-minded or IBM-minded employees. There are others. In retail trades, one look at average annual training hours per non-exempt (hourly) employee is a legitimate indicator of "getting their attention."

An example of customer service values guiding business performance lives in The Container Store. Headquartered in Dallas, Texas, The Container Store was named #1 on Fortune Magazine's list of top 100 Best Places to Work in America two years running, in 2000 and 2001, and was still #2 in 2002. (In 2013 it is still in the top 25. Google is ranked #1.) The company's web site, www.containerstore.com, tells only the surface of the story about their success, but there are some nuggets. For example, the Learn About Us page[xli] notes:

"Customer service is The Container Store's core competency, so hiring people who are self-motivated and team-oriented with a passion for customer service is key. We place so much importance on service that every first-year, full-time salesperson receives about 235 hours of training – in a retail industry where the average is about seven hours. And training continues throughout an employee's career. The Container Store has full-time employees who are dedicated to training all store employees on the features, advantages and benefits of each product, as well as specific training on how to best service and sell to our customers. At The Container Store, service equals selling. Our trainers are in the stores every day ensuring that store employees are knowledgeable and empowered to offer the unparalleled customer service that we are known for in the industry."

There are several things going on here. First, 235 hours of training, in U.S. Air Force 7-hour work days, is just about as long as Air Force boot camp, or between six and seven weeks. In the retail world, that's an enormous expense, but it pays off generously in greatly reduced turnover and higher employee loyalty, performance and morale. The Container Store reports turnover as 24%. In similar types of retail companies, annual turnover can be 100% or more for non-salaried staff on a store-by-store basis. At what cost? After you do some math on your 1.75% to 2.5% shrink in retail (employee theft and customer shoplifting), calculate what it costs to recruit and hire a constant turnover of new employees.

Second, note that the value-heavy statements ("service equals selling," "employees are knowledgeable and empowered," "unparalleled customer service," "customer service... core competency," "passion for customer service...") are woven through this brief paragraph about training. Those 235 hours is not only a lot of time to teach knowledge and skills, but company values at the same time.

In the business world, managers often wonder, after having an in-house training department or some contractor teach their work force new processes, skills or knowledge, why employees quickly return to doing business the way they used to. Perhaps it's because they didn't teach attitudes or values with skills and knowledge. You can teach people the facts about how a new process is supposed to operate, but if there is no motivation for embracing the new process, true change will not come about.

What of enron, or any company striving to become COMPANY? enron had propaganda; they had a propaganda *machine*. Vice presidents and directors spent freely, providing employees with enron-embroidered gym bags, hats and shirts, enron-printed golf balls, toys and games, plaques, coffee cups and insulator cups, and all of the same kinds of gadgets printed with the words proclaiming enron's core values: Respect, Integrity, Communication and Excellence. But it was the cups by the water coolers and coffee makers that told the real story. Like the two- or three-line fillers an editor might use to fill white space at the end of a newspaper column, enron printed the paper water cups with the real message: "Did you know enron's stock has split 3 times since 1985?"xlii

By definition, enron had *great* propaganda in every sense of the word, but the message embedded in that propaganda was currency that only traded in stock price, and enron was manipulating its stock. The most effective propaganda starts with a believable message rooted in truth, which is why intelligent adults believe they are least susceptible to propaganda in any form. The stock value myth was indeed true. For a while. Everyone who touched enron benefited, further confirming the myth. Stock prices tumble; *QUALITY* as an ideal cannot. Quality just is.

Focus, as a First Principle force multiplier, is essential to maintaining organizational excellence. The moral authority (the sergeant major) in any given organization must ensure that *focus* works with the other first principles, starting with QUALITY. If the CEO doesn't have a sergeant major to whisper in his ear, or a Good

Witch of the North to focus a team on the path to a vision, the CEO must assume that role and be prepared to live it.

My quest now becomes a search for evidence that an organization has lost its focus. What I find is stakeholders at odds with each other. Customers want quality for the least money possible, free if they can get it.

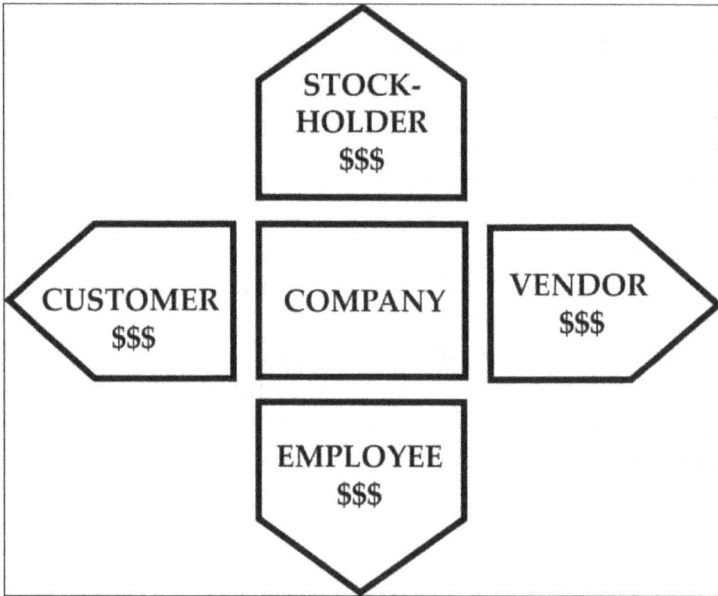

Figure 1.

The company seeks to increase wealth, which means getting as much money as possible from the customer after finding the lowest possible cost to provide a "quality" product or service (which includes not only raw materials and overhead, but salaries as well). Employees see that everyone else is in business for themselves, so want to expend the least amount of labor for as much money as possible, which is exactly the model presented by the organization they work for. Vendors catch on, and mirror the business climate they serve. The end result is that every player plays to maximize his own profit. This is pretty much how business has operated for thousands of years, with some exceptions.

Somewhere out there are employees who declare they

have found the ideal job and derive maximum satisfaction from doing what they do best, in the interest of serving customers. *Some* vendors maximize revenue by focusing on quality as defined by the business they serve; *some* businesses do the same. But often, we see a climate of *me first*...everyone trying to suck money out of your company:

If it were *MY* business, I'd start with the stockholders: "You want stock in my company? You now own a stake in customer satisfaction." Then the Employees: "Our vision is customer satisfaction. Employees are customers. If you're not satisfied, let's find out why and fix it. If you don't fit, it may be time to move along. If you can fit better, let's find out how." Vendors: "Don't bring me schlock. If your goods and services don't serve my customers' needs, don't bother calling." Now we get focus. Vendors bring value to the company; employees bring value to the company; stock-holders bring value to the company; and customers, of course, bring cash...value to the company. Everyone is focused on a customer. Idealistic? In some ways – but there are companies that embody this ideal. (I didn't find out that this was a Peter Drucker mindset until nearly 10 years after I wrote it.)

When the organization faces the *truth* about focus, propaganda becomes culture; the team becomes invincible. We are now meeting our customer's needs; we deploy *engaged* employees down the path toward self-discipline. We have a team relationship with our vendors and a healthy business climate that offers a stable platform for a return to investors. That return is never guaranteed in commercial enterprises because of unknown, uncontrollable variables, including war, politics, weather, competition, technology and other factors. But at least we've built an organization where all of the stakeholders should be capable of singing in harmony. A variation on this is to put values in the middle, focus the team on those values, and create a team that can then accurately target customer needs for quality. In either model, *revenue is still a result and profit is a potential derivative of revenue.*

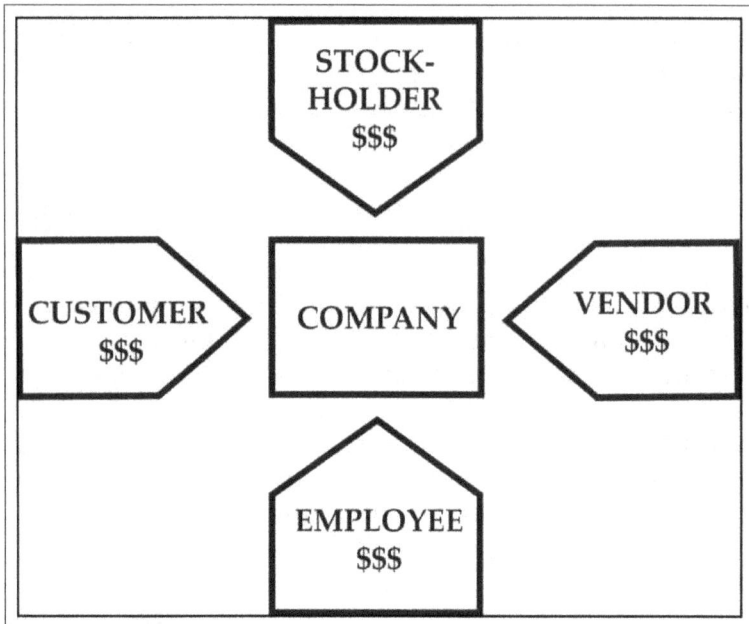

Figure 2.

If within your own organization you believe you have done all of this, but are still not meeting your objectives – there must be a reason you're not hearing the song. Another story suggests strategy:

While I was supporting General Motors as a contract training manager in the mid-1990's, a colleague and I were discussing the challenges of merging the talents of engineers with the talents of liberal arts-educated training designers. Richard and I got into philosophical discussions about quality and quantity, following the rules and coloring outside the lines. In one of these mental exercises, Richard described the process of making guitars by hand, a hobby of his.

"There is a mathematical formula that dictates the spacing of the frets on the guitar," he explained.

I thought about this a moment, as I had had some experience in music years earlier. "Makes sense," I agreed.

"But did you know you can get a sweeter sound if you

play around with the spacing of the frets? Of course you have to try different combinations, but every handmade guitar is unique."

I understood the idea, and we discussed that and similar concepts again over three or four sessions before I transferred out of Michigan.

Before discussion, I would observe in retrospect that while the guitar builders and musicians might know it when they hear it, and the audience might appreciate it more as well, not one of them could quantify the concept of 'sweeter.' Yet, everyone who listened to Richard explain the process understood exactly what he meant.

Your organization may have imposed just enough order on things to make it seem like you should be hearing harmony. Sweet harmony. But what if you played around with the frets on your guitar a little. In Richard's universe, the note A just above middle C vibrates at 440 cycles per second. Always. The "A" an octave higher vibrates at 880 cycles per second; the A just below middle C vibrates at 220 cycles.

Richard worked within the order imposed on "what constitutes a guitar" and the "relationship between notes" to produce a sweeter sound. He was talking about moving frets a tiny fraction of an inch. In your organization, this "playing around with the frets" may be as simple as removing a single disruptive employee from a department, praising failures that lead to invention and innovation, turning the organizational chart sideways on paper *and* in spirit so that even junior employees can embrace the reality that their leaders are leading from the front (instead of being "higher management").

Remove "higher management" from your vocabulary and replace it with "senior leaders." Then train those people to *be* leaders. Respect people. Rotate managers through departments so they can appreciate finance and accounting, shipping and receiving, sales, operations, design, assembly, security and maintenance – you'll have much better qualified managers in the long run.

Teach senior people that junior people have good ideas; teach junior people to respect the foundations laid by their seniors and to constantly and tactfully look for ways to improve. Teach leaders that their positions are on loan and that their primary jobs are to prepare the next generation of leaders and clear obstacles for today's team so they can get today's job done. Give people an opportunity to have ownership of products, processes and solutions.

The list of minor tweaks is endless.

Let's be REALISTIC

As my daughter continues riding her bike, her focus shifts from acquiring the skill to the needs for transportation and improving performance. My supporting role shifts from providing balance and encouragement to encouragement alone, with a continuing eye on safety now that she is capable of riding on streets in the neighborhood. Just as she has internalized the value of putting on her seat belt in my pickup truck, and does that subconsciously, she is internalizing the value of wearing a bicycle helmet and looking both ways before riding her bike into the street.

The bike is a means to an end, gradually changing in purpose over time. Early in her bike-riding career, the skill is a medium of exchange in social acceptance from her peers. Later it may serve her in recreation, competition or a means to maintain physical fitness. For adults, work is a means to an end. The vast majority of adults (minus those 30-year-old kids who hang around home, freeloading off mom and dad) see work as a transaction: input for output. Whether the adult sees work as drudgery or a means to personal satisfaction depends in part on which version of the *Work Ethic* he ascribes to. Likewise, a version of the *Work Ethic* can justify work for the sake of amassing wealth. Most people enter the job market with the expectation that they will in fact profit financially as a result. Entrepreneurs may believe they can meet some market need for a quality product or service better than any other provider – but will not enter that market without some reasonable expectation of profit. It is a short extension to admit that I, personally, will not enter the business of Industrial Training without some expectation of profit. Input-Output. No Problem.

We're still investigating focus, but the question arises: how is *work ethic* related to evolutionary ethics, discussed earlier? And short of Classic Philosophy, what of *ethics* alone...that set of morals that is supposed to guide people in the conduct of business. enron provided employees with a Code of Ethics handbook. enron's written ethics ostensibly emerged from "Principles of Human Rights," with the stated values of Respect, Integrity, Communication and Excellence, and the lofty vision:

> ...to become the world's leading energy company – creating innovative and efficient energy solutions for growing economies and a better environment worldwide.[xliii]

enron was certainly capable of achieving this vision. There is no doubt that money moves mountains, and natural gas, water, paper and pulp, and a lot of other commodities, including people. When enron made deals, customers usually benefited on the way to enron's profit. That's the way business should work. Working with engineers in Energy Asset Management, I saw this in enron's energy savings and maintenance programs. Show the customer how to save a million dollars a month on electricity and share the savings. What could be better?

Where this concept was co-opted, I hypothesize, was in the *work ethic.* The root for all three concepts is found in the Greek base word *ethos:* "the distinguishing character, sentiment, moral nature, or guiding beliefs of a person, group, or institution."[xliv] Hill's compact essay on the history of the work ethic tells that well past the ancient Hebrew, classical Roman and Greek periods, medieval times, work was viewed as demeaning and degrading.[xlv] The Hebrew biblical tradition, influencing Western thought, held that work was a punishment from God for the disobedience of Adam and Eve. It was not until the Reformation that Martin Luther and John Calvin offered contrasting views: that people could serve God though their work (Luther) and work was the will of God (Calvin).

According to Hill's analysis, Luther not only turned the Roman Catholic Church on its dogmatic head, he inserted a contrary explanation for work as a human endeavor: "He believed that people could serve God through their work." Yet Luther only helped initiate change:

> Luther still did not pave the way for a profit-oriented economic system because he disapproved of commerce as an occupation. From his perspective, commerce did not involve any real work. Luther also believed that each person should earn an income which would meet his basic needs, but to accumulate or horde wealth was sinful.[xlvi]

It was John Calvin, a French theologian, whose perspectives mingled with Luther's to set the stage for a modern philosophy that would support big business and eventually global commerce:

> Calvin taught that all men must work, even the rich, because to work was the will of God. It was the duty of men to serve as God's instruments here on earth, to reshape the world in the fashion of the Kingdom of God, and to become a part of the continuing process of His creation. *Men were not to lust after wealth, possessions, or easy living, but were to reinvest the profits of their labor into financing further ventures.* Earnings were thus to be reinvested over and over again, *ad infinitum,* or to the end of time.[xlvii] (my italics)

And there it is. Naked. Exposed. The prevailing social, religious and economic norms for nearly 500 years not only allowed but encouraged the *ethic* of creating wealth and reinvesting profits into new ventures, a la enron. New ventures create the need for new employees. As the company grows, local and national economies expand. More and more individual laborers benefit because their jobs are the means to their own ends. But exposure reveals the blemishes in enron's ethic: profit as an end in itself (wealth, possessions, or easy living) is inferior to quality (job satisfaction) as a motivator.

When profit is the prime motive for an individual or a company, failure is inevitable because there is never enough profit to achieve satisfaction. And in parallel – artificial economic growth based on government taxation is a falsity as well. Taxes suck money out of the engine of growth and the total value of what welfare recipients receive is paltry compared to what they might earn if employed...their right to create their own wealth (not borrowed from taxpayers).

The concept of government "taking care of" citizens who can't earn as much as "rich" people (whether because of education, talent or any other factor) leads to some artificial notion of relative poverty. In other words – if some football, basketball or baseball player, or corporate CEO, is earning $10 million a year and I'm not – then I'm poor and that's not fair. There's a pile of logic around this that explains why this mentality is skewed – including the reality that the relatively poor people 1.) Don't have the talent to play professional football, baseball or basketball, and 2. The professional athlete didn't take anything away from the poor person on the way to his or her professional athletic career (other than the cost of tickets to a game or $200 Air-Something shoes), and 3.) The *relatively* poor person doesn't typically castigate the professional athlete – but the corporate CEO who is not necessarily earning $10 million a year. (The relatively poor person doesn't have the talent or education to do that job either, *AND* the corporate CEO didn't prevent the relatively poor person from achieving that talent or education.)

In the end, enron's senior executives are the same thing I am – an ex-enron employee. And to those former executives I say: I have no problem with your right to create wealth. But you took your eye off the ball. You lost focus. You ended up denying others the right to create wealth by preventing them from focusing on their versions of quality. And if you measure job satisfaction in power – I deny that power. You have no control. And you can't fire me – I quit.

Twenty-Five: Laser Chapter 9

Murdoch's watch signaled the end of rest. Uninvited, the late afternoon sun poked through the wooden slats of the ancient barn, urging Sergeant Murdoch to close his eyes again and wish for a few more minutes of sleep. "All set, Captain?" he asked.

"Skipper?" Murdoch bolted upright and turned to the empty barn. Next to the laser canon, Steele had left a note: "You might need this. I've got one. If I can pick up Kathryn, there won't be room for three. Head for Corpus. I'll find you later. Semper Fi!"

"Great! This is just great...Steele doesn't need me anymore. Well I hope you have a good time out there, Skipper. I guess I'm back to doing what sergeants do best. Humpin' hills."

Fifty kilometers northeast, Steele silently maneuvered the enemy fighter at 50 feet off the deck along the Houston ship channel. Hugging the water's edge and moving slowly west by northwest, Steele nosed the fighter around tanker and container ships, under bridges and out from behind the massive petrochemical storage tanks, one by one, making his way to the center of the city, kilometer by kilometer. Turning due west under the Main Street bridge, Steele reflected that he hadn't been downtown Houston in years. New facades...same old Houston.

With the transponder scanning through thousands of frequencies that could be used for anything from radio to television, voice to radar, the only static continued to emanate from VHF, and triangulated to his west, then southwest as he inched along the steamy bayou. Eyes and ears open for any sign of unwelcome guests, Steele hovered into position under the interstate highway, northwest of Sam Houston Park, turned the agile bird and checked the charging pump indicators on the fighter's laser.

Steele keyed the mike: "Kathryn. It's Daddy. You

okay?"

Nothing.

Painfully aware that he was inviting a horde of alien fighters, Steele risked another burst: "Kathryn. If you've got comm., signal me.

Steele's receiver crackled...

"Daddy! They're waiting for you. I'm okay – I'm on the top of the building. Those freaks are sitting in their planes on the street, on the other rooftops."

"What building are you on, Kathryn?"

"The old enron building. It's like some kind of headquarters or something."

"Any guards?"

"No. I think I'm supposed to be the bait or something."

"How'd you get a radio?"

"It's a long story, Daddy. Could you just, maybe, like, swing by and pick me up?" Her voice sounded confident and calm, if a bit impatient.

"Stay where you are. I'll be there in a minute. The bad guys know we're here now, so this could get ugly. When I clear the top of the building, just run for the plane and hop in. Got it?"

"Got it."

It stood to reason that if the alien fighter could hover horizontally using inverted gravity as a source of energy, as well as climb vertically in a dogfight on the same energy, the same principles should allow Steele to stand this bird on its tail and hover, hugging the west façade of the building. Life had been too easy the past 24 hours, and Steele was getting nervous about the lack of enemy participation in the battle space. Smelled like a rat trap.

Gliding silently up the vertical façade of the old enron building with the fighter's nose straight up, Steele checked his six. But this was no six o'clock on a watch dial; there was a hemisphere of opportunity west of the tower. I'm communicating but maybe they're not listening. The bad guys couldn't be so stupid as to just be watching the sky, or looking south toward Corpus Christi, singularly fearing one possible outcome. Or could they? But then again...they hadn't really been especially nimble in tactics, so far...just overwhelming power.

As the nose of the alien fighter cleared the horizontal rooftop at the 50th floor, Steele pulled back on the stick, punched on the gas and pulled a tight, inverted 270-degree loop, easing the belly of the bird onto the roof top as the canopy eased open. As he turned to call out, Kathryn was already sprinting *away* from the fighter. "What the...? Oh shitake mushrooms. I didn't tell her what I was driving!"

"Kathryn! Wake up, will ya! Look..."

Twenty-Six: Energy. Anxiety.

August – December, 2003
Opportunity rings

Things often are not what they seem, including job offers. Easing away from the Diversity workshop and back to marketing the Leadership Skills seminar, I settled into a routine of e-mails, phone calls, presentations and painting to fill the 168 hours in a week. In the multitude of job applications overlapping the end of 2002 and the first several months of 2003, one of the gems looked to be contracting overseas for a government agency. Like the others, I put my best foot out and waited for the door to slam...but it never really did. We exchanged e-mail and telephone calls off and on for nearly a year. By August 2003, six months or more had passed since the last communication.

The phone rang. It wasn't the government; it was a head-hunter. Dear Friend with the Valentine had passed along the information on a job prospect. It sounded like a strong possible. That OODA-loop thing demanded my attention to opportunities, no matter how remote. Here was the chance to return to the corporate world in a position tailor-made to my resume and work history, working on the development of a corporate university. A solid paycheck; vision, dental and other benefits. Predictability. Security. Promising myself I was always open to the concept of taking a legitimate salaried position, I applied.

The phone rang. "A government agency has selected you as one of the top five finalists to work on this program abroad. Would you be kind enough to submit a capabilities statement?"

"Sure," I said, two weeks before the first delayed interview with the corporate university. The two options snowballed into a busy August, with a University of Phoenix class and one of my own Leadership seminars. Suddenly the endless free time had dissipated and I was, at last, working. I wasn't making nearly as much as I had at enron, but I was indeed bringing in a paycheck. Anticipating results on the government contract, I entered the rituals of interview with the local boss, interview with the boss' lieutenant. Wait a week and talk with the government in Washington, DC. Wait another week and interview with the local boss' other lieutenant, then the boss' boss. By the time an offer came in, I was sitting on a pending offer to contract with the U.S. government in Egypt. The local offer became an offer to contract on a trial basis for about three months, which would suit their needs and mine, if they would allow me the hiatus should the Middle East contract come in.

Observe. Orient. Decide. Act.

By the first of October, I was well on my way to visiting the Great Pyramids. Or so I thought. The government contract came through and I informed the supervisor I was supporting locally. She was gracious, and penciled in the dates I anticipated being out of the office. Averaging four days a week locally, I had the time to complete the passport and visa process, but in the interim I was nearing closure on my OODA loop on the corporate university. They wanted to formalize the relationship, turning the contract into a job offer. The people were right; they are internally motivated, smart, cohesive. The offer was fair, generally in line with market salaries. The boss was right; she is brilliant, experienced, both demanding and nurturing. The mission made perfect sense: director of curriculum development, working with a superior director of leadership and organizational development. The company was wrong. The store-front window says: "We care." The thick cloud hanging in the back office says "Sell." The company's president didn't believe in the core product the company was selling to the consumer masses (he wouldn't buy one), so it was obvious the core product was only designed as a money maker, not a response to consumer need. (The customer comment cards indicated the consumer base was not enamored of the packaged product anyway.) The company's stock was in the toilet (had dropped from $22 a share to $2.20 a share in two years), and the company was facing a class-action lawsuit growing from a lack of focus on customer service. Sounded too familiar.

By now I was getting pretty good at this counter-intuition thing. The day my government contact in Washington e-mailed to inform me the Middle East contract had been unexpectedly canceled, I had been through Observation and Orientation on the local gig. I had already decided. Time to act. It would not be fair to continue working the local contract for the final month – and then walk away. This team had a mission to accomplish and I would not be part of it. After 400 job applications, half a year on unemployment, much of the year on a ramen noodle diet...I walked in to the boss' office and calmly, politely declined the offer.

In what could have been the bonehead decision of the year in a parallel universe with predictable people, I felt complete relief. Freedom. It could have been easy to get sucked into the corporate domain and parrot what the corporate vulture wanted me to parrot. But I'd seen this parody before: bring in outside consultants because they are expert, as soon as you take a job, your voice gets very, very tiny, no matter how loud you squawk about changing the culture. I walked away from *that.* But if I would make it on my own until the *right* corporate opportunity should surface, I would have to put all my energy into survival. So – for the first time in more than two years...I played a round of golf. In Disney's animated children's story, *The Lion King,* the song goes: "Hakuna Matata. It means no worries, for the rest of your days. It's our problem free...philosophy. Hakuna Matata." In French – it's *sans souci.*

Lessons from four days in survival training, years back in Naval Aviation Officer Candidate School, included the concept of conservation. Isolated in a frigid climate, the survivor must concentrate on conserving body heat. Isolated in an arid climate, the survivor must focus on conserving water. Approaching Christmas of 2003, I had less worry about conserving water and the pantry was respectably stocked for the first time in two years, but now I had to conserve the financial resources I had banked during the local August-to-October contract. One of my fears in that local contract, because *they* offered it as a "test drive" relationship, was that I would lose momentum with my existing business. What if I busted my tail and liked the work, but they opted out? What if the corporate leadership should have a change of heart and pull funding for the corporate university initiative? I needed to keep the flywheel spinning so that no matter what might lead to the end of that relationship – if it did end – I would need to be able to pick up where I left off. I was probably more than a little gun-shy in a post-enron reality.

Timing is another matter. Not only does it become increasingly difficult to get a company to commit employees to training seminars during the holidays, which is any time from about mid-November through the second week of January, the Houston business community was still not increasing its own momentum in late 2003. The stock market was still searching for historic highs; job growth was apathetic. We weren't suffering a bust economy, but national corporate scandals, the wars in Iraq and Afghanistan, energy costs, periodic news on companies shipping jobs overseas and a handful of seemingly unrelated vices painted an anemic picture for much of the market that would be my client base. I booked no seminars in September. None in October or November. December was out of the question.

Hakuna Matata.

Daughter and I ran the Susan G. Komen 5K cancer fund-raiser in Houston's Galleria district in October. Sort of. As the gun sounded, my now-7-year-old and I jogged together for about a mile, dodging walkers and wagons. Turning the first corner, Daughter reached up for her "free ride." From stoplight to stoplight, Daughter rode on my shoulders; next stoplight to the one following, she ran. We followed this pattern to the finish and both worked up a good sweat, satisfied with a finish under 40 minutes. We drove home, cleaned up and talked about the "race."

Now it was time to track down the biggest pumpkin we

could find for a jack-o-lantern, then scan the local markets for bits and pieces of a "smoky the cat" costume, and break out the sewing machine again. Daughter found black tights and leotards. We added black gloves. Then came a tail, stuffed with cotton, and a set of ears, constructed on a black headband. We survived the goblins in both our neighborhood and her mom's, then retreated to our own again as Halloween disintegrated into a sleep-over for Daughter and several of her neighbor friends.

November melted into December, with plenty of time on the road in preparation for my fourth Houston Marathon. I wasn't getting any younger, but the qualifying time for Boston was getting closer. With the Boston Athletic Association handing us an extra 5 minutes, my age group now only had to reach a 3:30 qualifying time. Approaching 50, I would enter a new age group in two years and get another 5 minutes. If I could keep my time headed south as the qualifying time headed north – I might just make it before I turned 99. The only things I was worried about were the knees and hip sockets.

When Number One Son called in December to let me know he was headed south for a business conference in Houston, I was elated. We covered the usual business – his work; my work. But running always comes up, and the knees did too.

"Have you tried glucosamine-chondroitin?" he asked me.

"Never heard of it."

"You're a runner and you've never tried glucosamine-chondroitin?"

"Is this a drug or something?"

"No, Dad...it's a natural supplement, for your joints."

"I'll check it out," I replied, but didn't give it much more than a passing thought.

Twenty-Seven: First Principle - High Energy

By now the laser is nearly complete. All we really need is for someone to flip the switch, turn it on and aim it accurately. I realize from the corporate university experience it's the CEOs I need to get to, they are the ones I need to turn the laser over to. But there are usually too many layers of management – directors of this, executive directors of that, vice presidents of something else.

At 5 a.m., as I head into downtown Houston for the 2004 marathon, the January 18th morning air is holding around 45 degrees. Close to the edge of adding a few layers of throw-away clothes – a shirt, sweat pants, gloves. But I pass. The jog from the Four Seasons parking garage is enough to keep me warm on the way to the George R. Brown Coliseum. Number One Son and his wife had arrived three days earlier, allowing time enough for a round of golf, two rounds of philosophy and three rounds of my favorite carbohydrates. We did indeed track down glucosamine-chondroitin, giving me three days to get in nine doses before the race, and a 10th on the morning of. Son One and his wife, with my Daughter, would be waiting at the finish of today's marathon.

Matching up Daughter with either of her East Coast brothers is a rare treat, and we wandered off to Katy Mills mall together in search of Gu for me and some Texas souvenirs for my Son. With months at a time with Ramen noodles and an apple for my single daily meal, I'd shed enough weight, nearly 20 pounds, in the two years since that enron running club lunchtime seminar on *train heavy- run light* that I knew I was well past the net-zero situation on carrying six ounces of liquid energy.

Two days before Son One arrived, Washington called and the Middle East contract was back on. In less than a week, I'd be settling into a 14-hour flight on Air France with an empty notebook and two years of mental notes.

Against the still-black morning sky, the George R. Brown monolith is the center of a black hole. The pavement crossing the front of the building is the event horizon. Only those with enough energy to counter the gravitational effects of sleep will escape the tug. As the scene comes into focus, doors open and close, spilling intermittent light into the darkness, attracting runners like moths from parking garages and deserted streets in all directions. I start scanning the swarms for familiar faces. There's a guy from NASA, but I don't remember his name. He doesn't remember mine either so we exchange predictable nameless pleasantries and move on. I run into that Dutch engineer who now works for one of the local energy companies. We trade *guten tags*. I never did learn his name – just the back of his shirt from a dozen 5k races in 2000 and 2001.

Table after table, corner after corner, anonymous runners stretch in impossible gyrations, chat with running buddies about past races, and breakfast on Gatorade and bagels, or bananas and yogurt. No Atkins disciples in this bunch.

Still missing...and now perpetually missing...is the crooked E. There was no finer feeling than to assemble with friends at dawn under a banner with a team identity, warming up for a 5k, 10k or 20k race, or the next marathon. That team identity lingered in the remnants of an enron running club, but the banner would never reappear, shamed. I miss those faces – Jim, Cindy, Ricky, the rest...The road trip to Corpus Christi for the Armed Forces Day Marathon Relay. The carbo-loading parties. enron took my buddies away, cut me off from a circle of friends. They – enron – had the power to prevent it, but failed to act.

As I stow my bag with water bottles and a warm-up jacket, I run into another familiar face – from one of the other Houston-based energy companies. He left enron before I started, but had maintained his enron running club status. As we exchanged questions and answers about life after enron, I found it amusing that he referred to his new employer as "the power company."

Is it possible that enron's executives, wanting to shed the moniker of *energy company*, thought of themselves as a

"Power Company?" Is that what the banner was intended to read? "To Become the World's Most Powerful Company." In a literal sense it didn't happen this way. But it doesn't take a metaphor or a moron to understand that people who translate money into power might also think of *knowledge* as power. They're lost. Knowledge is *energy!*

As the morning chill welcomes the first hint of blue sky, runners straggle toward the starting lines. Some men walk brazenly half-naked through the crowd, unimpressed by temperatures in the 40's, as if they had been training in Anchorage since November. Other runners sport throw-away jackets, gloves and knitted caps. A local TV station has a helicopter overhead to televise the start.

Once the race begins, they will focus mainly on the leaders, and 20 minutes into the race, those leaders will already be three miles ahead of my anonymous position a third of the way back. We're supposed to position ourselves with our pace groups – 7-minute milers, 8-minute milers, 9-minute milers and so on – but once collected at the starting line, working through the crowd in either direction is less practical than trying to drive out of downtown Houston at 5 p.m. on a Friday. I hang on to my almost random position with the 7-minute crowd. The lead echelon will thin quickly.

The National Anthem is followed by a few announcements, unintelligible over the din of 5,000 conversations. Then at 7:30 a.m., "Runners...Take your mark." POP!

I'm an extra in what for me has been once-a-year theater. I never meet the leading man or leading lady, not even at the stage door. As a dim but aspiring track star in high school, I might have gone out of my way to meet milers Jim Ryun or Marty Liquori. I wanted to tell them how I was going to get my 4:20 / 4:30 mile down to 4 minutes. Those memories seem so far distant they have a red Doppler shift. Now I'm content to marvel at the costumes and messages printed on runner's shirts, or trade wit with spectators looking for their champions.

7:38:30
One mile. On target.

Dodging occasional elbows and feet, I settle into a relaxed pace, focused on a 3:30 finish. My target is negative splits, picking up the pace slightly at the half-way point so my second half will be faster than the first. This year's race offers perfect weather. For those willing to challenge the 46-degree start without layers of extra clothing, a cool, low-humidity morning is ideal. I've had so many targets over the years I can't run through them all. Some I hit; some I missed. Some things came so easily and naturally I never even considered a plan – I just made the best of whatever situation came along.

When I was good, I wanted to be the best. When I was bad, I was the worst. As class president in Navy OCS, it took me three tries to swim a mile in a flight suit under the maximum allowable time. I was last. When I was wrong I had a hard time coming to terms with my own failings. What had once seemed to be the end of my career was merely the start of a different set of options.

When enron fired the starter's pistol, there were no options and it seemed like anything *but* a race into unemployment. My first response was that I was unprepared. I didn't have a plan. I wasn't trained for unemployment. In a tangible, financial sense that was true; I wasn't prepared. But denial doesn't put food on the table.

7:46:50
Two Miles

Back in February or March, 2002, two to three months into my job search, one of my phone calls landed a meeting with an engineering company in the Houston area. There was no immediate prospect for either a salaried position or contract work, but the meeting did lead to a referral. I was to contact this fellow, Mike, in Canada, working HR and Training for a $5 billion joint venture shale-oil mining operation, about the dilemma with his workforce. It seemed that as the pace of activity increased, the excitement leading up to commissioning this massive operation also increased. Graphing the anticipation would show a steep rise to the top of a mountain. The problem was, and Mike had seen it before, after the construction project would be commissioned, the high-energy workers would drift away in search of the next high-excitement, high-feedback construction project, shunning the daily grind, the fall from the top of the mountain. Could I come up with a solution to keep the most valuable construction engineers at the plant?

I'd try. Mike pointed me to fragments of his own research on the topic, a national clearinghouse for research on *post-traumatic stress disorder* on the web site of the Veterans Administration. Initially I thought this was a little strange; my mental image of the syndrome was imbedded in the process of comforting survivors of major accidents or counseling Vietnam veterans who are still trying to subdue demons from the war of a past generation. But one phrase rang out – separation anxiety. Mike's hypothesis was that the high-energy construction engineers were so attached to the *pace of the project*, not the people specifically, that when the danger, excitement and challenges of construction were replaced by the monotony of a 9 to 5 job, those engineers were experiencing a form of separation anxiety. Lost relevance.

7:55:10
Three miles

The deeper I read on this concept of separation anxiety, the more I realized I was looking in a mirror. I wasn't financially prepared for unemployment and an extended job search. That little seminar by the Texas Employment Commission at the end of the first week, post-enron, included the wisdom about a time-salary relationship. The bigger paycheck you want, the longer it takes to find the job. But I did come to realize that I *was* prepared for separation anxiety. At least on the surface, that element of grief I was experiencing over the loss of my job was fundamentally equivalent to the death of both parents, divorce, waving goodbye from the flight deck of the USS NIMITZ to my family on the pier as I headed off to the Persian Gulf theater, graduation from college, entering the empty nest when my sons graduated from high school in 1993 and '94, and retiring from the Marine Corps.

I had already done these emotional push-ups. I had already run these emotional miles. I had not always turned to God for spiritual support, but this time was different. Dad's death was inevitable; Mom's was difficult but not a surprise...more difficult because she lingered through the pain of lung cancer for nearly a year. In each case the results were predictable months or years before the final outcome. Separation in the military seemed to be something I was born into and at least somewhat prepared for. And releasing grown sons into the world comes with a little pain, a little pride, but also a little freedom. What made the enron experience different was the suddenness, the shock of getting screwed by my employer, the Respect-Integrity-Communication-Excellence employer. This was a marriage that led to an ugly divorce.

8:03:30
Four miles

The barriers are down between metaphors. Everything is fair game. If I could write the time travel story that would take me back to that marriage with enron, back to the beginning of the relationship, I would have been looking for a corporation that conducted business as if all transactions were relationships – especially relationships with employees:

Love is patient. Love is kind. Love isn't jealous. It doesn't brag or get conceited. It isn't indecent. It isn't selfish. It doesn't get angry. It doesn't plan to hurt anyone. It doesn't delight in evil but is happy with the truth. It bears everything, believes everything, hopes for everything, endures everything. Love never dies.[xlviii]

It must not have been true love with enron. We split. This wasn't irreconcilable differences. enron cheated.

8:11:50
Five miles

We seem to be living in a cheating society. As the final pages of this essay seem to write themselves, I hear of a book espousing that observation. I'll read it when I'm done. People who cheat must not be *happy with the truth*, yet most of these people would deny any association with evil. There's got to be some major cognitive dissonance going on there. Justification, I would propose, lives in the culture, the values of a society or organization. If society says it's not technically illegal, it must be legal. If others will make more money too, it must be a good decision. If everyone in the organization is doing it, I should be able to also.

I fire up my laser to melt this culture, this edifice of arrogance that has preserved counter-values in a grotesque, frozen block of cultural ice. Somewhere in the core of this pursuit I naively hang on to the notion that people have the ability to do good. Companies *can* proclaim core values focused on *quality, integrity, respect, customer service, diligence* and the like, and *can* live and work, corporately and collectively according to those ideals. These values I want to leave on ice. I know those organizations are out there. I've seen them.

Freedom is essential to innovation, competition, creativity. However: Everything is permissible but not everything is beneficial.[xlix]

8:20:30
Six miles

Losing a few seconds over six miles doesn't worry me. I'd walked through a water station, gulping down one cup of PowerAde and another cup of water. Internal combustion is gradually working on my reserve of carbohydrates. No friction so far in the knees or hips, but the real test will come after 15 miles.

Laser surgery on a cultural monolith is certain to cause friction. Some people won't want to back away from their power positions. I need to demonstrate that they are sitting in a nuclear pile. The knowledge they hoard is only potential energy. It has no kinetic energy until we coax the molecules away from the core. Like Occam's Laser, I take aim on every dead end, every failed simulation of the right way to run a business. I target every company that wants to become COMPANY, every organization with sights set on ORGANIZATION, and set them free, molecule by molecule.

Some friction is good. We get heat, steam, energy; the block of ice begins to melt and the phase change is under way.

8:28:30
Seven miles

Enron's natural gas wasn't energy; neither were the derivatives of natural gas' future value. Coal isn't energy either, nor are books. The energy is locked inside. The lights don't come on until the energy starts flowing. I take aim at the last bit of enron's ice castle: stock price. I will allow that the stock market is in fact a market. Investor capital is essential for corporate expansion...but expansion of what? Stock value? That's where enron was and it proved to be a failed hypothesis on the way to theoretical ENRON. Investor capital only fuels expansion of a commercial enterprise's ability to meet or exceed customer-defined *quality*. That's *liquid thinking*. In anticipation of a return on investment, the wise investor will base market picks on the company's *real* values, the genuine focus on quality – both internally and externally.

As the phase change is complete, knowledge becomes energy and starts flowing.

8:36:50
Eight miles

Approaching the coming water station I reach for my Gu. Son One had suggested he buy me a pouch to clip to the waist-band of my running shorts. I didn't want a fanny pack or anything that would bounce, rub or cause friction. This

Gu holster wasn't ideal either so I ended up carrying the whole thing, Gu in holster, switching from right hand to left every half mile or so. I'll have to find a different solution next race. Just in case, I down 1000-milligram tablet of Ibuprofen even though I'm only a third of the way home and don't expect the crunch for another eight miles or so.

I've got new energy, but now I need to harness it. Pirsig runs along, but now is decision time. After five readings over 25 years, do I swallow his hypothesis, his *Zen and the Art of Motorcycle Maintenance* metaphysics of quality, or not? As a professor, Pirsig dispensed knowledge, thus energy, like so many packages of Gu or BTU's worth of natural gas. But what Pirsig never fully accounted for in his research was the imposition of observer bias on the experiment. When a nuclear physicist takes a picture of a subatomic phenomenon in order to determine whether it's a wave or a particle, the observer has affected what he is observing. Pirsig was imposing order – training wheels – on his students by asking them to write quality papers. He would still have been imposing order if he didn't use the word "quality." He would have been imposing order if he had asked them to sing. Just being there influences the results.

I decide Pirsig was on the right track – that Quality is Good, and Quality *just is*. But if Quality is the cause of form and function, it must also be the cause of quality and quantity. In the Principia Cyberntica's Metasystem Transition Theory, there is no rule that says "S" cannot be a subset of itself. And so, accepting quality as a subset of QUALITY, I look for qualities and quantities that emerge from QUALITY. Stock price is a quantity. Units sold is a quantity. Number of employees and salaries are both quantities. But the total corporation is more than quantities; it's qualities too. This is Pirsig's Romantic Logic.

Quality is potential energy in respect, integrity, communication and excellence, in customer service, in leadership, in job satisfaction. Business operations don't focus on these values, these qualities, in too many organizations because qualities are wrapped around people.

Understanding people is not a core competency. Too hard to understand. Too hard to convert potential into kinetic energy.

8:45:20
Nine miles

The lady ten paces in front of me for the past two miles suddenly stops, turns, and heads straight for me. I jump to the right and adjust my stride to avoid a collision. Crazy woman! Or is she? People seem to be unpredictable, but if I had been paying attention I would have seen that she had dropped something and had just turned to retrieve it. People usually do things for a reason, but some reasons are invisible. Chaos theory, applied to river deltas, clouds, trees and sea shells helps us understand emerging, predictable patterns in nature, like hurricanes. But people are fractals too. One by one it may seem impossible to understand human behavior, but there are predictable patterns. My favorite professor, dear friend and mentor at Ball State University, Jim, once asked, "If human behavior can be changed, why predict it?"

It makes sense that Jim had little time for the computer psychologists who were intensely focused on observing, recording and analyzing laboratory behavior, then creating mathematical models to predict future behavior. But even the process of *changing* behavior means changing it *from* something *to* something. Attempting to harness the energy in my employees means I must assert a measure of control; I must impose order over chaos. My employees need a paycheck and job satisfaction – quantity and quality – on the road to their vision of QUALITY. The people who buy stock in my company expect a return on investment, but they should be watching that I create that wealth they seek by focusing on my own customers' version of QUALITY. I can predict both sets of behaviors and I can also change both sets to predictable new behavior.

People need freedom to innovate and be creative, but not all tasks are fair game for innovation. Burger King, McDonald's, Wendy's and Arby's are all assembly lines. We don't want team members adding ketchup to milkshakes or plopping ice cream on French fries – in the spirit of innovation.

Applying sufficient external pressure I can get people who don't want to – to do push-ups, and with a change in direction I can get the same people who don't want to run to change that behavior to running. But to get people to *want* to run, to *want* to do push-ups, to want to conduct business ethically, I need to mentor them, work with them, coach them. It takes time to cause people to internalize a working set of values that guide behavior. Like boot camp. Unemployment was my new boot camp...a new sort of self-discipline.

8:53:50
Ten miles

Recovering from the near collision with the lady runner, I regain my balance. Checking my watch I'm two seconds a mile off-pace. I'm okay, and cruise through a water stand. On the sidelines are a dad, mom and little sister, desperately seeking someone named "Becky" amidst the thousands of runners, now spread out across miles of Houston streets. Their sign reads: "Go Becky!"

I quip back, "Thanks, but I'm not Becky."

They laugh.

I run.

The whole thing with Pirsig is about balance. Freedom is essential. People crave it in all its manifestations. But like my daughter's triumph over the bicycle, freedom is not enough, and it takes work to get there and to keep it. The F-117 is a good fighter because it's maneuverable, but it can only maneuver if it's got motion. Without motion it falls out of the sky. Without forward motion, the bicycle falls over. Best in class never *is*, it's always in a state of becoming. Every day. Energy that creates forward motion is not enough. Someone must provide balance. Once externally imposed discipline, with a guiding, non-threatening hand, has created self-discipline, my daughter on her bicycle is ready to balance on her own.

Pirsig is done. Dropped out of the race. It's good stuff, but his metaphysics is incomplete without Leadership. Leadership provides balance, maintains focus and imposes order, but at the same time allows autonomy, freedom to create. A leader who doesn't know where we're going is lost. Like all ground-breaking ideas, there is value (dare I say quality) in Pirsig's work. Bell's telephone paved the way for today's picture phone with digital images and televised NFL games, and both were, or are, possible because of freedom and order, balance and leadership, vision and focus.

9:02:15
Eleven miles.

I see the light, but am I deluding myself? Do others see the same light? I had realized before that enron's fall was not a simple matter of greed, and I'll stick by that. Something else spelled that doom, that certain entropy. My laser has disintegrated enron's culture, but I am now obligated to rebuild it, or at least the remnants.

I put a portion of my hypothesis to a test. Over the past three days I explored the possibility of trading my trusty Ford pickup in for a brand new truck. Ford Dealership: "I'm a credit challenge. You've discounted this old body style so much that I can now buy a new F-150, with triple rebates, for $17,000. I owe $15,000 on my 1999 and Kelley Blue Book tells me it's worth $9000 at most. On top of that, the bank will run a credit report on me and pull up a score – a quantification of the computer's assessment of my predictable credit worthiness. I would like you to have a discussion with your bank about the *qualitative* aspects of my ability to pay for this new truck – based on the fact that I've never filed for bankruptcy and all my bills are paid on time. I am not a statistic; I'm a person.

"Got it."

Chevy Dealership: I'm a credit challenge. I owe

$15,000 on my 1999 Ford and Kelley Blue Book tells me it's worth $9000 at most. On top of that, the bank will run a credit report on me and pull up a score – a quantification of the computer's assessment of my predictable credit worthiness. I would like you to have a discussion with your bank about the *qualitative* aspects of my ability to pay for this new truck – based on the fact that I've never filed for bankruptcy and all my bills are paid on time. I'm not a statistic; I'm a person.

"Got it."

I drove home in a new truck from one of these two dealerships, with 2.9% financing. I'll leave the denouement for the backyard barbeque stories. (In 2013 – I still have that truck. It's a good truck, and has 202,000 miles on it.)

9:10:40
Twelve miles

Excising the last of enron's cancer from my memory tells me to point the laser back to enron's risk models. Mathematically they appeared sound. We could send an enron-trained team into a store, manufacturing plant, university or office building and come back with gigabytes of data: how many square feet, how many cubic feet, the age, model and maintenance record of every energy-using asset, the percentage of compressed air used for tools compared to electrical tools (air tools cost a lot more to operate), type and age of lighting hardware, size and location of windows, who had done the maintenance on this equipment, where it was manufactured and what the warranties were – just about anything anyone could imagine that would impact how an organization spent money on energy. With all of these numbers plugged into a computer simulation, that Monte Carlo model, and matrixed across futures prices for natural gas or electricity, our team would dump a probabilistic model that should allow the energy traders to more precisely calculate enron's risk, thus discount rate to fund the project, and ultimately enron's profit and enron's offer to the customer. Mathematically, it was hypothetically ideal. But it's the same kind of model that predicts my credit score, based on mathematical probabilities. What if gas prices surge? What if the customer's employees don't stop using compressed air, or turn off the lights, or *continue* to change air filters monthly because the "manufacturer said so," and refuse to apply our de-scaling techniques on chill-water towers because they think their processes work better?

Qualitatively, in retrospect, the model was less than ideal. Sysco, J.C. Penney, The Limited and the scores of other clients were not statistics alone. We could install more energy-efficient lighting, but if people didn't turn off the lights, the model wouldn't work perfectly. We could tell the manufacturer that air costs seven times as much as electricity to operate tools, but if we can't get the people weaned off air, the model wouldn't work perfectly. People do not respond to the laws of physics.

Oddly, people were at the *top* of the risk model in one of the sub-teams I worked with: Risk-Quantified Maintenance. The core of this model was focused on the golden fleece of maintenance – no maintenance at all, on HVAC, chillers, boilers, air compressors and other energy-using capital assets. The idea was, the decision to perform or not perform maintenance of any type would be weighed against four risk factors: threat to human life or health, threat to the environment, the value or cost of lost production, and the value or cost to replace the equipment if maintenance is not done. If required for human safety – do the maintenance. If required to preserve the environment – do the maintenance. If maintenance costs less than lost production – do the maintenance, and so on. Why couldn't enron's business model reflect a risk model with an interest in the threat to human welfare? It could have.

9:19:15
Thirteen

Half-way home and everything was working perfectly. Knees, hips, ankles, toes. I was feeling like I could do this all day, and it was the first time I had pushed the wall past 12 miles.

Kicking through the charred remains of enron's culture, looking for salvageable elements with which to build my own World's Best Company, I find people first. It's people I will need to focus on, people I will serve as my customers, people I will lead and who will be my leaders, my mentors.

My business mission in the business community is not to convert these people to Christianity or teach them Lutheran "stuff." I have a business mission. I need never say words like "church," "Jesus," "God," "heaven," "sin" or "forgiveness" on my business mission. There's a time and place. If people ask, I'll be more than happy to share what I believe. God gives us a secular world to make sense of, to impose order on. In this environment, I am *free* to live my life so that my actions alone <u>demonstrate</u> Christian ethics. Sometimes I will fail. Sometimes it will be too much work, too hard:

> But those who depend on the Lord get new strength. They lift up their wings like eagles; they run and don't get tired; they walk and don't get tired.[1]

9:28
Fourteen

When people internalize the values of an organization, culture becomes a living thing. If we compare the human body as a system to the organization as a system, we see that the human body can lose a finger or toe and still function. An organization can lose an employee or two and still function. Many amputees, including heroic athletes and soliders, have demonstrated that it is possible to surrender an arm or leg and continue to lead productive lives; organizations sell subsidiaries and lay off masses of employees all the time – and thrive.

Where does it end? What makes a person a person? How many organs or cells constitute a living person? Just as organizations replace retiring employees, the human body regenerates cells that die off at irregular rates. According to the New York Public Library Science Desk Reference[li], "There are between 50 trillion and 75 trillion cells in the body; each second there are about 6 trillion reactions taking place within each cell." Red blood cells "live" about 120 days; white blood cells more than a year. Skin cells last a month, liver cells six weeks, and cells in the colon are replaced on the order of about every 4 days. None of these cells individually or collectively owns human consciousness (as far as I know, although I could venture a couple of thoughts on people I've met who seem intent on proving this theory wrong with their 4-day consciousness). Brain cells, on the other hand, can live upwards of 90 years.

I want to get the organizational culture into my employees' heads – their brain cells. By extension that means the organization's self-awareness as an organism resides in the collective intelligence of *all* employees. I can't inspire organizational patriotism with an *us versus them* chasm between executives and line workers.

What I'm looking for is a team.

9:37
Fifteen

A quarter-mile ahead I spot an Enron Running Club team member. I can see I'm gaining on him, and take the challenge to recapture some of the seconds that have been fading from my time. I was supposed to be picking up the pace at the half-way point. I start doing the math to calculate how far I'm off 3 hours and 30 minutes, but the numbers get jumbled up in my head. I work better with words.

"Richard! It's you!"

He looks over with a tired smile. "Yup. What's left of me. How's it going?"

"So far so good. No problems with the joints this year," I reported. "I tried that glucosamine-chondroitin stuff for the first time. Seems to be working...helping, anyway."

"Hmm..."

"Still at Enron?"

"Yup. What's left of it."

I can see the whole organization's morale in this one soul. "Well, good luck!" I took off and left him to his pace.

That summer I had moved into my new home, six months before bankrotten I was to join the enron team for a corporate track competition at Rice University. My morale was in running, but it would be my weekend with Daughter, so I bought a large picnic cooler, snacks, bottles of water, and a huge umbrella so she could relax in the shade and watch old people race. As the Wednesday and Thursday ahead of the weekend grew increasingly questionable because of the weather, I called around the team phone numbers to find out if we were on or off. Tropical Storm Allison was flooding Houston. We didn't get a final decision from track meet organizers until Saturday morning. Washed out.

9:46:10
Sixteen

With ten miles to go, I could more easily calculate the delta between my pace and what I needed to qualify for Boston, and it wasn't going to happen this year. That realization didn't erase my vision of making Boston in the future, nor would it deter my focus from this race. I'd faced challenges in the past where I'd quit when I realized I wasn't going to win. That kind of attitude wouldn't get me anywhere.

A new attitude – a new pitch, yaw and roll – would allow me to see that I had to disprove the null, that I couldn't win, and the only way to do that was to keep on trying. Not trying would be tantamount to living life as a slug. If I kept on trying, I might not make enough money this month to pay all of my bills for three months, but I might make enough to pay all of my bills for *this* month, or maybe two months. But I won't know if I don't try, and I won't try if I don't have a vision and maintain focus. So I keep at it, seeking to disprove that I have to declare bankruptcy and lose the house.

Not one test has yet proved that null hypothesis. I pull vision, mission and goals from the wreckage of enron's crash and move on.

9:55:15
Seventeen

Switching the polarity on enron's gravity, the focus swings around from profit and share price to quality. But now I must articulate exactly what all of this means to my team and my junior leaders in a coherent message. Respect, Integrity, Communication and Excellence are a great start. I can add as many values as I want or the team needs. Fewer is probably better. The *form* of Marine Corps Leadership Traits incorporates merely 14 words to define a set of standards for an organization of 200,000 warriors. The *functions* written in Leadership Principles are merely guidelines; the Corps expects Marines to do whatever it takes to accomplish a combat mission (within the rules of engagement, ethics and laws of armed combat). Like any bureaucracy, the Corps has endless laws, rules and regulations, yet the expectation is that leaders make decisions based on the values that created those regulations. Combat, and training for combat, can always be counted on to deliver scenarios not covered by the regulations. That's where "progressive" (liberal) government-heavy governments go wrong, and where some corporations go wrong. They think they can legislate human behavior. Write enough rules and you've got it covered. All those rules do is restrict freedom and the ability of independent thinkers to find positive answers.

On the far end (the "end-state") of many Marine Corps *missions* is often the concept of *freedom.* But Marines, soldiers, sailors and airman are not the only ones fighting for freedom – patriots wear the uniforms of police and fire departments, school teachers, computer programmers, boiler technicians, bus drivers, accountants and farmers. We all work for the vision of Freedom, and paramount in Freedom in the United States is Freedom of Speech. Most people (minus a few disc jockeys) seem to agree Freedom of Speech comes at the price of some measure of self-control. We hoard Freedom. We cherish Freedom. We valiantly defend every freedom in our Constitution, starting with the Bill of Rights. What we don't have is a Bill of Responsibilities. The commander in chief with the stained blue dress certainly wasn't one.

Freedom as quality is mission enough to generate energy. Megawatts of energy. Terawatts. The energy is there but people cannot and do not maintain accelerated performance over sustained periods. World-class sprinters cover 100 meters in less than 10 seconds, but those same sprinters aren't built for marathons. I need a mix of both types on my team, and I need something to sustain both types during and between performances. I need to guarantee their situational awareness when the going gets slow, dangerous, hard and thankless. I offer balance to guide self-discipline, based on internal values and financial rewards, tailored to performance and measured in quality.

10:04:15
Eighteen

The going's getting a bit harder, and even though the knees and hips aren't complaining this year, keeping an 8-minute or even 8:20 pace into 20 miles is proving to be tougher than I had hoped. I know what the last hurdle is. I've known it since 1978. I've covered the shoes routine, the training regimen, nutrition, and now diet supplements. I've got one last hill to climb. The biggest hill.

I reflect on another unanswered question – about whether the military demands more from their leaders than do commercial enterprises. On the surface this seems a stupid question to ask myself. The obvious answer should be "no." Proof comes in the form of people who leave the military and enter the civilian, often commercial, workforce, and the citizen soldier who normally spends one weekend a month and two additional weeks in a year on active duty in the National Guard or Army, Navy, Air Force or Marine Corps Reserves. There's no brick wall between the two.

Then I consider the training. Many corporations spend no more than a week, sometimes two weeks per year, training their employees. Others invest as little as 7 to 10 hours per year on training an employee. Some of this training covers mandatory "values" infused training such as Diversity Skills. Much of the rest focuses on operations – the technical aspects of a job. More senior people tend to get more so-called soft-skills training, focusing on fuzzy things like visioning, delegation, strategic planning and anger management. I've seen the foundations in person or pulled up the research to get a statistically valid, or quantitative sample of what's going on out here. Qualitatively, I hear the same thing from my college students, in North Carolina and Virginia, Michigan and Texas. They too must be close enough to a randomly generated sample to represent America's workforce, with the (statistically) significant distinction perhaps being that those who self-selected themselves into adult education programs may have a different point of view than their peers at work.

In contrast, while I may trade jabs with my brothers and sisters from the Army, Navy and Air Force, all of the military services do a credible job of indoctrinating their troops – both officer and enlisted. I admit bias toward believing that the Marine Corps' method is superior. Ten weeks of close supervision, immersed in a new culture without distracting external influences equates to nearly 1680 hours. If we subtract 8 hours of sleep a night (which is not always the case) – 560 hours over 10 weeks – the typical enlisted Marine will have been exposed to 1120 hours of *Marine Corps* in three months, at the still-impressionable age of somewhere between 17 and 24. That 1120 hours is more than all of the classroom time for two master's degrees. (Do the math.)

For the retail store that spends 7 hours a year on training for each hourly employee, that means it would only take 160 years to get that goofy clerk at the cash register indoctrinated in the ways of a corporate culture. Those 17- to 20-year-old clerks at the cash register are the same ages as the young men and women going into combat. Indoctrinating store clerks in customer service is not an impossible task, but the company that wants to be THE COMPANY must be willing to invest the time. MORE time than 160 hours.

10:13:15
Nineteen

Houston's Memorial Park is within reach. Crowds in the Galleria district offer encouragement, beer, loud music, belly dancers and lots of signs. Encouraging signs. My pace is fading, but I'm feeling okay. Not great. I'll live with okay. There are "delighted with," "happy with," and "satisfied." If I can beat 3:50 today, I'll be very happy – a new PR. Anything under 4 hours is "satisfied."

I need to be satisfied that the null is void. The null is: ENRON never existed. ENRON was a zero. Scientific inquiry would look for validity, reliability, generalizability. The first question would be whether enron's corporate decisions defined survival ethics. Did these decisions constitute valid hypotheses to test the theory of a perfect corporation? Guilty pleas and pending indictments suggest the answer is *no.*

Are the results reliable? Could enron's experiments be repeated by other corporations seeking to become CORPORATION – with parallel results? Tyco International Ltd, WorldCom Inc., Parmalat and others provide the answer. In the antithesis, reliable findings suggest that companies like Southwest Airlines, W.L. Gore, The Ritz Carlton, Chick Fil-A and many others get it: focus on values, treat employees right, and turn this machine on to delight customers.

In the end, I find no evidence that ENRON ever existed. Generalizing the results from enron to other organizations will now become a full-time job.

10:22:20
Twenty

Too many times in both the Marine Corps and the corporate domain I had worked with people simulating

LEADER whose work demonstrated a shortsighted focus on just "satisfied." While the Marine Corps may offer some lessons for the business community, the question has been asked if a given military unit could demonstrate a profit.

Battlefield commanders, squadron COs, commanding generals do *not* stop to calculate how much a bullet costs, how much a jet fighter or cruise missile costs or what the overhead is to get a company, battalion or division from North Carolina to Iraq, Vietnam, Germany or Haiti. But their profit, like NASA's and any other non-profit, college or government organization, is measured in *mission accomplished.*

(Yes – somewhere in the strategic planning process, someone is doing the math to determine in advance what it will cost (and how to purchase the materiel to accomplish assigned missions), but when the call comes to *send in the Marines* they don't hesitate with a calculator.)

Some Marines enter the Corps as a calling; some don't. Conducting periodic surveys intended to help shape recruitment advertising for the Marine Corps, marketing giant J. Walter Thompson (now JWT) finds that enlisted Marines may indeed be seeking to fulfill a calling, but some are just looking for a job or an education, or searching for a way to prove themselves or prove something to family or friends. Some have had no father figure growing up and the Marine Corps appears to offer that.

There's a saying in the Corps: A *lifer* is someone who can't live without the Corps; a *career Marine* is someone the Corps can't live without. Those career Marines are the ones I wanted to work with. The Marine Corps was a calling for them. Perpetually aware that their civilian counterparts earned 20 to 50 percent more, or even double the income, these career Marines weren't in it for the money. The armed services reward superior performance with medals and ribbons. Financial bonuses include incentives to enlist, to re-enlist, or for retention in job categories with chronic shortages – pilots, doctors, computer technicians.

10:31:25
Twenty-One

Five miles to go. My favorite radio station is set up with trailers, outside, along the boulevard in Memorial Park, blasting away with Aerosmith. The belly dancers undulate with a different tune in their heads.

In a naked comparison, I decide it's not as simple as thinking Marines serve as a calling (not all do) and civilians *don't* serve their trades as a calling (many do). I've worked with countless civilians who would have made great non-commissioned officers, or captains or colonels... Fate has merely drawn them into construction, aerospace, real estate or engineering, and they generally become front-runners in their trades.

But what of those higher standards? If I base *standards* on the abstract of Leadership Traits, as an example, not one commercial enterprise would deny that their leaders should come pre-packaged with Integrity, Decisiveness, Judgment, Knowledge and the rest. The problem is, those leaders *don't* necessarily come pre-packaged. I can target this. Marine Corps leadership concepts, in *civilian terms*, filtered through organizational psychology, are appropriate anywhere. Cultural differences set the military aside; directors and vice presidents in corporate America would never stop by the homes of their employees to ensure cleanliness and habitability; nor would they stop by the restaurants their employees eat at to guarantee the food is of good quality...both common practice in the uniformed world of the armed services. But there are principles that apply anywhere. In the opening chapter of an older version of The Marine Officer's guide, a single paragraph from a past commandant of the Marine Corps illustrates the mentor relationship sought for in an ideal Marine Corps:

Relations between officers and men:

The relation between officers and enlisted men should in no sense be that of superior and inferior nor that of master and servant, but rather that of teacher and scholar. In fact, it should partake of the nature of the relation between father and son, to the extent that officers, especially commanding officers, are responsible for the physical, mental and moral welfare, as well as the discipline and military training, of the young men under their command...[lii]

In the end, I decide we expect just as much from leaders in commerce and non-profits as we do from military leaders. We expect merchants to be honest, to be able to make decisions, to be intelligent, fair, and so on – the Marine Corps leadership traits. The Army, Navy, Air Force and Marine Corps may send people to some thankless jobs with comparatively smaller financial rewards, but so do police and fire departments, or teachers in school districts with rough neighborhoods.

10:40:30
Twenty-Two

Standards of conduct are part of the equation. Quantitative standards are easy to measure, easy to observe. The Boston Athletic Association sets standards for five-year age groups, but qualifying for the Boston Marathon not only requires meeting the standard *time* in a given age group, the qualifying time must be certified in a qualifying race. Houston's race, sponsored by Hewlett-Packard this year, is well-organized and expertly monitored, meeting Boston's standards.

Job performance – quantitative standards – are readily observable. Standards of conduct, ethical standards, are difficult to see. Not impossible, just more difficult. Standards of conduct take us to accountability.

In the Marine Corps, privates are accountable to corporals and sergeants, sergeants to senior NCOs, and senior NCOs to officers. Generals are accountable to the Commandant of the Marine Corps, and he to the Secretary of the Navy, who reports to the Commander-in-Chief, the

President of the United States. But the chain of command doesn't stop there – the president is (or should be) accountable to the people. Joe Private, the Marine, is accountable to the people of the United States.

And corporate officers? More laws? More Sarbanes-Oxley? Give me a break. I want fewer rules, more freedom and ethics training starting in kindergarten.

10:49:50
Twenty-three

The answer to the question of accountability is up to each corporate officer. The decision comes down to purpose. As president and CEO of my global corporation I can determine that my purpose is to increase personal power, wealth and influence, that my purpose is to focus my attention on delivering quality lemonade to my customers, or that my purpose is to appease stockholders. Decisions are based on values.

Where does the *real* energy come from?

Allow me to hypothesize the reader's response to the following scenario: I find a corporate CEO making $10 million a year making peoples' lives better by providing commercial solutions in a given industry, then offer this CEO $10 million to leave his or her company to work for my company, mucking the corporate horse stables. The requirement is that this former CEO *must* be the one shoveling manure, and *cannot* subcontract the work or have anyone else do it. Would he or she take the new job? Ten million bucks is ten million bucks. If the goal is truly money – what difference does it make how it's earned, as long as it's honest? Plow the answer to this question back into every earlier argument on ethics and human motivation.

10:59
Twenty-four

In two miles and 385 yards, I'll be back where I started. This is the best part of the race – finishing. Not because I get to rest, eat and replenish fluids, but for the personal satisfaction. I'm close to downtown Houston. Running the streets I used to trek on my lunch hours at enron, I get the same feeling I have when I cook-out after a race. Good memories. Pictures in a photo album.

Anger over enron has dissipated. In the end, what I got out of it was freedom, a chance for a new start, a fresh race with a new attitude. Freedom itself, like quality, is impossible to define. Freedom is odorless, colorless, weightless. It just is. Maybe freedom *is* quality. I don't know...but freedom is *my* energy. *You'll know it when you see it.* I just didn't see it. Until now. If it weren't for enron, I probably would have talked about starting my own business for years, without taking the fatal step. enron threw us out in the middle of an ocean...we had to learn to swim. Thanks, enron!

Nearing downtown, I run past one of those Monday through Friday handout hotspots, where panhandlers proliferate on each corner during morning and evening rush hour. I think back to the first week I was working the local corporate university consulting contract near this intersection less than six months earlier, disappointed in my performance on the way in to work one morning. As I neared the stoplight, I read the fellow's hand-lettered sign: "Veteran. One Eye. Homeless and hungry. Wife and three kids. Anything helps. God Bless."

Sitting there at the stop light in my crisp, starched blue shirt and yellow power tie, I thought, "Get a job." As I drove on, my second thought was that if I could find work, he could too. My third thought, by the next stop light, was disappointment. I'm just as disgusting as the next guy. In World War II, the Marine Corps motto *Semper Fidelis,* shortened to *Semper Fi,* is storied to have been perverted to "Semper Fi, Mac," meaning, "I got mine, get your own."

The next morning, the same guy was there. We never know if they're legitimately incapable of work, drug addicts, alcoholics or professional scammers, but it's gotta take something significant to drive someone to that level of desperation, and I had almost considered his job as a potential career. I had packed two lunches, and when I got to the corner, I handed the guy two bagels, two bananas and a plastic storage container full of spaghetti. If he was hungry, he ate it. If he was scamming and looking for a buck – he got a carbo-loading lunch.

11:09
Twenty-five

Turning the corner into the final mile brings the most incredible feeling of exhilaration. I'm a hero coming back from the war. I've circumnavigated the globe. Landed on the moon. Invented a cure for cancer. All the music is playing for me. I'm weightless once again (though not quite odorless).

Heading into the final hundred yards, running buddy Lisa steps from the sidelines and runs along, offering words of encouragement until one of the race marshals tosses her out. She said she might be there. I'm buoyed even more seeing a friendly face. I start scanning the spectators for Son One with his wife and his little Sis. I spot Daughter and run over to get my kiss, my reward, then sprint the final 50 meters to beat 3:50, twenty minutes faster than last year.

11:19:36
The Starting Line

Rewind. It's never over.

The end is just the beginning of training for the next race. We never get to see how it ends because it doesn't end; we just hand over the desire to compete to the next generation. The landscape remains constant, as do the obstacles and the choices.

And I still have Boston to shoot for.

Twenty-Eight: Laser Chapter 10

"Kathryn...wake up. Look at the time."

"hmpf...."

"It's time to wake up. Time for school. Time for Second Grade."

"Not now Daddy; I'm dreaming. I wanna finish my dream."

"What are you dreaming about?" I ask as I lift Kathryn from her bed and carry her down the stairs with her eyes closed. *Animal Planet* on the TV will get her eyes open.

"Remember when enron was broken?" she asks with one eye open.

"Uh-huh."

"I dreamed you went back. But you were in the Marine Corps again. You were a captain, and you were made out of steel!"

"Really?" I asked, as I navigated down the stairs.

"Really. And you had a big laser and you went to blast enron..."

"That's a pretty crazy imagination you've got there, little one...Maybe you've been watching too many cartoons."

"...and you zapped the bad guys and..."

"Whoa... Wait a minute. There weren't any bad guys at enron, just good people who made bad wizards."

"What are you talking about, Daddy?" she looked at me oddly.

"Remember in the Wizard of Oz, when Dorothy tells the Wizard that he's a bad man?

"Yessir."

"He says, 'Not a bad man, just a bad wizard.' It's a metaphor."

"Oh. Dad?"

"What?"

"You're so weird sometimes."

"I know. So how does your dream end?"

"You rescue me, over and over and over, but the dream never ends. It just rewinds and starts all over again."

"Oh good. I'm glad I rescued you."

"Dad?"

"What's a "meta" for?"

"It's for target practice. Just something to shoot for, little one."

Twenty-Nine: Epilogue

February 1st, 2004
10:30 a.m.
<u>Paris</u>

The Panthers and the Patriots will kick off Super Bowl XXXVIII in Houston in a few hours, but I'm missing it. Trying to book the return flight from Cairo through Paris into Houston on January 31st was so outrageously expensive as to be impossible. The government would have paid the ticket, but I'm a taxpayer too, and if I can cut the fare in half or more by spending a 2-day lay-over in Paris, I'll just have to suffer through it. The Frogs haven't been very friendly of late, because of the war in Iraq, but I'd always wanted to visit and after enron, every chance is a last chance. Half of my ancestry is French. Mom never got to make the trip, so I'm visiting for her.

Before leaving Houston on January 21st I had booked – via the Internet – a cozy, single tourist room a block from La Louvre. My four-hour flight from Cairo gets into Paris at 6 a.m., and by the time I ride out the shuttle bus routine and the Metro, and emerge from the subway tunnels near L'Arc du Triomphe, it's still dark. One thing I had not planned for was getting to my hotel with 150 pounds of luggage. None of my bags has wheels. From Houston to Cairo to Paris – I had had paid "bag boys." By now I have camels, pyramids, Hard Rock Café T-shirts, books and other goodies tucked into the voids in my bags. With my laptop computer and both business and leisure clothes in a total of four bags, I'm hard-pressed to get three to four blocks from the metro near La Louvre to my hotel on foot. I hesitate to take a cab because I sense the hotel is close by (and I don't want to give that pleasure to the Parisian cab drivers leaning against their Citroens, smoking French cigarettes and drinking Euro coffee). Complicating my problem are the short side streets in Paris. I'm literate enough in French to survive forever in Paris, but am not familiar with the city, so the map confuses me. The sun isn't up and I'm not certain where North is. Taxi drivers watch in amusement as I sling one, then two, then three bags over my shoulders, then grab the fourth to carry by hand – across the tiny square for another rest. Finally turning the corner to my destination, I stop at a *patisserie,* now open with the sun, for croissants, yogurt and coffee, then struggle to the end of the block, check into my hotel, coax my bags into the tiny room, and sleep.

"Bon jour?" The hotel maid wakes me politely. It's early afternoon.

"Juste un moment. S'il vous plait attente," I ask her to wait a minute while I change. I can't miss an opportunity to run a few miles on a fourth continent, and as I emerge from my room, the maid looks strangely at my bare legs, running shorts and shoes. "A bientot," I tell her as I jog down the creaky, narrow staircase..."See you soon."

Out the door, left, and across the street I'm in the shadow of La Louvre. At the pyramidical entrance to la sprawling *musee*, I turn right and head for L'Arc du Triomphe. Plenty of time to reflect on the previous two weeks in Cairo and the past two years that led to this experience. The Egyptians were curious and kind, many asking if I were an American. There is a sizable, mostly Coptic, Christian community in Cairo. Aside from those manufactured conversations intended to get me to visit a jewelry shop, souvenir perfume salon or papyrus art gallery, many people expressed sadness at the terror attacks of 9-11. In contrast to the predictability of panhandlers in Houston, I saw no beggars in Cairo. Everyone was an entrepreneur, even if they were selling bread or pocket tissues on the sidewalks. From the balcony at my 10th floor hotel room at the Sheraton on the Nile I can see the Great Pyramids to the west-southwest of the city, and plan a morning trip on a tourist bus for the next day off work.

The contract goes well, and too-quickly I am back in the air, headed home. A week after scrambling to the depths of a crumbling pyramid to view a pharaoh's tomb, and riding a camel for the photograph I can take home to Daughter, I'm running the sidewalks of the Champs Elysees. The contrast from December 3rd, 2001, exiting enron's crumbling tower, to today is so totally bizarre I think I'm on a different planet. My own science friction story. Crossing the stone-paved city streets of Paris, dodging strange-looking, synthetic cars that would fit in the back of my Ford truck, I almost believe I *am* on a different planet. Two years and two months after enron had dismissed me, I could at last dismiss enron. It never existed. Enron had pushed me into the race, God had pulled and patiently coached me to the finish. The grief cycle had run its course and I was emerging at the starting line of the next race with enthusiasm. In the distance, La Tour Eiffel signals, and I head back to the hotel room to clean up, rest, find a sidewalk café and work on my elevator speech.

Paris
February 2nd, 2004

Standing in line at the Eiffel Tower, I compose my elevator pitch notes for the 10-Euro trip to the summit. Two days from my first months at enron flash to the front of my memories. On the first I had just left my pickup in the parking garage and was walking toward enron's lobby when the old man himself intersected my path. It was early; no one else was around and Mr. Lay greeted me. We had two to three minutes of pleasant but idle conversation on the brisk walk to the lobby, and separated at the elevators. Lay would head for 50 in one bank of elevators; I would push the button for 6 at another.

Arriving in my team's maze of cubicles, I commented that I had run into the boss. Justin, my hiring manager and mentor, asked if I had given him my elevator speech.

"We didn't ride the same elevator," I said. "And what's an elevator speech?"

"Doesn't matter if you ride the elevator or not. When you get 30 seconds with the old man," Justin explained, "that's your chance to tell your story, your big ideas, like that Enron University pitch you've been mumbling about."

"Ah..."

A week later, it happened again. Mr. Lay and I seemed to be on the same schedule, but the opportunity happened only twice in my eighteen months at the company. This time I was ready. Joining Mr. Lay in the executive elevator, I hit the button for 47 and waited for my chance. Lay asked what I did for enron, so I told him I was a training manager, and working on a concept for a corporate university. The corporate university wasn't even close to my job description, just something I could envision as my ticket to the top in a yet-to-be-written future. Lay asked a polite question or two about the concept and I described the salient ideas before my opportunity expired and the elevator doors opened to 47. Lay was headed to 50. It wasn't Lay who would make decisions on something like a corporate university, but if the seed I had planted led him to comment about the idea to some vice president of HR, I might get some traction. It never happened that way, but you can't win the lottery if you don't buy a ticket.

As the line snakes around toward the Eiffel Tower's north entrance, I spot a crowd of tourists headed for the front of the line with a group ticket. The delay is reasonable, and gives me the chance to read the warning notices in French, English and German on the side of the street-level souvenir shop and ticket window: "Beware of pickpockets."

Two years seems like 10 minutes, and now it's my turn, my chance to deliver an elevator speech one more time. This time is different. The corporate university for enron is a faded memory; this time it's about first principles. I imagine the CEO emeritus from some failed corporation boarding the elevator with me and I begin:

I've been working on a model for the ideal organization. It works well for corporations, but may be applied equally well to non-profits, educational institutions, government agencies or, with some adaptations, even to personal relationships. The model is based on a laser – light amplification by stimulated emission of radiation. A LASER is intense, focused, coherent, high-energy light. That LIGHT is your vision and values. Light is illumination, awareness, enlightenment. Your goal is Light Amplification by Stimulated EMPLOYEE Radiation. Your company is the LASER, the crucible of vision and values. Your message is the electrical charge. Your customer's needs for quality products and services are the FOCUS. Your employees are the HIGH-ENERGY, excited photons. Your leadership sets the example and gives order to chaos, creating the COHERENT, single wavelength beam of light. That SINGLE WAVELENGTH is your company, division or team's product or service. The level of INTENSITY depends on how efficiently you release the energy in your corporate values.

That laser beam is your team. They must be unified, coherent, in phase and in step. The only way to do that is to have a single message they can all believe in. Yet based on that faith, they must also have the freedom to navigate, to innovate, to create and invent, and forgiveness when they fail. Your junior leaders must have the confidence to break down barriers to success, and all team members must have confidence in a survival ethic in order to compete and win. That survival ethic emerges from your goals, expressed in values.

One of your goals as a leader is to ensure your team can operate without your direct supervision. Sooner or later you'll have to delegate, but to get to this point, your team will have to absorb your organization's values. You must ensure they do this accurately. Values guide decisions. Some team members will have to work harder and sweat more than others to get to this point. When you delegate, deliver not only responsibility but enough authority to get the job done. Build all-terrain junior leaders, but just remember that the responsibility you delegate is a *derivative* of your responsibility. You cannot abdicate.

Shared success in the face of adversity will lead to closer bonds for your team, but adversity will also detract from focus. Temptations will prey – glory, fame, power, wealth. Your team's race to their target is long. Training, dedication, focus and desire are required to reach the target and avoid temptation, and these require energy. Energy comes from knowledge, from freedom, from the satisfaction of accomplishing a mission. The laser works best in the hands of a mature, self-disciplined leader. Pick your targets as if you have one shot; if you miss – you may not get another chance. Miss your target and your organization may not survive.

You have *five* choices: Values, Employees, Customer Defined Quality, Share Price or Personal Profit. The option you select will shape your responsibility to the other four.

"So, CEO emeritus...," I continue, as the elevator reaches the pinnacle, "Here's the laser. It works. What's your target...?"

The erstwhile CEO considers the options for a moment and replies, "I'll take the 5th."

Thirty: The Post Post Script

February 2013

By the time I had this story in my head – using writing as a catharsis to rid myself of ENRON and enron – I was returning from a real five-day contract in Cairo, Egypt, (part of the surreal, science fiction-like nature of that whole experience), working as a consultant for the US Commerce Department. My assignment was to assist the *Insurance Supervisory Authority of Egypt* in the process of "marketing" insurance to a predominantly Muslim nation. A growing middle class was buying Egyptian-built FIAT cars (and wrecking them) and "car insurance" was a relatively easy sell. Homeowner's insurance was more difficult, culturally, but our hardest task was "life insurance." It seemed that contrary to Shariah law, life insurance was something akin to "betting God when you're going to die." Our goal – with my several Egyptian colleagues – was to paint this, through advertising media, radio, television, pamphlets and billboards, as "you're going to die someday anyway... who's going to pay the mortgage?" Interesting week. Great colleagues in Cairo!

I had two travel days each at the start and finish of the week and I did indeed visit The Great Pyramids. I visited the Sphynx (and when I got off the tourist bus from our hotel, and turned around in the parking lot – there was a Popeye's Fried Chicken and a Coca Cola sign). I was still under-employed, if the gauge was either achieving my previous income level or at least being able to pay my bills. I had hoped to string together many such contracts with the government, but it didn't happen that way.

The contract in Cairo was good for $10,000: $2,000 a day for five days as a consultant in a field for which I was uniquely qualified. The paycheck was enough to cover my bills for a few more months. Although we discussed it, the Commerce Department never called me for another such contract.

Returning from Cairo, I had a two-day layover in Paris. (More surreal. I had never been there before, and of course I saw the mandatory tourist things in two short days.) On the Air France flight from Paris to Houston I took up conversation with a fellow who had just published a book. The details are unimportant, but the discussion offered a flood of ideas and ignited my motivation to finish writing the draft manuscript for MERATHON in February and March, 2004.

The water under the bridge since then includes the court trials of Jeff Skilling and Ken Lay. In May 2006, Lay was convicted on 10 counts, Skilling on 19 counts of fraud and conspiracy. Lay died of a heart attack in July 2006; his conviction was vacated. My condolences to his family. As of late 2009, Skilling, still in prison, had approached the courts to evaluate his assertion that he didn't get a fair trial. In 2002, I had opted "in" to a class of former ENRON employees who asserted that *we* didn't get a fair severance package. My fraction of the $230,000 severance I didn't receive in 2002 paid out in 2010...pennies on the dollar ($7800). Lawyers in the cases against Enron collectively grabbed $688 million.

Through 2002, 2003 and 2004, I had developed, marketed and delivered ½ day to 2-day workshops in Leadership, Conflict Management, Time Management, Diversity, and Value-Based Pricing Sales Leadership. My audiences included a handful of Houston-based Fortune 500 corporations in energy, aerospace and manufacturing, several small and mid-size companies, as well as government and higher education audiences. With growing success at wedging my way into a market dominated by national professional development companies with established reputations and local Houston independents who were years ahead of me with their business networks, I was perpetually hopeful about the prospect of climbing out of debt.

– until one contract went unrealized and the next postponed for three months. In early 2005 I had added the Marine Corps back in to my job search.

Yes – I had just turned 50. And yes – I had been

retired from the Corps almost 10 years. The wars in Afghanistan and Iraq had started in October 2001 and March 2003; by 2004 the Marine Corps had already posted a recall of retired officers and senior non-commissioned officers, asking for officers and senior NCOs who had been retired within the previous five years. The first time I had responded, by phone, I had left a message saying that I had only been retired about 3000 days. It was likely a major or lieutenant colonel who picked up the message and probably thought I was a smart-ass, or just blew me off because I truly had been retired more than five years.

(The concern for the Marine Corps, or Army, Navy or Air Force in recalling retirees is that people do indeed get old; their bones get creaky and some get fat; they lose touch with their job specialty's current doctrine, tactics, technology and processes.)

Through the Spring and into Summer of 2005, I worked the phones with the Marine Corps. Finding an active duty command to request my services wasn't difficult; my old running buddy was soon to assume command at the duty station I had retired from in 1995. The glitch was that I would need security clearances...clearances that had effectively expired nearly a decade earlier. We finally worked out the details and I found myself headed back to the United States Marine Corps in August 2005.

My return to active duty as *the oldest captain in the Marine Corps* is really another story. Considering my background, the 7 months of 2006-'07 that I spent as an economic, cultural and political intelligence analyst in Anbar Province in Iraq gave me fodder for a different analysis. Another book. Suffice it to say – in order to close this chapter, that it was an honor to serve, first as the academics officer at the Navy and Marine Corps Intelligence Training Center in Virginia, then with the 2nd Intelligence Battalion in Fallujah. When I returned from deployment, I finished those two extra years and seven months in uniform as the officer-in-charge of enlisted training back at the intel school. During the nearly three years back on active duty, I took to running a marathon nearly every month (two of those during the seven months in Iraq), and a couple of 50-milers. Much time to write more stories in my mind, and...

Before I shipped out to Iraq, I had met an incredible woman in Virginia Beach – a gal with two children close to my daughter's age. We corresponded while I was deployed, and although we have much in common we also had a few details to work through before we realized we were discussing a wedding date. We were married in 2008. If I were to consider dusting off that consulting business and trying to pick up where I had left off – I would need a running start, a year's worth of working capital to live on while I knocked on doors and made phone calls, and a healthier economy. Too much risk for a new family...

As it turned out, the economy was already headed south as I hung up my uniform and the kind of service I would have been marketing is one of the first things companies cut back on when they start tightening their belts and laying off employees. I was fortunate to land a job as a government contractor. In many ways I'm still doing what I did in the Marine Corps...same general line of work, but now supporting the men and women in combat – but as a civilian.

If there's a summary to the lessons I would offer – it's wrapped up in the encouragement to be flexible, adaptable. Persevere. Focus. Learn to live with less...a lot less. When you do get back on your feet, be generous to those who are struggling and remember what you learned when you were in that nightmare. If there was ever a time to resurrect a trite expression, this is it: Necessity is in fact the mother of invention. Some numbers of people unemployed in 2007, '08, '09 and rolling in to 2010 started new businesses, many for the first time. Some of those will fail. Some will move into entirely new career fields. Others will eventually get hired back with their former employers, or at least in the same industry, when the demand picks up. And unfortunately, some will evolve into chronic unemployment.

Think about it like this: If you're the victim in a car accident, a robbery or the result of a faulty drug or commercial product, you might hire an attorney and sue for compensation. You would have the moral standing to think of yourself as a victim. If you go to court, you might break even, you might not. On the other hand, if you're a victim of *the economy*, there's no one to sue. You can't take on *the economy* in a courtroom. But...if unemployment eventually leads to *nothin' left to lose,* that means freedom – to start a business, take a different job (any job) or learn a new trade. What's there to lose?

Oh yeah – I did finally get my qualifying time for Boston. In Iraq. I imported the Houston Marathon to Camp Fallujah for the 35th Annual Houston running, in parallel with the hometown race in January 2007. We had about 40 runners, mostly Marines based at Fallujah, in Anbar Province. My certified qualifying time from that race was 3:18 – almost good enough for two age groups younger than me (the 40-44 year-olds) – and I ran the Boston Marathon in 2007 when I returned from Iraq, and again in 2008. In all – 22 MERATHONS between 2002 and 2011, plus two 50-milers and a boat load of 5k and 10k races.

Another *by the way...* Has Sarbanes Oxley prevented corruption? Bernie Madoff....?

Citations and References

[i] © Robert M. Pirsig, William Morrow and Company, NY, first published 1974.

[ii] Retrieved from: http://www.caib.us/news/report/

[iii] NASA headquarters sought proposals to rebuild NASA's management culture, as recommended by the Columbia Accident Investigation Board. My proposal did not make the cut; my financials were weak and incomplete. Improving my proposal writing and financial estimates will be new missions for me. Interestingly, NASA Administrator Sean O'Keefe met with a similar fate when submitting NASA's plans for Moon and Mars exploration. NASA's plan and financials were incomplete, according to Rep. John Walsh, R-New York, chairman of the House Appropriations Veterans Affairs, Housing and Urban Development and independent agencies subcommittee. Walsh told O'Keefe he would give the space exploration vision a fair hearing, but was reluctant to approve the money NASA says it needs to set off in the new direction. "I cannot commit this Congress and future Congresses to a program that is undefined," Walsh said. (http://www.cnn.com/2004/TECH/space/04/27/nasa.budget/index.html.   retrieved April, 2004.)

[iv] The NeverEnding Story, © 1984 Neue Constantin Film Productions GmbH. Released in the U.S. by Warner Bros. Home Entertainment, 1984.

[v] DiSanto, R.L. and Steele, S.J., William Morrow and Company, Inc., New York, 1990

[vi] Warfighting. FMFM 1. U.S. Marine Corps

[vii] Dictionary of the History of Ideas, Ancient Roman Ideas of Law. Charles Scribner's Sons, New York. 1973, Vol II, pp. 686-687.

[viii] F. Heylighen, C. Joslyn, V. Turchin (Oct 1, 1993, modified Oct 27, 1999) "What are Cybernetics and Systems Science?" in: F. Heylighen, C. Joslyn and V. Turchin (editors): Principia Cybernetica Web (Principia Cybernetica, Brussels), URL: http://pespmc1.vub.ac.be/REFERPCP.html.

[ix] F. Heylighen ibid. Feb 17, 1997 (modified) Aug 1993 (created).

[x] C. Joslyn, F. Heylighen, V. Turchin, ibid. July 7, 1997 (modified), Jan 1992 (created).

[xi] V. Turchin, C. Joslyn, ibid. July 19, 1999 (modified), Aug, 1993 (created).

[xii] F. Heylighen, C. Joslyn, V. Turchin, ibid. Jun 29, 1995 (modified) Aug 1993 (created)

[xiii] Grieder, W., May 13, 2002. The Nation. Retrieved from http://www.thenation.com/doc.mhtml?i= 20020513&s=greider
[xiv] F. Heylighen, V. Turchin, ibid. Oct 24, 2000 (modified), Aug 1993 (created).
[xv] Dawkins, R., 1976. Oxford University Press, Oxford, England.
[xvi] National Public Radio (NPR). Hosted by Susan Stamberg: *Gingrich discusses Life After Power.* www.npr.org. Oct. 28, 2003. Retrieved from www.npr.org/archives/ on March 15, 2004.
[xvii] Beck, W. F., ibid. Mark 9:35.
[xviii] Retrieved from: http://www.fortune.com/fortune/investing/articles/0,15114,5257 55-2,00.html
[xix] Aronson, Elliot. The Social Animal, 5th ed. Wh. H. Freeman and Company, New York. 1988. Aronson periodically refers to Festinger's work a generation earlier, much of which is rooted in the analysis of how blond, blue-eyed German farm boys could be overcome by propaganda and how they would come to justify their roles in the atrocities of World War II.
[xx] Beck, W. S., The Holy Bible, An American Translation, Romans 12: 5-8. Leader Publishing Company, New Haven, MO. 1976.
[xxi] Beck. Ibid. Matthew 6:25.
[xxii] McCall, M. September 18-24, 2003, *Nashville Scene: Freedom's not just another word.* Retrieved from http://www.ohboy.com/media/kris.nashvillescene.pdf Retrieved March 24, 2004.
[xxiii] Kowalski, B., cited in Human Resources Executive, Dec 3, 2002. Retrieved from workindex.com.
[xxiv] Retrieved from http://channels.netscape.com/ns/careers/package.jsp?name=fte/slackers/slackers, March 4, 2004.
[xxv] F. Heylighen, Jul 7, 1997 (modified) Sep 19, 1995 (created)
[xxvi] Deal, T., and Kennedy, A. 1982: Corporate Cultures: The rites and rituals of corporate life. Reading, MA: Addison-Wesley Publishing Company.
[xxvii] Peters, T., and Waterman, R. (1982): In Search of excellence. New York: Harper & Row.
[xxviii] Heinlein, R. A., *Time Enough for Love.* Ace Books edition, 1988 (p. 248): New York: The Berkley Publishing Group.
[xxix] Declaration of Independence.
[xxx] Retrieved from: http://www.blankrome.com/publications/emplbenlabor/PDFs/update1003-6.pdf

xxxi Taxonomy of Educational Objectives, Handbook 1: Cognitive Domain. Benjamin S. Bloom, ed. Addison-Wesley Publishing Company, 1984.

xxxii Beck. Genesis 1:1

xxxiii Beck. Genesis 1:27-28.

xxxiv SARGE! A&E Television Networks. The History Channel, © 2001.

xxxv Sergeant. In the Marine Corps, a sergeant is a sergeant. Although there are ranks with names like staff sergeant, gunnery sergeant, master sergeant, first sergeant, sergeant major and master gunnery sergeant, each of these is addressed by their proper title. That is, a Marine is addressed by his rank, as in "First Sergeant Bnotz." In the Army and Air Force, any ol' sergeant (master sergeant, first sergeant, sergeant first class, etc.) may be addressed as "sergeant," with the exception of the senior ranks of chief master sergeant in the Air Force and (command) sergeant major in the Army.

xxxvi N. E. Thing Enterprises, (1994). Andrews and McMeel, Kansas City, MO

xxxvii Ellul, J. *Propaganda: The formation of men's attitudes*. New York: Alfred A. Knopf (1966)

xxxviii Aronson, E. *The social animal*. New York: W. H. Freeman and Company (5th ed. 1988)

xxxix Perrow, C. Complex Organizations: A Critical Essay, 1979.

xl Wilkins, p. 6.

xli www.containerstore.com

xlii (or words to that effect. It's hard to track these things down, with so much enron memorabilia disappearing over e-Bay.)

xliii enron, Code of Ethics. July, 2000.

xliv Merriam-Webster online, retrieved March 14, 2004.

xlv Hill, R. B. *History of Work Ethic*. The University of Georgia, Athens, GA. Retrieved from: http://www.coe.uga.edu/%7Erhill/workethic/index.html Dec 20, 2003.

xlvi Hill, ibid

xlvii Hill, ibid.

xlviii Beck, ibid: I Corinthians 13: 4-8.

xlix Beck, ibid: I Corinthians 10:25

l Beck, ibid: Isaiah 40:31.

li Barnes-Svarney, Patricia, Ed. The New York Public Library Science Desk Reference. Stonesong Press (MacMillan), New York. © 1995.

[lii] Marine Officer's Guide, page 4. United States Naval Institute, Annapolis, MD. Third edition, second printing. 1975. (The gender specific reference to enlisted *men* can be inferred as referring to *troops,* a gender non-specific noun, including men and women.)